SUE WHITING

The Crochet

Bible

D&C
David and Charles

About the author

Sue Whiting is an accomplished crochet and knitwear designer. She graduated from the London College of Fashion and has been involved in the needlecrafts and fashion industry for more than 30 years. She has written many books on subjects such as embroidery, dressmaking, knitting and crochet, and works regularly for most of the major British spinners.

A DAVID & CHARLES BOOK

Copyright © David & Charles Limited 2008

David & Charles is an F+W Publications Inc. company
4700 East Galbraith Road
Cincinnati, OH 45236

First published in the UK in 2008

Text and designs copyright © Sue Whiting 2008
Photography and Illustrations copyright © David & Charles 2008

A catalogue record for this book is available from the British Library.

ISBN-13: 978-0-7153-2488-2 paperback
ISBN: 0-7153-2488-8 paperback

Printed in China by SNP Leefung
for David & Charles
Brunel House   Newton Abbot   Devon

Commissioning Editor Vivienne Wells
Senior Editor Jennifer Fox-Proverbs
Desk Editor Bethany Dymond
Project Editor Nicola Hodgson
Art Editor Sarah Underhill
Designer Sue Cleave
Production Controller Ros Napper
Photographers Lorna Yabsley and Karl Adamson

Visit our website at www.davidandcharles.co.uk

David & Charles books are available from all good bookshops;
alternatively you can contact our Orderline on 0870 9908222 or write to us at
FREEPOST EX2 110, D&C Direct, Newton Abbot, TQ12 4ZZ (no stamp required UK only);
US customers call 800-289-0963 and Canadian customers call 800-840-5220.

contents

Introduction	**6**	
How to use this book	6	
Equipment	7	
Yarn textures	8	
Yarn weights	9	
Yarn fibres	10	

Techniques	**12**
Basic stitches	14
Placing the crochet stitches	18
Making crochet fabrics	21
Tension	24
Combination stitches	26
Relief stitches	28
Picots	32
Bullion stitches and clones knots	33
Linked stitches	34
Crossed stitches	35
Branched stitches	36
Fur stitch	37
Solomon's knots	38
Joining in new balls of yarn	39

Changing colour of yarn	40
Multi-coloured designs	42
Shaping in crochet	44
Following a crochet pattern	50
Filet crochet	53
Joining pieces of crochet	56
Making crochet motifs	60
Pressing crochet items	66
Borders and edgings	68
Decorative details	74
Working with beads	76
Embroidery on crochet	78
Tartan effects	80
Fringes, tassels and pompons	82

Stitch library	**84**
Basic stitches	84
Textured stitches	86
Chevron and wave stitches	88
Spike stitches	91
Lacy stitches	92
Edgings	96
Motifs	98

Projects	**102**
Band of bunnies	104
Sunny day stripes	107
Precious pastels baby set	109
Pretty in pink cardigan and shawl	112
Autumn colour coat	115
Corsage	118
Glorious glamour scarves	119
Peruvian-style bag	120
Solomon's knot wrap	123
Circles and stripes set	124
Seaside and shells set	127
Tartan-style set	130
Summer sky mesh top	132
Bead-edged beauty	134
Flower-trimmed cardigan	137
Multi-coloured motif shrug	140
Lazy stripe wrap jacket	142
Casual comfort sweaters	144
Pot pourri sachets	146
Rose-red heart rug	147
Three-colour baby blanket	149
Rainbow ribbon throw	150
Picture-perfect cushion covers	152
Heirloom bedspread	156

Yarn details	**158**
Yarn suppliers	**159**
Acknowledgments	**159**
Index	**160**

introduction

Crochet is fun, it's versatile, and it's quick to learn – it's nowhere near as difficult as many people think! With the help of this book, you can learn to crochet even if you've never picked up a hook before. Or, if you already know the basics, this book will help you to improve your skills and learn new ones.

How to use this book

This book is divided into three main sections.

The **Techniques** section (pages 12–83) gives you all the basic information you need. Complete with diagrams, photographs and helpful hints, this section will take you step by step through the basic stitches and techniques you need to start to crochet – from choosing yarns and selecting hooks, to how to work the basic crochet stitches that form the foundation of all crochet work. This section then takes you on to the next stage, giving you details of how to combine the stitches and skills you now have to create your very own crochet masterpieces. Fully illustrated throughout with diagrams, photographs and tips, this section will show you how to combine basic stitches to make exciting new combinations, how to work the more unusual stitches, such as Solomon's knots and bullion stitches, and how to complete your work to obtain a truly professional finish.

The **Stitch Library** (pages 84–101) contains full instructions, both written and diagrammatic, for some of the basic 'old favourite' stitches, and for some new and exciting stitches you can try out to create your own unique crochet items.

In the **Projects** section (pages 102–157) you will find the patterns to make the items that are featured within the other sections. Some are simple, some are more complex – but you will find all the techniques you need to complete the projects within this book. If you want to make a quick and easy project to try out a new technique, why not try the little Pot Pourri Sachets (pages 146–147) or the Corsage (page 118)? Or, if you want to create your very own heirloom, you could make the exquisite Heirloom Bedspread (pages 156–157). Among the 24 projects, there is bound to be something you would simply love to try out – for you, your home or your family! Finally, on pages 158–159, we detail the exact yarns that we used to create all the projects in the book, and provide a list of international suppliers of yarn and crochet equipment.

Whatever your skill level or whatever you want to make, this book will become an invaluable reference book to keep by your side whenever you decide to crochet.

So what's stopping you? Get some yarn and a hook and start crocheting now!

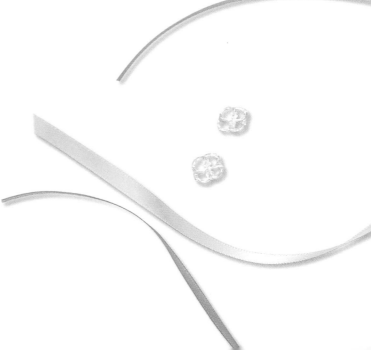

Equipment

Crochet uses surprisingly little equipment, which makes it a wonderfully portable craft – for the main bulk of the work, you basically just need a crochet hook, some yarn and a pattern! When it comes to finishing a project, you will need some other essential items, such as scissors, a tape measure and some pins. None of this equipment is expensive, and all is easy to get hold of – although you will probably need a useful box or tin to keep all your tools together.

Crochet hooks

These come in a range of sizes and can be made from a variety of materials – most commonly metal, plastic, wood and bamboo.

The size of hook needed is directly related to the thickness of yarn being used: a fine yarn will use a small hook, while a thick yarn will need a much chunkier hook. There are two basic sizing schemes for crochet hooks: the metric system and the American system. (There is also an old imperial sizing system that is now very rarely used, and we don't mention it in this book.) Throughout this book, you will find metric sizes quoted first, with American sizes given in brackets. Consult the chart shown right to convert between the systems.

Other equipment

Apart from the essential crochet hook, there will be a selection of other items that you may need to complete your crochet project.

- Scissors – to cut the yarn.
- Tape measure – to check that the work is the correct size.

- Ruler – this is useful to measure smaller pieces, such as tension swatches.
- Pins (large glass-headed or decorative-headed) – to secure pieces together before joining them. As ordinary pins can easily be lost in the surface of crochet, use large pins instead – these will be much easier to find later.
- Darning needle – to sew your crochet item together. It is best to use a blunt-pointed needle with an eye large enough to easily thread the yarn through – like those designed for sewing up knitting and for tapestry and cross stitch. The blunt point means that the fibres of the yarn are eased apart, rather than pierced and broken, which can weaken and damage the yarn.
- Notions – if the project you are making needs any ribbons, buttons or other fastenings, your pattern will give you details of exactly what you need to buy. It is a good idea to collect everything together before you start a project.

Crochet hook conversion chart

METRIC SIZES	AMERICAN SIZES
2.00mm	B1
2.25mm	B1
2.50mm	C2
3.00mm	D3
3.25mm	D3
3.50mm	E4
3.75mm	F5
4.00mm	G6
4.50mm	7
5.00mm	H8
5.50mm	I9
6.00mm	J10
6.50mm	K10½
7.00mm	–
8.00mm	L11
9.00mm	M13
10.00mm	N15

Yarn textures

There are three aspects that make up any crochet yarn: its texture, its fibre (natural or synthetic; plant- or animal-derived), and its thickness. Almost any hand-knitting yarn is also suitable for crochet. On these pages we explore yarn texture. The best yarns to use for crochet are usually those that are fairly smooth, such as classic wool, cotton or mixed yarns. More exotic or fancy yarns may be a little trickier to work with, but don't let that put you off experimenting with them.

Bouclé A bouclé yarn consists of loops of fibre held in place by a core thread. These loops can be quite large or very small, and the yarn can be difficult to crochet with – the larger the bouclé loops, the more difficult it will be to place the stitches in the correct place. However, if you can manage the snarls, this yarn produces a fascinating loopy, bubbly texture.

Chenille A chenille yarn is made by securing lots of short fibres to a central core – like a very thin strip of velvet. Depending on the length of the pile, chenille can be quite tricky to handle, as the 'fluff' of the yarn can hide the stitch definition, making it difficult to place the stitches correctly. On the plus side, chenille has a lush, dense and velvety texture when worked up.

Classic This type of yarn is what you would normally regard as a knitting yarn – quite tightly twisted and fairly smooth. Available in all sorts of weights, from 3ply to super-chunky, these yarns can be made in any type of fibre, from silk to wool.

Crepe Crepe yarns are perfect for crocheting with – they are smooth and easy to handle. The crocheted stitches are clearly visible so are easy to place, and the resulting crocheted fabric is clean and crisp. These yarns can be made from any type of fibre, but they are most commonly found in easy-care synthetic fibres.

Fancy Modern technology means that yarn producers can combine different sorts of yarns within one yarn. These

One of the greatest joys of crochet is the glorious array of yarns that are available to explore.

fancy, or speciality, yarns can be easy or difficult to crochet with depending on the combination of yarns they are constructed from. The only way to find out whether you can crochet successfully with a fancy yarn is to experiment with it! Some will work; others won't.

Fluffy These are exactly what their name suggests – fluffy! These yarns can be made from any naturally fluffy fibre, such as mohair or angora, or they can be fluffy because the yarn has been brushed to give it a fluffy appearance. Either way, they can be tricky to use; the hook can catch the fluff of the yarn, not its core, and stitches can be missed or misplaced. If you persevere, such yarns can produce a beautifully light fabric with a soft haze of colour.

Perle Normally made of cotton, a perle yarn is the classic fine crochet yarn. Its name derives from the way the yarn is constructed: it is tightly twisted, giving the effect of a string of beads or pearls.

Ribbon As their name suggests, these yarns are simply ribbon! Generally made of lightweight synthetic fibres, they can also be made of cotton or silk, or combinations of fibres, and are quite easy and quick to crochet with.

Roving Sometimes referred to as lopi yarns, a roving yarn has almost no twist to it, with the fibres just laying neatly next to each other. Generally made of woolly fibres, these yarns can be tricky to crochet with. They have a tendency to split, and the hook can catch on the fibres of previous stitches, leaving a messy appearance to the work. If you can get the hang of working with them, these yarns produce a pleasingly chunky and robust texture.

Slub A slubbed yarn does not maintain a consistent thickness along its length. Instead, the yarn features stretches of thin fibre and then areas of thicker fibre, known as slubs. Slubbed yarns can be made from almost any fibre. They are often constructed from a combination of fibres – one fibre that is used to create the smooth core that gives the yarn its strength, and a second fibre that forms the slubby thread twisted around the core. These yarns produce an intriguing fabric with a lot of depth, but it can be difficult to pull a slub through one of the thinner areas.

Tape These yarns consist of a tube of very finely knitted yarn. Lurex yarns and many summer-weight cotton yarns have such a construction. The yarn's smooth texture makes it ideal for crochet. One drawback is that, unless the ends are well secured, the knitted tube itself can unravel.

Yarn weights

The thickness of a yarn is referred to as its 'weight'. Any type of yarn construction and any type of fibre, or fibre combination, can be made into any thickness of yarn. Originally, the names given to the weights of yarns related to the number of strands, or 'plys', used to make it. However, nowadays modern yarn construction has rather thrown this out of the window. Although a yarn may still be referred to as a '4ply' yarn, it may appear to be made of only two or three strands of twisted fibres.

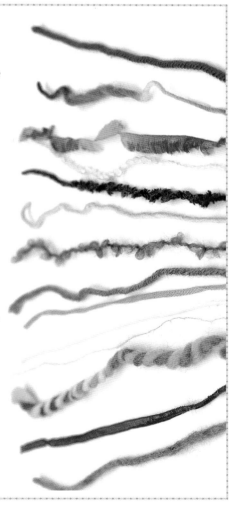

Crochet cotton These tightly twisted cotton yarns are more like a sewing thread than a crochet yarn. Traditionally used for the ultra-fine crochet of our grandmothers, their popularity has waned in recent years – but they are still widely available.

2ply and 3ply These are both very fine yarns, traditionally used for baby clothes and Shetland lace knitting.

4ply This fine yarn is possibly the most common thin yarn currently available, and it is one of the best weights for crochet. 4ply yarns are ideal for little tops, baby clothes and an assortment of household items.

Double knitting Often abbreviated to 'DK', this weight of yarn is possibly the most commonly used and best-known of all yarns. Suitable for almost any end use, it is another ideal yarn for crochet.

Aran Based on the weight of yarn used for traditional fishermen's sweaters (also known as aran sweaters), this weight of yarn is slightly thicker than a DK yarn. It is easy to crochet with and makes a good, firm fabric that is ideal for jackets and coats.

Chunky This weight of yarn, as its name suggests, is very thick – roughly two or three times as thick as a DK yarn. Although suitable for crochet, it can be a little tricky for a beginner to handle, but it works up very quickly and makes wonderfully warm coats and jackets.

Super-chunky and mega-chunky These are yarns that are even thicker than a chunky yarn. Although they work up very quickly, they can be tricky to use and often you may spend as long searching for the correct size hook as making the garment!

Fancy weights Apart from the basic yarn weights, there are many weights that fall between the standard weights. Shetland-weight yarn is a slightly thin DK weight, for example, whereas the once popular baby quickerknit is halfway between a DK and an aran weight. Many of the fancy fashion yarns available now come in their own idiosyncratic weights.

Yarn fibres

There is a wonderful array of yarns available for crochet, both natural and manmade or synthetic in origin. Natural yarns can be sourced from either plant fibres or animal fur, ranging hugely in texture, thickness, weight and elasticity, from the fluffy lightness of angora, to the sleek fluidity of silk, to the warmth and robustness of chunky sheep's wool. Natural yarns are not always hard-wearing and robust, and items made from them often need special care. Consequently, many manufacturers produce blends of natural and synthetic fibres to get the best of both worlds.

Alpaca, camel hair and other 'wools' Any animal that has fur can be shorn and the resulting fibres made into a yarn, but some are more commonly used than others. Alpaca, camel hair and llama are rather exotic yarns, but becoming increasingly easy to find. Alpaca, a llama-like animal, is native to the highlands of Peru, and has evolved a very dense fleece to keep it warm in those cold, harsh conditions. The resulting yarn is rather like sheep's wool in texture but is much warmer.

Angora Angora comes from rabbits – and we all know just how soft a rabbit's fur is! However, the fibres are quite short and an angora yarn will often shed these fibres both when you work with it and when it is worn. It is not particularly strong and is fairly expensive, so it is often combined with other fibres to make it more affordable and stronger – and also less prone to shedding.

Cashmere Cashmere is taken from the extremely soft fur of the cashmere goat. It makes the softest, lightest, cuddliest yarn that simply hugs you with warmth and luxury – in fact, this fibre makes the ultimate in luxury yarn! Regrettably, its price often reflects this, so manufacturers often combine it with other fibres to produce a more affordable yarn.

Cotton This plant-based fibre makes a yarn that lends itself perfectly to summer garments. However, cotton can be heavy and has no stretch or elasticity to it. As such, anything made from a pure cotton yarn may sag and grow once it is made. As with wool, there are many different finishes that can be applied to a cotton yarn, the most common being mercerization. Mercerized cotton has a glossy sheen that stays there wash after wash.

Linen, ramie and bamboo These plant-based fibres are lightweight and breathable and often best-suited to summer garments. Linen has a cool, dry texture with a lot of drape. Like cotton, it has little elasticity by itself and is often found in blends with other fibres to make it more resilient and easier to work with. Bamboo has a silk-like texture. It is promoted as an eco-friendly yarn, as bamboo is very fast-growing and needs no pesticides, unlike cotton. Ramie yarn comes from the nettle plant family, and the fibre has a lovely lustrous texture.

Manmade and synthetic fibres

The major difference between these fibres is that one starts from a natural product and 'man' makes it into a fibre, whereas the other is totally synthetic. Many manmade fibres, such as viscose and rayon, are derived from material such as wood pulp. On the other hand, synthetic fibres, such as acrylic and nylon, are often petro-chemical derivatives and basically consist of a very fine thread of a plastic-like substance. Names such as 'acrylic' and 'nylon' are generic names that relate to the type of fibre, but each manufacturer will give their fibre its own brand name, such as Lycra®. Manmade and synthetic fibres can be soft or coarse, economic or expensive, cool or warm, thick or thin – they can be virtually anything that the manufacturer chooses! These yarns are generally strong and hard-wearing, and are often combined with a natural fibre to create a more versatile yarn than the natural fibre alone could produce.

Mohair This yarn comes from the hair of the angora goat. It is very fluffy, but, as the mohair fibres are quite long, it is a very different fluff from an angora or wool fluff. Mohair yarns generally consist of a fine core of yarn with long fluffy fibres extending from the core. To show off the fibres to their best effect, mohair yarns are best worked very loosely – the central core creates a mesh and the loose fibres fill out the holes.

Silk As with silk fabrics, there are many different qualities of silk yarns. The smoother yarns have a wonderful sheen and lustre. However, one thing that they all have in common is that, as silk fibre takes dye very well, the colours will generally be clear and strong. This natural fibre can be delicate and needs to be looked after carefully. It has little elasticity so the finished item can sag.

Wool Wool is perhaps the classic yarn. There are many different types of wool and many different treatments that it can be given. Lambswool is the softest type and gets its name from the fact that it is the first sheared wool taken from a lamb. The fibres are particularly soft as one end of each fibre is not cut, but is the naturally soft, rounded end the lamb was born with. The quality of wool is also dictated by the breed of sheep it comes from: manufacturers now sell woollen yarns made from specific breeds of sheep, such as Herdwick and Jacob. Merino wool is often considered the Rolls-Royce of wools, as it is very smooth, sleek and soft, making it the perfect choice for a good yarn. It is also widely available and good value for money. Once the wool has been sheared from the sheep, it can be given all sorts of treatments to change its appearance and the way that it behaves as a yarn. Most untreated woollen yarns need to be washed very gently to stop the fibres matting together, or felting, and to stop the yarn shrinking.

Easy-care wool

In today's easy-care society, you will generally find that woollen yarns have been treated during their manufacture to stop them shrinking and to allow them to be machine-washed. There are now even felted wool yarns available! These have been especially treated to give a felted, or 'washed and well-worn', appearance that will stay exactly as it is without shrinking or felting further.

These four GLORIOUS GLAMOUR SCARVES are crocheted to the same pattern. However the different types of yarn used for the four variations (tweedy yarn, cashmere blend, silk and super kid mohair) show just how significantly your choice of texture and fibre for a yarn can affect the look of the finished item.

techniques

Basic stitches

Unlike when knitting, crochet only ever has one stitch in work at any time, making it far easier not to drop stitches! Each stitch is made by forming a loop of yarn and drawing this loop through existing loops. In this section, we look at the basics of holding the hook and the yarn, and introduce the most commonly used crochet stitches. When you are learning the basic stitches, it is a good idea to use a classic yarn – a DK wool yarn, for example. The yarn is smooth, so will be easy to handle, and you will be able to see each stitch clearly as you form it.

Holding the hook and the yarn

Before you can make any crochet stitches, you need to know how to hold the yarn and the hook.

The traditional way is to hold the hook in the right hand and the yarn in the left hand. However, many crocheters who also knit find it easier to hold the yarn in their right hand too, leaving just the work and the working loop to be held in their left hand. There is no right or wrong way; just find the way **you** feel most comfortable with!

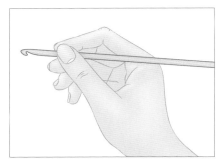

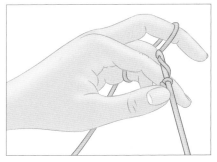

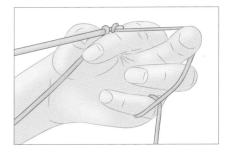

The traditional technique is to hold the hook as though it were a pen, gripping it between your thumb and first finger just near the actual hook section – the same way as you would hold a knitting needle.

The traditional method to work is by holding the yarn and the base of the working loop in your left hand. Start by gripping the base of the starting slipknot underneath the hook and between the thumb and first finger of your left hand. Leave the cut end of the yarn to dangle free and take the ball end over your fingers, wrapping it round your little finger.

To make each stitch, you either twist the hook clockwise around the yarn, or loop the yarn over the hook to wrap the yarn around the hook, ready for the next stitch. Extend your middle finger to regulate the flow of the yarn, taking care not to pull the yarn too tightly.

The starting loop or slipknot

Before you begin, you will need to make your first stitch. This will form the basis for all the following stitches.

Make a loop near the cut end of the yarn and insert the crochet hook into the loop, picking up the end of the yarn leading to the ball.

Draw this new loop of yarn through the existing loop, and gently pull on the cut end to tighten this new loop around the hook. This is your first stitch.

Make this now!

This classic cardigan is given a new twist when decorated with pretty flowers and leaves. Simply made using a combination of double crochet and chain stitches, the clever denim yarn makes the cardigan both sporty and casual while remaining feminine. The flower and leaf decoration is applied afterwards, so you can add as many or as few pieces as you want.

The **FLOWER-TRIMMED CARDIGAN** is made in a DK-weight denim yarn (which will fade in colour just like real denim fabric when you launder it), while the flowers and leaves are made in 4ply cotton. The main body of the cardigan is made with a 4.00mm (G6) hook, while the border is made with a 3.50mm (E4) hook and the trimmings with a 2.50mm (C2) hook. See pages 137–139 for the pattern.

Chain
(abbreviation = ch)
Almost all crochet items start with a length of chain stitches, and they also often appear within stitch patterns. Wherever the chain is required, it is made in the same way.

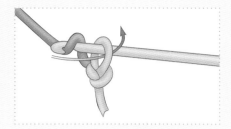

To make a chain stitch, take the yarn over the hook, wrapping it from the back, up over the hook towards the front, and then down and under the hook (every time the yarn is taken over the hook it should be done in this way). Now draw this new loop of yarn through the loop on the hook to complete the chain stitch.

Double crochet
(abbreviation = dc)
A double crochet stitch is one of the most commonly used and easiest crochet stitches to make.

To make a double crochet, start by inserting the hook into the work at the required point. Take the yarn over the hook and draw this new loop of yarn through the loop on the hook – there are now 2 loops on the hook.

Take the yarn over the hook again and draw this new loop through **both** the loops on the hook. This completes the double crochet stitch.

Treble
(abbreviation = tr)
This is the other most commonly used crochet stitch: while a double crochet stitch is a very short, compact stitch, a treble stitch is taller and will add more height to the work.

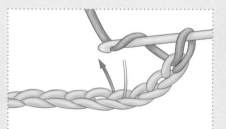

To make a treble, wrap the yarn around the hook **before** inserting it into the work.

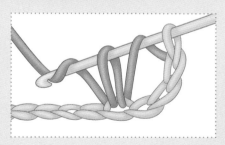

Wrap the yarn around the hook again and draw this loop through the work – there are now 3 loops on the hook. Wrap the yarn around the hook once more and draw this new loop through just the first 2 loops on the hook – the original loop and this new loop.

Wrap the yarn around the hook again and draw this new loop through both loops on the hook to complete the treble stitch.

Half treble
(abbreviation = htr)
A half treble stitch is a variation of a treble; its height is halfway between that of a double crochet and a treble stitch.

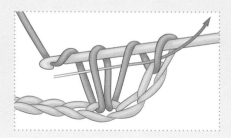

To make a half treble, start in exactly the way a treble is made until there are 3 loops on the hook. Wrap the yarn around the hook once more and draw this new loop through **all 3** loops on the hook to complete the half treble stitch.

Double treble

(abbreviation = dtr)

Another variation of a treble is the double treble stitch. This gets its name from the fact that the yarn is wrapped twice around the hook before it is inserted into the work.

To make a double treble stitch, start by wrapping the yarn around the hook **twice** before inserting it into the work.

There are now 3 loops on the hook. Wrap the yarn around the hook again and draw this new loop through the first 2 loops on the hook, leaving just 2 loops on the hook.

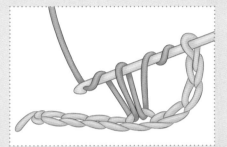

Wrap the yarn around the hook again and draw this new loop through the work. There are now 4 loops on the hook. Take the yarn around the hook once more and draw this new loop through just the **first 2** loops on the hook.

To complete the double treble stitch, wrap the yarn around the hook once more and draw this new loop through both the remaining loops on the hook.

Taller treble variations

Triple treble (abbreviation = ttr)
Quadruple treble (abbreviation = qtr)

A double treble is formed by wrapping the yarn around the hook twice before it is inserted into the work, and taller treble variations can be made by wrapping the yarn around the hook more times before inserting it into the work.

For a triple treble, wrap the yarn around the hook 3 times before inserting it. For a quadruple treble, wrap it round the hook 4 times.

However many times the yarn is wrapped round the hook, the stitch is completed in the same way: insert the hook into the work, wrap the yarn around the hook and draw the new loop through. Now complete the stitch by wrapping the yarn

around the hook and drawing the new loop through just the first 2 loops on the hook. Repeat this last process until there is only one loop left on the hook. The stitch is now completed.

Slip stitch

(abbreviation = ss)

This stitch adds virtually no height to the work and is generally used either to move the hook and working loop to a new point, or to join pieces.

To make a slip stitch, insert the hook into the work at the required point. Take the yarn over the hook and draw this new loop through **both** the work **and** the loop on the hook to complete the slip stitch.

Placing the crochet stitches

Although different effects can be created in crochet by working the different crochet stitches, you can also vary the fabric that each stitch forms by varying exactly where each stitch is placed in relation to the previous stitches. It is most common to work stitches into the top of stitches on the row below. However, it is also possible to work between existing stitches, or to work into chain spaces. We examine the various possibilities over the next few pages.

Working into the top of stitches

This is the most common position for the new stitches to be worked and, unless a pattern states otherwise, this is how all stitches should be placed.

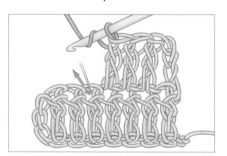

Across the top of crochet stitches there is a 'V' shape, formed by two bars of yarn. To work into the top of the existing stitches to make the new ones, insert the hook through the work by sliding it from front to back under this 'V'. Working stitches in this way encloses the whole of the 'V' in the new stitch.

Working into a foundation chain

The foundation chain is the name given to the string of chain stitches that will form the base, or foundation, for the rest of the crochet. Each chain stitch consists of 3 bars of yarn – 2 forming a 'V' and a third running across the back of the work.

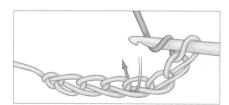

When working into a foundation chain – or any chain stitch – it is best to insert the hook through the middle of the stitch. Insert it

from above and from front to back between the 2 bars creating the 'V', keeping the hook in front of the third bar underneath the 'V'. Working stitches in this way encloses 2 of the 3 strands making up each chain stitch, leaving just the front bar of the 'V' free.

Working into one loop only

Working into just one of the two bars that form the 'V' of the previous stitches can create yet more effects.

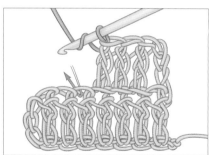

To work into the **back loop only** of the previous stitches, slide the hook through the work between the 2 bars forming the 'V', picking up just the back loop.

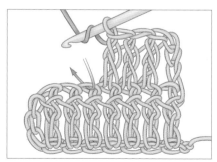

To work into the **front loop only** of the previous stitches, slide the hook through the work underneath just the front bar forming the 'V', bringing it up in front of the back loop.

Working in this way encloses just one bar of the existing stitch in the new one. If a row of stitches is worked in this way, the remaining 'free' bar of the 'V' will form a line across the work. This line of threads can be used to create a particular effect. It will also tend to make the work 'fold' along that line, making it a useful tool when working three-dimensional items.

Working between stitches

Sometimes the new stitches of the crochet are not placed on top of the previous stitches but worked between them. This creates a more lacy effect to what would otherwise be a very solid fabric. When working with fancy textured yarns, this can be a simple way to place the stitches as it is easy to see where to insert the hook.

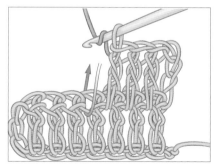

To work a new stitch between the previous stitches, simply insert the hook through the work, from front to back, between the stems of the 2 existing stitches. Although this method can be used with any type of stitch, it is much easier to work in this way when the existing stitches are tall stitches, such as trebles, where the stems of the stitches are quite long and obvious.

Working into chain spaces

Some fancy stitch patterns are made up of a combination of different types of stitches and little strings of chain stitches, known as chain spaces (abbreviated to 'ch sp').

To work a stitch into a chain space, simply insert the hook through the work through the hole below the string of chain stitches, inserting it from front to back. Working stitches into a chain space will enclose the whole of the chain stitches in the base of the new stitches.

crochet craft

Sometimes a design that is made up of lots of chain spaces will NOT have the next batch of stitches actually worked into the chain space, but into one of the chain stitches that makes up this chain space. This is likely to be the case for clusters, puffs and bobbles where the base of the stitch needs to be kept tight and narrow – to work into the chain space would allow the base of the stitches to fan out and would not create the desired effect. Ensure you read the pattern carefully and work the stitches above a chain space in the correct way.

Make this now!

This stunning throw is simply worked in blocks of glorious colours of fancy textured yarns. This type of yarn can be difficult to crochet with, as it is not that easy to see the tops of the existing stitches. However, this fabric is simply made up of trebles worked between the trebles of the previous rows.

RAINBOW RIBBON THROW is made in a selection of four vibrantly coloured yarns. Two of the yarns are 90% merino and 10% nylon; one is 50% wool and 50% cotton; and the fourth yarn is 50% cotton, 40% rayon and 10% nylon. The varieties of fibre create a throw with a wonderfully rich and diverse texture, and the yarns are hand-dyed so no two hanks are the same. These are chunky yarns that work up quickly on a 6.00mm (J10) hook. See pages 150–151 for pattern.

Combining stitch placements

Many crochet fabrics will not place all the stitches in exactly the same way, and it is often this variation in the way the stitches are placed that will create the different textures. It is therefore vitally important that you read the pattern and place the stitches exactly as stated in the pattern. If they are not placed correctly, you will have serious problems matching the required row **and** stitch tension for that particular design.

Although the widths of the stitches will probably remain the same, their heights will more than likely vary as different placements of stitches will alter their heights. A treble placed between stitches of a previous row will add less height than if it were worked into the top of a stitch. Similarly, if it is worked into just one of the 2 loops, more height may be created as the base stitch will 'stretch', adding to the treble's height. This variation in height may not be that apparent over one or two rows, but it will become far more obvious as more rows are worked, making it very difficult to achieve the correct row tension for a design.

Make this now!

This beautifully feminine, lacy scarf will add some glamour to your wardrobe. One version is shown here, but we offer four alternatives on page 119. The scarves are crocheted to the same pattern, but the different types of yarn used for the four variations show just how significantly choice of texture and fibre for a yarn can affect the look of the finished garment.

GLORIOUS GLAMOUR SCARF is shown here in a tweed yarn. This has a felted effect, and is made from merino wool, alpaca and viscose. The scarf was made with a 3.50mm (E4) hook for the DK-weight yarn. See page 119 for pattern.

Making crochet fabrics

Once you have learnt how to make the various crochet stitches and how they should be placed, you can start to make crochet fabrics. As crochet only ever has one stitch actually in work at any one time, it is easy to join the stitches together either in rows, to make a flat sheet of crochet, or to work the stitches in rounds, to make flat disks of crochets (like the traditional doily) or to create 'tubes' of crochet fabric – like the sleeve of a garment, for example. Crochet is a truly versatile craft!

Working in rows

Working in rows consists of piling lots of rows, or strings, of stitches on top of previous rows or strings of crochet.

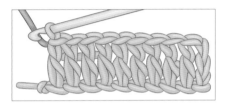

A flat piece of crochet will be formed by making a foundation chain and then working back along this chain. The stitches worked into the foundation chain form the first row.

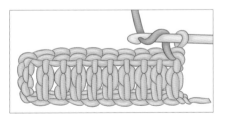

Once this first row is complete, the second row can be worked. But, as almost all crochet stitches are worked from the right

crochet craft

At the end of each row of a pattern, it will say 'turn' so you are ready to work the next row. To turn the work, you do exactly that – turn the work around so that the side that was away from you now faces you and the hook is now at the right-hand side of the work, not the left.

towards the left, the fabric needs to be turned at the end of each row so that you can work back across the stitches just made to form the next row.

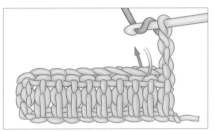

The working loop for any piece of crochet sits at the top of the stitches. Therefore, to start the next row of crochet you need to raise the hook and working loop up to the required point. This is done by working what is called a turning chain. The length of this turning chain will vary depending on the type of stitch being worked. Below is a guide to the length of the turning chain equivalent to the most commonly used crochet stitches.

stitch	length of turning chain
double crochet	1 ch
half treble	2 ch
treble	3 ch
double treble	4 ch

Sometimes the turning chain will be there to replace the first stitch of the new row, and sometimes it will simply be used to raise the hook to the right place. Most crochet patterns will tell you which is the case for this particular row.

If the turning chain counts as the first stitch of the new row, the first 'real' stitch of this row that you work will effectively be the second stitch. To ensure this stitch is placed

correctly, you need to miss the stitch sitting at the base of the turning chain and work it into the next stitch.

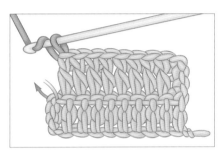

If the turning chain does count as the first stitch of a row, it is vitally important that you work into this 'stitch' at the end of the next row! If you do not work into the top of this length of chain, you will accidentally decrease a stitch and your crochet fabric will be spoilt.

Take care, as sometimes the length of chain at the beginning of a row will be there to replace more than just the first stitch of this new row – but this should be detailed in the pattern!

Fastening off

Once the last stitch of the last row or round of a piece of crochet has been completed, there will still be the one working loop, or stitch, on the hook. To complete the work, this stitch needs to be fastened off.

To fasten off the work, cut the yarn and simply draw this cut end of yarn through the loop on the hook. Pull gently on the yarn end to tighten the stitch so that it does not unravel.

Working in rounds

Due to the way a crochet fabric is formed, it can also be made in rounds to create flat disks or three-dimensional tubes. Working rounds of crochet is a quick way to make items as it can avoid the need to sew seams afterwards.

To start a piece, you will need to join the ends of the foundation chain to make it into a ring. This is generally done by making the required number of chain and then working a slip stitch into the first of these chain stitches. Take care not to twist the chain when joining the ends, as this could distort the work.

The first round of crochet can either be worked into the centre of this ring as though it were a chain space (as will generally be the case with flat disks of crochet), or into the chain stitches themselves as you would normally do with a foundation chain (as will generally be the case with tubes of crochet).

At the end of the first round of any crochet piece, the first and last stitches need to be joined together to complete the circle. This is usually done by working a slip stitch into the top of the first stitch – but consult your pattern to be sure, as this can vary for fancy stitch patterns.

To make the second and every following round of crochet, the hook must, as when working in rows, be raised up to the height of the new stitches. So each new round of crochet will start with a turning chain, exactly as when working in rows.

crochet craft

If you are working into the centre of a ring, it is quite likely there will be more stitches to work than it would appear will fit in! As you work the stitches, gently ease them along the chain so that they all sit neatly next to each other.

To turn or not to turn

Crochet stitches look different on one side from how they appear on the other side. So, when working rounds of crochet, you can create more types of fabrics by choosing to either turn or not turn the work at the end of each round.

If the work is turned at the beginning of each new round of crochet, the resulting fabric will look exactly like one made using rows of crochet. Therefore, if an item combines sections made in rows **and** in rounds, this is the best way to work to ensure that all sections match. Generally, crochet fabrics made where the work is turned before beginning each new row or round will look exactly the same on both sides of the fabric.

If the work is not turned at the beginning of each new round, the fabric created will be totally different on one side from on the other side – and totally different again to one made where the work has been turned! To make sure your crochet looks as it should, take care to read the pattern and check whether you should turn the work or not at the end of each round.

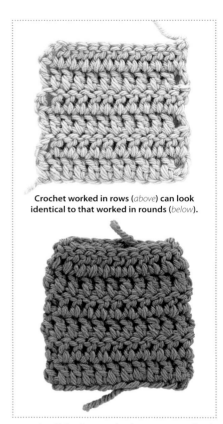

Crochet worked in rows (*above*) can look identical to that worked in rounds (*below*).

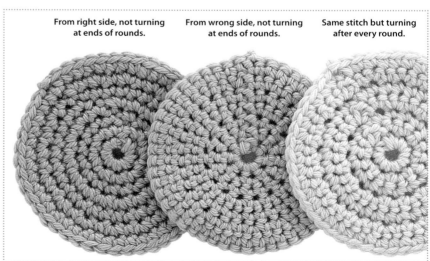

From right side, not turning at ends of rounds.

From wrong side, not turning at ends of rounds.

Same stitch but turning after every round.

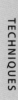

Make these now!

This hat, bag and belt set all use the same stitch pattern – but the hat and the bag have been worked in rounds, while the belt was worked just in rows. To make sure that the stitches look the same on all three pieces, the work was turned at the beginning of each round.

SEASIDE AND SHELLS SET is made in an ocean-blue 4ply mercerized cotton. The mercerization process helps the cotton to take the dye, so such yarns have a particularly strong depth of colour. All the pieces in the set are made to the same tension, using a 2.50mm (C2) hook. See pages 127–129 for pattern.

Tension

The size of crochet stitches is described as the 'tension' they are worked to. In a crochet pattern, tension is usually expressed as the number of stitches and rows that measure a certain amount – generally 10cm (4in). For example, the pattern might tell you that you need 10 stitches and 14 rows of double crochet to make a 10cm (4in) square. It is vitally important when crocheting any item that you achieve the exact tension stated. If your tension does not match that stated, your final item will not look like the guide picture and will not be the correct size.

Effects of incorrect tension

To ensure success, you **must** check your tension before you begin every project! If your tension is out, you will face several problems:

- The resulting crochet fabric will not feel the way it should.
- The tension of the crochet governs the size of the finished item; if the tension is incorrect, the item will not fit as it should.
- The tension will affect the amount of yarn required. If your tension is tight, you could have yarn left over; if your tension is loose, you may require additional yarn.

Making a tension swatch

Before starting to crochet any item, take time to check your tension by making a tension swatch.

1 To make a tension swatch, look at the pattern and find out what hook size you need to use and what stitch pattern the tension is measured over.

2 Once you have sorted out what stitch and hook to use, make the tension swatch. Although the tension will normally be given as a number of stitches and rows to 10cm (4in), it is best to make the tension swatch larger than this – ideally, your tension swatch should be about 12–15cm (5–6in) square.

3 Calculate the number of stitches you will need: for a tension swatch 15cm (6in) wide you will need one and a half times the number of stitches stated if the tension is measured over 10cm (4in).

4 Make your foundation chain the length required, adjusting the number of chain to fit in with any pattern repeat, and then work the stated stitch pattern until you have a square of crochet. Fasten off the work but do NOT press it.

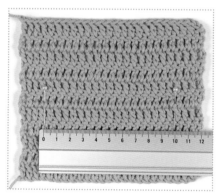

Measuring the tension

Once your tension swatch is complete, lay it flat and mark out, with pins, the number of stitches stated for the tension. Now measure the distance between these pins. If this measurement is the same as stated for the tension, you are crocheting to the correct tension.

If the distance between the pins is less than stated in the tension, your crochet is too tight. Change to a larger size (thicker) hook and make another swatch.

If the distance between the pins is larger than the tension states, your crochet is too loose. Change to a smaller size (thinner) hook and try again.

Continue making swatches until you achieve the correct number of stitches to match the tension.

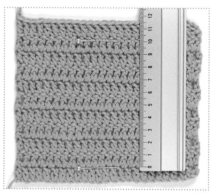

Checking rows

Once you have made a swatch that has the correct number of stitches to match the tension, check you are achieving the correct number of rows. In the same way as before, mark out the number of rows stated and measure the distance between these pins. Generally, if the number of stitches is correct, the number of rows will be too – but you do need to check.

crochet craft

Occasionally you may find you cannot exactly match both the number of stitches **and** the number of rows. If this is the case, try working one row (or round) with one size hook and the next row (or round) with a size larger (or smaller) hook.

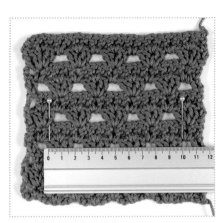

Fancy stitch pattern

When the item is made in a fancy stitch pattern, the tension will often be expressed as a number of pattern repeats, not stitches, to a measurement. If this is the case, make the tension swatch with at least 2 more pattern repeats than stated for the tension. Once the swatch is made, measure the tension as before, but now count the number of pattern repeats, not stitches or rows.

Motif tension

If an item is made up of lots of motifs, the tension section will often give you the size that one motif should be.

To check the tension, make one motif and check its size. If it matches that stated, then your tension is correct. If too big, start again with a smaller hook. If too small, make another with a larger size hook.

Circular disks

Flat items made in the round and large circular motifs often have their tension expressed as the size of the first few rounds. If so, work the stated number of rounds and then measure their diameter.

crochet craft

Crochet 'shrinks' the larger the piece you work, so the tension of a swatch may be different from that of a large piece. Always double-check your tension while working the large pieces to ensure they are the correct size.

Make these now!

These cute toy bunnies show just how much tension can affect the size of the finished item. Each bunny is worked to the same pattern – it is just the yarn and the hook size, and therefore the tension, that has changed.

MISS PINK is worked in an aran-weight yarn with a 3.5mm (E4) hook.
MR GREY is in a classic DK-weight yarn with a 3.00mm (D3) hook.
SPARKLES is in a glittery lurex 4ply with a 2.50mm (C2) hook. FLUFFY is in a very fine kid mohair yarn with a 1.75mm (5) hook. See pages 104–106 for pattern.

Combination stitches

The basic crochet stitches can be combined to form groups of stitches that create different effects. They can add texture to a plain base, or simply add visual interest to the work.

The types and quantities of stitches used for these combinations will vary depending on the effect required – but the abbreviation used within the pattern may be the same as that used for a similar stitch group in another pattern. However, the abbreviations section of the pattern should clearly explain how each of these stitch groups should be made for this design.

Shells

The finished appearance of this stitch group is exactly as its name suggests – it looks like a shell. Shells look most effective when worked in the longer crochet stitches, such as trebles and double trebles. A shell does not add any extra surface interest to the crochet fabric but, if worked along an edge, will create a scalloped effect.

Shells are formed by working lots of the same type of stitch into one point. This point is usually a stitch, rather than a chain space, as the shell effect is created by all the stitches fanning out from one point.

To work a shell, simply work the required number of stitches into the same place.

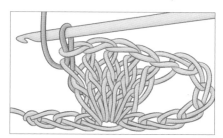

This sample shows a shell fabric with a shell edging added afterwards in a contrast colour. One row of the fabric has also been worked in the contrast colour to show how each shell 'sits' neatly on top of the previous row of shells.

Clusters

Clusters are basically the reverse of a shell. For a cluster, lots of stitches are worked into lots of points but all these stitches are joined at the top, creating a shell-like effect that fans out downwards, not upwards. Again, they are best worked using the longer crochet stitches.

To make a treble cluster, work each treble into the relevant point until just before it is completed – to the point where the last 'yarn over hook and draw through last 2 loops' is about to be made. Make all the necessary trebles that will form this cluster in this way – you will have the original loop on the hook plus one extra loop for each treble that has been nearly completed.

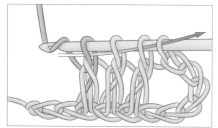

To close the top of the cluster, take the yarn over the hook and draw this new loop through all the loops on the hook. The finished cluster has one stitch at the top point.

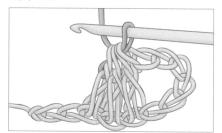

Bobbles

Bobbles are a combination of a shell and a cluster. They are worked in virtually the same way as a cluster, but all the stitches that form the bobble are worked into the same point, as for a shell.

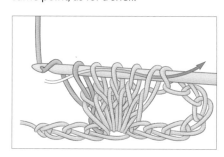

Bobble stitches will add texture to the surface of the work. As the stitches that make up the bobble are often longer than those of the surrounding crochet fabric, and many stitches are squeezed into one place, the group of stitches will stand proud of the work, thereby causing a small, protruding bobble.

Sometimes a bobble will be secured at the top by a chain stitch. This closes the top of the bobble, holding all the stitches securely together. Always check the abbreviation section of the pattern to find out whether this is the case for the bobble you are working.

Puff stitches

A puff stitch is basically a bobble worked using half treble stitches. Because of the way a half treble stitch is made, the resulting 'bobble' consists of lots of strands of yarn lying next to each other, rather than separate stitches.

To make a puff stitch, make each stitch to the point where the new loop of yarn has been drawn through the base position for the stitch. To accentuate the effect, the pattern will often specify that each new loop drawn through the base stitch should be pulled up taller than it would normally.

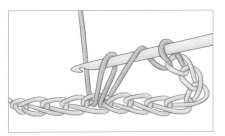

Once the required number of half-worked half treble stitches have been made, complete all the stitches by taking the yarn over the hook and pulling this new loop through all the loops on the hook.

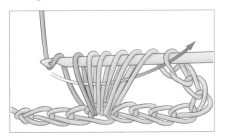

As with bobbles and popcorns, there may be a chain stitch worked at the end of each puff stitch to close the top. Check the abbreviation to see if this is the case.

Popcorns

These stitch combinations are similar to a shell but, because of the way the 'shell' is drawn together at the top, they create added surface texture.

To make a popcorn, work the first part of the stitch combination in the same way as if working a shell, by working a group of stitches all into one point. Now take the hook out of the working loop. Insert the hook through the top of the first stitch that makes up this group and then back into the working loop.

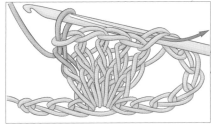

Take the yarn over the hook and pull this new loop through both the working loop and the first stitch of the group. This completes the popcorn.

A completed popcorn forms a tiny 'bell' of stitches that sits away from the surface of the work.

PICTURE-PERFECT CUSHION COVERS, below, in plum, soft green, gold and taupe, are worked in classic DK-weight yarn with a 3.50mm (E4) hook. See pages 152–155 for patterns.

Make these now!

These aran-effect cushion covers show exactly how much extra texture can be added to a simple double crochet fabric. The trellis effect is created by travelling lines of relief treble stitches; each diamond has a bobble sitting inside it. The flower heads of the panelled cushion covers are formed by popcorns; simple loops of chains create the leaves and stems. The textured border is again created by relief stitches, with added interest created by the bobbles that sit next to the zig-zag lines.

Relief stitches

Extra surface texture can be created by working what are called 'relief' stitches. These stitches do exactly what their name suggests: they add extra surface relief, or texture, to the work. They are sometimes also known as 'raised' stitches. You can use these to create fascinating patterns, including ones that look like basketweave and ones that look like ribbing. Almost any type of stitch can be worked as a relief stitch but, as there needs to be a 'stem' of a stitch to work around, they are generally only worked as treble stitches.

Working relief stitches

Relief stitches can be worked from either the front of the crochet or the back. The abbreviation normally used for a relief stitch is a combination of the type of basic stitch being worked, the fact that it is a relief stitch and the side from which the hook is inserted. For example, a relief front treble stitch is often abbreviated to 'rftr' – a combination of 'r' (meaning a relief stitch), 'f' (meaning it is worked from the front) and 'tr' (as it is a treble stitch that is worked).

   The actual stitch being worked is made in exactly the same way as that type of stitch would normally be worked – it is just how the hook is inserted through the work that changes. Instead of the stitch being worked into another stitch or a space, it is worked around the stem of one of the previous stitches.

Working a relief back treble

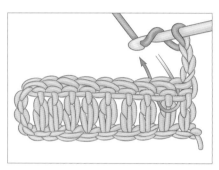

To make a relief back treble, start by taking the yarn around the hook as you would to start any treble stitch. Once the yarn is wrapped around the hook, insert the hook through the work, from the back, just to the right of the stem of the stitch this relief stitch is to be worked around. Return the hook to the back of the work just to the left of the stem of this stitch. The hook is inserted from the back of the work, and from the right to the left around the stem of the stitch.

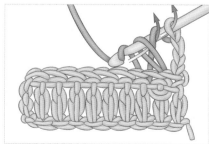

Take the yarn around the hook and draw this new loop through the work so that there are 3 loops on the hook. Complete the treble stitch in the usual way. A relief back treble leaves the whole of the top section of the stitch it is worked around visible on the front of the work.

Working a relief front treble

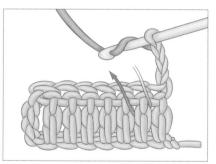

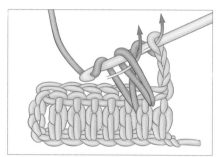

Take the yarn around the hook and draw this new loop through the work, behind the stem of the stitch. There are now 3 loops on the hook.

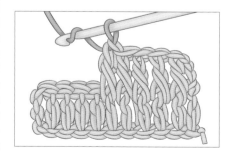

To make a relief front treble, start by taking the yarn around the hook as you would to start any treble stitch. Once the yarn is wrapped around the hook, insert the hook through the work, from the front, just to the right of the stem of the stitch this relief stitch is to be worked around. Bring the hook back through to the front of the work just to the left of the stem of this stitch. The hook is inserted from the front of the work, and from the right to the left under the stem of the stitch.

Complete the treble stitch in the usual way. A relief front treble leaves the whole of the top section of the stitch it is worked around visible on the back of the work.

Preparing to work relief stitches

As there needs to be a stem to any stitch that a relief stitch is worked around, it is really only successfully worked onto a base of stitches no shorter than half treble stitches. This allows there to be sufficient room and definition between the stitches to accurately place and work the relief stitch.

Generally, stitch patterns made up of relief treble stitches will start with a foundation row of simple half treble stitches. Once the stitches of the relief stitch pattern are worked, these base stitches become virtually invisible so do not detract from the finished effect.

Turning chains for relief stitch patterns

A relief stitch is not as tall as this type of stitch would normally be; some of the height of this new stitch is lost as its base is placed below the top of the previous row. It is therefore necessary to reduce the length of the turning chain required so that the edges of the crochet remain the same length as the body of the work.

Generally, the turning chain required in a relief stitch pattern will be one chain shorter than would normally be required for the type of stitch being worked. For example, normally a treble fabric would start with a turning chain of 3 ch (to count as the first treble), but when working a relief treble fabric the turning chain is reduced to 2 ch (to count as the first stitch).

crochet craft

When ending a row of relief stitches, take care that you work the last stitch around the turning chain at the beginning of the previous row so that the whole row remains the correct height. Although this stitch is a relief stitch, the effect created on this end stitch will not be as apparent as on the rest of the work.

Creating relief stitch patterns

Relief front and back stitches can be combined both with themselves and with all sorts of non-relief stitches to create a myriad of fancy stitch patterns.

Working a relief stitch leaves the whole of the top section of the previous stitch sitting on one side of the work so, to create a 'bar' of relief stitches sitting on one side of the work, the type of relief stitch must be alternated on every row. If the stitch is a relief **front** stitch on a right-side row, it needs to be worked as a relief **back** stitch on the following wrong-side row so that the top section of the stitch it is worked around always remains on the same side of the work.

If a relief stitch is worked on a base of non-relief stitches, it needs to be worked as a longer stitch than those around it. If the base fabric is a treble fabric, working a relief treble stitch will not add sufficient height to the work and you will notice that, once numerous rows have been worked, this insufficiently tall line of stitches will pull and pucker the work. To prevent this happening, you should always work the relief stitch one 'height' of stitch greater than those around it. On a half treble fabric, work relief trebles; on treble fabric, work relief double trebles.

Make this now!

The basketweave effect on this cute child's coat has been created using alternating blocks of relief front and back trebles. This stitch pattern is simple to work, and the fabric created is totally reversible, so it doesn't matter if the wrong side of the work shows. The resulting fabric has the feel of a woven fabric, and is cosy, warm and hard-wearing.

AUTUMN COLOUR COAT is made in a multi-coloured marled 100% wool yarn that creates a tweedy effect with a lovely depth and richness of colour. Although this is only a DK-weight yarn, worked on a 4.00mm (G6) hook, the relief stitches form a thick, dense fabric. See pages 115–117 for pattern.

Creating rib effects

Simple lines of relief stitches can be left sitting on the surface of the work by replacing a stitch with a relief stitch.

These bars of stitches can be placed close to each other, to create vertical textured stripes, or one can be worked on its own, to divide one section from another or to create a natural line along which the work will fold. Working a bar of relief stitches in this way leaves the fabric quite flat on the wrong side, with just the relief stitches sitting proud on the surface of the right side of the work.

A more 'true' rib effect can be created by alternating relief front and back stitches across a row – as you would if knitting a rib fabric. This creates a fabric that is textured on both sides.

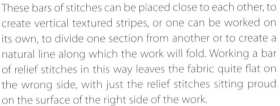

Creating woven effects

Working alternating blocks of relief front and back stitches will push the top of the previous stitches from one side of the work to the other. This line created by the tops of the previous stitches will form horizontal bars across the work, while the relief stitches themselves form vertical lines up the work on the other side.

Alternating blocks of relief front and back stitches will create alternating vertical and horizontal bands of texture on the surface of the work to give a woven effect that is totally reversible. It will also create a much thicker fabric than would normally be formed as there are, effectively, two layers of stitches sitting on top of each other. This means a much warmer, thicker and firmer fabric can be created with quite a fine yarn – but it also means that you will use much more yarn than you would normally.

Picots

Picots are little loops of chain stitches that are generally used to add interest to an edging or within an open lacy pattern. Picots are often used to trim garments; for example, adding a pretty edge to the neckline and the hem. A picot looks different on one side to how it looks on the other side, so try out both ways to find the look you prefer. If needs be, change the side the last row will be worked on to achieve the effect you want.

How to make a picot

A picot will sit on top of another stitch – so start by working up to the point where the picot is to be made.

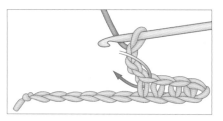

Make the required number of chain stitches for the picot. Usually picots consist of 3 ch – but check the abbreviations section to make sure this is correct for the design you are making.

To complete the picot, a stitch needs to be worked into the top of the last stitch worked before the little length of chain. To work this closing stitch, twist the hook back on itself and insert it down through the top of the last 'real' stitch worked. Picots can be closed with a slip stitch or a double crochet to create a tiny ring of chain stitches, and the effect created is slightly different. Completing a picot with a slip stitch keeps the ends of the chain tightly together, meaning it sits proud on the base stitch. Closing the picot with a double crochet increases the size of the tiny ring as the double crochet forms part of this ring. Check the pattern to ensure the correct closing stitch is worked.

Picots on edges

Picots can be used to create a pretty edging, either by working them at the same time as the foundation chain, or by adding them along the final row or round of the piece.

To add picots to a foundation-chain edge, simply replace the required chain stitch of the foundation chain with 1 ch and 1 picot. To ensure the edge remains the length it should be, it is best to close this type of picot with a slip stitch. When working back along the foundation ch, take care to work only into the foundation chain stitches and not those of the picot as well.

crochet craft

Take care when working into a picot that you actually insert the hook through the centre of the ring of chain stitches. If the picot consists of just 3 ch it can be quite tricky to find the centre.

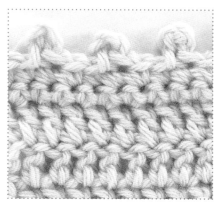

To add picots to any finished edge, simply work a picot at the required position. Working picots at regular intervals along an edge creates a classic edging that adds a pretty touch to an item – you will often find picots used to decorate the edges of baby clothes and lacy designs.

Working into a picot

As a picot is just a tiny loop of chain stitches, you work into the picot in the same way as when working into any chain space – simply insert the hook through the centre of the tiny loop and work the stitch so that the whole of the chain stitch is enclosed in the base of the new stitch.

Bullion stitches and clones knots

Crocheted bullion stitches look like bullion stitches (or large, long french knots) used in embroidery and are worked in a similar way. A clones knot is similar to both a picot and a bullion stitch – it starts with a length of chain and is formed by repeatedly wrapping the yarn around the hook. It is generally worked along a length of chain stitches, although it could be worked on any type of stitch.

Making a bullion stitch

To make a crocheted bullion stitch, start by wrapping the yarn around the hook as many times as specified in the pattern – usually anything between 7 and 10 times. Insert the hook into the work, take the yarn over the hook and draw this new loop through. Now take the yarn over the hook again and draw this new loop through **all**

the loops on the hook. This can be quite tricky; you may need to pick off each loop separately. Complete the bullion stitch by working one chain stitch to close it.

Working the chain stitch that closes the bullion stitch quite loosely will leave a wrapped bar of yarn in the work.

Working the chain stitch that closes the bullion stitch tightly will pull the ends of the wrapped bar together. This means that the resulting bullion stitch curls back on itself and forms a little looped knot on the work.

Making a clones knot

Start the clones knot in the same way as when making a picot, by making a short length of chain. *Wrap the yarn over the hook. Pass the hook under the length of chain, wrap the yarn around the hook again and bring the hook back up. Repeat from * as many times as required – usually 4 or 5 times, but your pattern should tell you exactly how many times. Now take the yarn over the hook again and draw this new loop through **all** the loops on the hook.

Carefully slide the wrapped thread towards the hook until the chain stitch at the start of the clones knot is visible, and complete the knot by working a slip stitch into this chain. The resulting knot forms a little ring of wrapped chain.

A clones knot adds an attractive loop of yarn to the edge of the crochet work.

Linked stitches

When you are making a fabric from tall crochet stitches, such as double trebles or one of the even taller stitches, you will notice that little vertical holes will appear between the stems of each stitch. If you wish to create a much more solid and densely packed fabric, it is possible to link the stitches together while they are being made. You can also use this method when you need to create vertical slits in a fabric, as explained below.

Making a linked stitch

A double treble stitch is started by wrapping the yarn around the hook twice before it is inserted into the work. When linking one double treble to the side of another double treble, these 'wrappings' are formed by drawing loops through the side of the previous stitch.

crochet craft

When working a series of linked stitches, try to make sure that you insert the hook through the side of each stitch in the same place. This will ensure that the look of the finished stitches is smooth and even. Also make sure you don't pull the yarn too tight as you make the 'wrappings', as this could cause the work to pucker and pull.

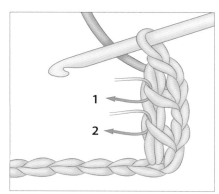

Start the linked stitch by inserting the hook through the side of the previous double treble near the top. Take the yarn over the hook and draw a loop through – this is your first wrap. Now insert the hook through the side of the same double treble again, but near the bottom. Take the yarn over the hook again and draw this loop through to create the second wrap of yarn around the hook.

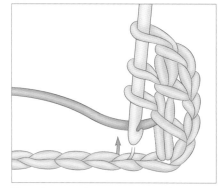

Now that you have your original working loop on the hook and the 2 wraps of yarn around the hook, the hook can be inserted into the work at the required position and the double treble can be completed in the usual way.

Making holes for ribbon

Rows of linked and unlinked double or triple trebles can be used in place of several rows of double crochet where vertical slits are required that are longer than the height of one row of double crochet. This is particularly useful if a wide ribbon is to be threaded through, as the yarn does not need to be repeatedly cut and rejoined as each section is worked backwards and forwards in rows between the slits. Here, 3 rows of double crochet have been replaced with one row of linked and unlinked triple trebles to leave the slits required for a wide ribbon.

Crossed stitches

When you are working with tall stitches, such as trebles, it is possible to cross them over each other in order to create a variety of different effects. These crossed stitches can either be totally separate from each other, or the second stitch can enclose the first stitch. You can create some interesting stitch patterns using this technique – try it out and see for yourself.

Separate crossed stitches

When working 2 double trebles that cross each other, but remain totally separate, it is a good idea to separate the 2 double trebles with one stitch to accentuate the cross. The completed cross will then sit on 3 base stitches and consist of 3 stitches.

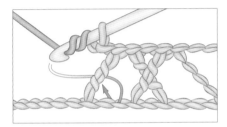

Start by working to the point where the cross is to fall. Miss the first 2 stitches across the base of the 3 stitches needed for the cross, and work a double treble into the next stitch. Work one chain stitch to separate the 2 crossed double trebles at the top.

Now work the second double treble that will complete the cross. Wrap the yarn around the hook twice, twist it back on itself and insert it into the first of the 2 missed stitches, passing it behind the previous double treble. Complete this double treble in the usual way to complete the cross. The stems of the 2 crossed double trebles remain totally separate, with one simply laying on top of the other.

Joined crossed stitches

To work 2 crossed stitches where the second stitch encloses the stem of the first stitch, it is really best to work with stitches no taller than a treble, as the stitches tend to cross near their base. With this type of crossed stitch, there is no real need to space them apart so the crossed stitches cover just 2 base stitches.

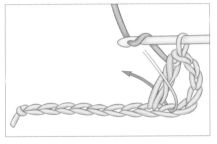

Start a pair of crossed trebles by missing one stitch at the base and working a treble into the next stitch. Then wrap the yarn around the hook and insert it into the missed stitch.

Draw the new loop through the work – the stem of the previous treble is now enclosed between the 2 loop strands of yarn at the front and 2 strands at the back. Take the yarn over the hook again and draw the new loop through the first 2 loops on the hook.

Complete the second treble by wrapping the yarn round the hook and pulling the new loop through both loops on the hook. The stem of the first treble is now firmly enclosed within the second treble.

crochet craft

As crossed stitches and branched stitches (see page 36) don't add as much height to the work as their simple versions, you may need to reduce the length of the turning chain needed. For crossed or branched double trebles, a turning chain of 3 ch (to count as first treble) is probably enough. Remember to replace the last stitch of the row with a correspondingly shorter stitch.

Branched stitches

Crossed stitches either enclose or sit on top of each other, and a similar effect can be created with taller stitches by working a branched stitch. The effect that these create can be a simple 'X', a 'Y', or an upside-down 'Y' shape. As the branched stitches need to have a definite stem in order to show the branches distinctly, they are most effective when based on double treble or taller stitches.

Making an X

In order to make the 'X' quite apparent, these are best worked over at least 3 base stitches so that the top and bottom branches are clearly visible.

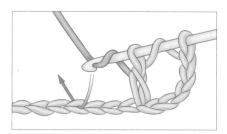

To make a branched X-shape of double trebles over 4 stitches, start by working half of the first double treble into the first base stitch. Wrap the yarn round the hook twice and insert the hook into the work.

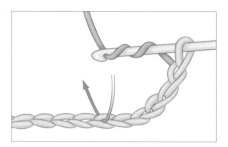

Wrap the yarn around the hook again and draw this new loop through, then wrap the yarn once more and draw this loop through the first 2 loops on the hook. There are now 3 loops on the hook. This completes the first lower branch of the X. Now start to work the other lower branch. Wrap the yarn around the hook again, miss 2 stitches and then insert the hook into the next (4th) stitch along.

Wrap the yarn around the hook and draw this new loop through the work. Take the yarn over the hook once more and draw this loop through the first 2 loops on the hook. There are now 4 loops on the hook. This completes the second lower branch of the X shape.

Now complete the first top branch of the X by repeating the (yarn over hook and draw through 2 loops) process until there is just one loop left on the hook. This completes the first upper branch of the X.

Before working the second upper branch, work 2 chain stitches to separate the upper branches. To make this last branch, wrap the yarn around the hook and insert it into the point where all 3 existing branches meet, picking up 2 strands of yarn.

Draw the new loop through the work and complete the stitch by repeating the (yarn over hook and draw through 2 loops) process until there is just one loop left on the hook. This completes the entire X.

Making an upside-down Y

An upside-down Y-shaped stitch needs to be worked over an odd number of stitches as there will be a branch only at the top.

To make the upside-down Y shape over 3 base stitches, start by working one chain. Now make the first 3 branches of an X shape, inserting the hook into the first and third stitches across the base. Complete the stitch by working one more chain stitch.

Fur stitch

A fur-like effect can be created in crochet by working lots of loops of yarn on a double crochet base. The fur, or loop, stitches leave a loop of yarn sitting on the back of the work, so they are usually worked on wrong-side rows.

Making a Y

As with an upside-down Y-shape, this needs to be worked over an odd number of stitches as there is only one branch at the base.

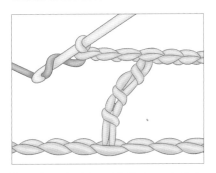

To make a double treble Y-shaped stitch over 5 base stitches, start by working a double treble into the third of the 5 base stitches. This will form the single lower branch and the first of the upper branches. Now work 3 chain stitches to separate the upper branches.

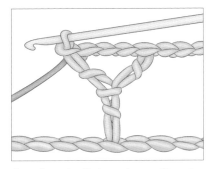

Complete the Y shape by working the third branch in the same way as for the final branch of an X-shaped stitch, inserting the hook through the work halfway down the existing double treble.

Making the fur stitch

As a fur stitch is a variation of double crochet, start with a base of double crochet stitches.

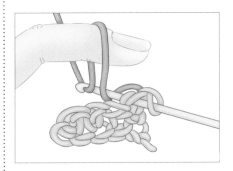

To make a fur stitch, insert the hook into the work. Wrap the yarn around the first finger of your left hand and draw this loop out to the required length – your pattern will tell you how long this should be. Pick up both of the strands of this loop with the crochet hook.

Draw both of these strands through the work. There are now 3 loops on the hook. Take the yarn over the hook again, as you would for any double crochet stitch.

Draw this new loop of yarn through all 3 loops on the hook to complete the stitch, leaving the loop of yarn on the back of the work. If the fur stitches are worked correctly, the loops on the back of the work will be quite secure. However, you may wish to gently tug on them to neaten up both them and the stitch.

Alternating right-side rows of double crochet stitches and wrong-side rows of fur stitches creates a densely packed fur effect. As the loops of the fur stitches are well secured, it is possible to snip these loops to create a really furry and fluffy fabric that is surprisingly hard-wearing.

Solomon's knots

A Solomon's knot is simply an elongated chain stitch that is secured with a double crochet. Each knot is made up of the 3 strands that form the elongated chain stitch and the double crochet stitch that secures it. When working into the knot, it is usual to work into just the double crochet securing it, leaving the elongated chain stitch free. This stitch creates a very light, open and airy fabric perfect for summer-weight accessories.

Start by elongating the working loop to the required length (your pattern will tell you how long this should be).

Take the yarn over the hook as though to make another chain stitch.

Now draw this loop through the elongated loop on the hook, leaving this loop the 'normal' size. There are now 3 strands of yarn running from the stitch on the hook back to the stitch at the base of the knot: the 2 original strands forming the first elongated loop and another strand at the back.

Insert the hook under this back strand of yarn and take the yarn over the hook again.

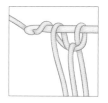

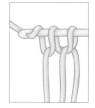

Draw this new loop through so that there are now 2 loops on the hook. Take the yarn over the hook again.

Draw this new loop through both of the loops that are on the hook to complete the Solomon's knot.

Make this now!

This lovely lacy wrap is made up of a simple mesh of Solomon's knots. The resulting fabric is gossamer-light and airy, making it perfect for cool summer evenings. And, as there are more holes than stitches, it's quick to make, too!

SOLOMON'S KNOT WRAP is worked in a drapy DK-weight pure silk yarn on a 4.00mm (G6) hook. This yarn has the wonderful lustre that is unique to silk. See page 123 for pattern.

Joining in new balls of yarn

Almost all crochet projects use more than one ball of yarn, so you are likely to need to join in a new ball of yarn at some stage. Ideally this should be done at the edges of the work. Simply complete one row with the old ball of yarn and start the new row with the new ball of yarn. Do NOT knot the yarn ends together as this knot could affect the texture of the finished work. Leave the two yarn ends free and darn them in once the work is completed. If the ends are left quite long, they can be used later to sew the seams.

Joining in new yarn

Sometimes it is not possible to join in new yarn at the edges of the work – especially with a circular piece of crochet as there are, quite simply, no edges!

If this is the case, simply change to the new ball of yarn at a point in the round where it will be most easy to darn the ends in, leaving both yarn ends hanging on the wrong side of the work. If a stitch pattern consists of lacy areas and solid areas, change to the new yarn within one of the solid areas as this will mean you have a solid area in which to darn in the ends.

If you are working in a solid stitch pattern (such as a simple double crochet fabric), it is possible to darn in the ends as the stitches are worked.

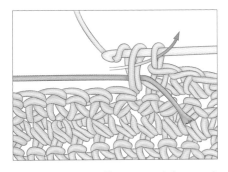

When you have sufficient yarn left to work only 6 or 7 more stitches using the existing ball of yarn, introduce the yarn from the new ball. Lay the new yarn across the top of the next stitches to be worked and work the last few stitches using the old ball of yarn, enclosing this new yarn in the stitches.

Once the new yarn end is well secured within the stitches, simply change to the yarn from the new ball. Lay the old yarn

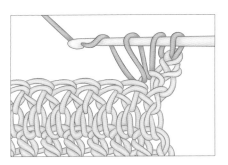

end across the top of the next set of stitches and work the next few stitches, enclosing the old yarn end in these stitches. Make sure both yarn ends come out of the stitches enclosing them on the wrong side of the work.

Once the next row or round has been completed, gently pull on the free yarn ends to secure the stitches where the old and new yarns meet, and cut off the two yarn ends. If worked correctly, the point where the two yarns meet should be virtually invisible on the right side of the work. The number of stitches you will need to work to safely and securely enclose the two yarn ends will depend on the type of yarn being used and how dense the crochet is but, as a general rule, enclosing the yarn ends in 5 or 6 stitches should be sufficient.

Rejoining yarn

Sometimes a pattern will require the work to be fastened off and the yarn rejoined at a different point along the top of a row or round.

To rejoin the yarn at a new point, insert the hook through the work at the required point. Wrap the yarn around the hook and draw this loop of yarn through the work.

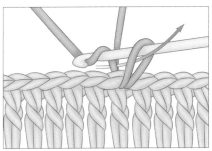

This loop becomes your new working loop. Make the required number of turning chain, remembering to use the yarn running to the ball, not the cut end, and continue across the row. Depending on the type of stitch being worked, the cut end can either be left free and darned in later or it can be laid across the top of the existing stitches and enclosed in the next few stitches.

crochet craft

When rejoining yarn, take care that you read the pattern to check exactly where the first new stitch needs to be placed. Depending on the stitch pattern being worked, the first 'real' stitch of this new section may also be worked into the stitch where you have rejoined the yarn. Working this first stitch in the wrong place will throw out of place the positioning of all future stitches.

Changing colour of yarn

Not all crochet items use just one colour of yarn, and care needs to be taken when joining in a new colour. The way in which crochet stitches are formed means that the last loop of one stitch actually sits on top of the next stitch, creating the 2 bars of yarn that form the 'V' across the top of this next stitch. It is therefore important to change to the new colour of yarn just before completing the last stitch in the old colour yarn.

How to change colours

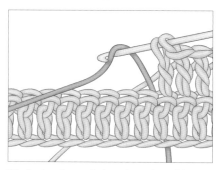

Work the last stitch using the old yarn colour up to the stage where the next 'step' to complete this stitch would be to wrap the yarn around the hook and draw this new loop through all the loops on the hook. For most types of stitch, this will be stopping at the point where there are only 2 loops on the hook. However, for some stitches, such as half trebles, there may be more loops on the hook. Let the old colour of yarn drop to the wrong side of the work and pick up the new colour of yarn, leaving the end of this new yarn on the wrong side of the work.

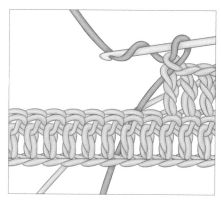

Wrap the new colour of yarn around the hook and complete the stitch using this yarn.

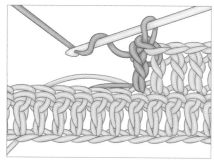

Now work the next stitches using the new colour of yarn. The two yarn ends left on the wrong side of the work can either be left free and darned in later, or they can be enclosed within the new stitches. As when joining in any new yarn, this will depend entirely on the type of stitch being worked, the thickness of the yarn and the types of yarn colours being used.

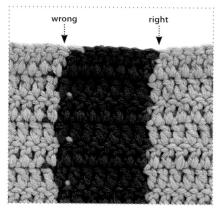

Changing the colour of yarn just before completing a stitch ensures that each complete stitch appears to be just one colour. Completing the last stitch in the old colour will create a broken-colour effect across the top of a row and can influence the positioning of any future stitches.

Working in stripes

When working in stripes, you will be changing yarn colour at the beginning of a new row or round.

Whether the turning chain at the beginning of the row or round counts as the first stitch of the new row, you should change to the new yarn to complete the last stitch of the previous row. Even if the turning chain does **NOT** count as a stitch, it will sit with the stitches of that row or round and should therefore be in the appropriate colour.

When working in rows of narrow stripes, the yarn not being used should be loosely carried up the side of the work from one stripe to the next. However, if the stripes are quite wide, it is best to cut the yarn once each stripe is completed and rejoin it for the next stripe. This avoids long strands of yarn 'floating' up the side of the work that may spoil the look of the finished item.

When working in rounds of narrow stripes, the yarn can still be loosely carried up the wrong side of the work from one stripe to the next. Make sure the yarn not being used is left free on the wrong side of the work at the end of each round so that the floats of yarn running between each stripe are not visible from the right side of the work.

If you are working in rows of stripes, try to make sure you work an even number of rows in each colour. This will mean that the yarn left for the next stripe will be at the right side of the work when you need to use it again. It also avoids the need to repeatedly cut and rejoin the yarn. Another way to avoid repeatedly rejoining yarn is

to work each first row of a stripe starting at the side of the work where that colour yarn has been left. However, this will mean that you will be working 2 rows in the same direction, so check that this will not affect the look of the work too much.

On the other hand, if you are working in rounds of stripes, each stripe can be made up of as many rows as you want. This is because the beginning and end point of every round is in the same place, regardless of whether you are turning the work or not before beginning each new round.

crochet craft

If you are stranding the yarn from one stripe to another, take great care not to pull the yarn too tight. If it is pulled too tight, this edge of your finished piece will be shorter than the other edge! The stranded yarn needs to be slightly longer than the edge it sits next to so that, in wear or use, this edge still has as much elasticity as the rest of the work.

Make these now!

Simple stripes of trebles are used to make this cute baby sweater and hat in fresh, cheerful colours. The sweater is worked in rows, while the hat has been worked in rounds. The stripes are fairly narrow, so it is quite possible to strand the yarn not being used up the side of the work from one stripe to the next.

SUNNY DAY STRIPES sweater and hat are worked in a 4ply-weight cotton yarn using a 2.50mm (C2) hook. This is a fine yarn, but the rows of trebles and simple construction make the sweater quick to make. See pages 107–109 for pattern.

Multi-coloured designs

It is possible to work designs in crochet that are similar to the Fair Isle or intarsia designs that appear in knitting. Instead of simple stripes, where each row or round is worked using just one colour, each row or round will have some stitches worked in one colour and other stitches worked in another colour. These designs can be as simple as patterns that feature single spots of a second colour, or they can be complicated multi-coloured designs, using several colours within one row or round.

Regardless of the quantity of stitches worked using each colour, the way the new colour is introduced will remain the same: it should be used to complete the last stage of the last stitch before the one to be worked in the new colour.

The crochet patterns for designs that feature rows or rounds worked in more than one colour can have this use of colour explained in two different ways: they are either written out within the pattern or shown on a chart.

Charted colourwork designs

If the colourwork design is fairly complicated, you will often find this is shown on a chart. This chart gives you a clear visual image of exactly what colours are used and where they sit in relation to the other stitches.

Charts for colourwork designs can be shown in two different ways: in colours that relate to those actually being used, or by using a different symbol for each different colour. Either way, the chart will consist of a grid of small squares. Each of the squares on this chart relates to one stitch on the crochet, with each row or round of the crochet being shown as a new row of squares. Within each square of the chart will be the colour or symbol that relates to the colour of yarn that should be used to work this stitch, and each chart will be accompanied by a key that explains exactly what colour of yarn you should use to work each stitch. When a chart is shown in colour, it is usually quite obvious what colour you will use and where, but if the chart features symbols you will need to refer to the key to find out what colour each symbol relates to.

Written instructions for colourwork designs

Where there are just a few stitches of each row, or round, worked in a different colour, you will often find that this is detailed within the instructions for the particular rows, or rounds, where this colour change occurs.

Along with details of exactly what crochet stitches should be worked and how these should be placed, you will find your pattern will tell you what colour of yarn to use for each set of stitches. Remember that the pattern will tell you to work, say, 2 trebles using a second colour, but you **must** change to this second colour to complete the stitch **before** these 2 trebles.

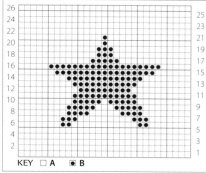

Pattern repeats

Sometimes a colourwork design will repeat a group of stitches using a set of colours. This is called a pattern repeat.

When the colourwork design is written out within the instructions, this colour pattern repeat will be expressed in exactly the same way as any stitch pattern repeat would be. An asterisk appears at the beginning of the pattern repeat and, once the whole pattern repeat has been explained, the pattern tells you to repeat the section from this asterisk across the rest of the row or round. The colourwork pattern repeat may also appear within a set of brackets, with details as to how many times you repeat this section.

On a charted colourwork design, the pattern repeat is indicated at the edge of the chart. This may be a set of stitches repeated across a row, or a set of rows that are repeated up the work, or both.

If it is a stitch repeat, repeat the indicated area as many times as possible (or as indicated) across the row, working the stitches at the beginnings and ends of the rows as shown on the chart.

If it is a row repeat, work the rows that form this repeat, then start again and work these rows once more. Continue in this

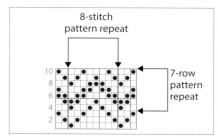

way, working all the rows that make up the pattern repeat again and again, until the work is completed.

Following a colourwork chart

Each square on the chart relates to one stitch of the crochet and the key tells you what colour to use.

To use a colourwork chart, work the first row by working across the first row of squares on the chart, changing colour as required. To work the next row, work the next row of squares on the chart. Generally, the first row of squares on a chart is a right-side row on the work; read the row of the chart from right to left. For the next row, you will work back across the crochet, so you need to work back across the chart, reading the next row of squares from left to right.

If you are working in rounds, you may find that every row of the chart should be followed in one direction. Or, if some sections are worked in rows and others in rounds, you may need to vary the way in which you follow the chart accordingly. Your pattern should tell you exactly how to read the chart to achieve the effect desired for this design.

Shaping in a charted design

A colourwork chart shows you what colours to use for which stitches. It will not tell you to increase or decrease any stitches – there will just be more or fewer squares on the chart where any shaping occurs. If the design has shaping while the chart is being worked, this will be explained in the written section of the pattern. You must refer to both the written pattern and the chart while working a design such as this.

Carrying yarn across

A colourwork design that uses more than one colour in each row will require the colour of yarn not in use to be carried across the wrong side to the point where it is next needed.

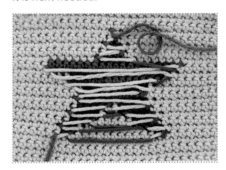

To move the yarn not in use to where it is next needed, simply strand the yarn loosely across the wrong side of the work. Make sure these strands, or floats, of yarn are not pulled too tightly as this can distort the finished work. Stranding the yarn across the back of the work will result in a fabric that has lots of floats of yarn at the back.

If the stitch pattern being worked is quite solid – such as a double crochet fabric – and the colours of yarn are fairly similar in tone, the yarn not being used can be laid across the top of the stitches and enclosed within these stitches as the next colour is used. Carrying the yarn between the different areas of colour in this way will result in a fabric that looks virtually the same from both sides, with no visible strands of yarn on either side.

Make this now!

This bag, based on an ancient Peruvian textile design, is worked in a combination of rounds and rows of simple double crochet. The colourwork design is quite complicated, with quite a few colours in use at any one time. To make it easy to see exactly what colours are used and where, the colourwork design for this bag is shown on a chart (see page 120).

PERUVIAN-STYLE BAG made in five shades of DK-weight mercerized cotton with a 4.00mm (G6) hook. See pages 120–122 for pattern.

Shaping in crochet

Very few crochet items are made up of just simple rectangles or tubes of crochet; at some point, you are going to need to know how to alter the number of stitches in each row or round – either by increasing or decreasing stitches – in order to shape the section as required. Note when increasing that the 'distortion' sometimes created by working lots of stitches into one base stitch is required to achieve the shape needed, such as when shaping a toy – so always work the increases as the pattern states!

Shaping a simple crochet fabric

If you are making a crochet item in a simple crochet fabric – such as rows or rounds of just double crochet or trebles – the shaping is easy to work.

● *Simple increase*

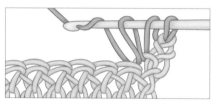

To increase one stitch in a row of basic stitches, simply work 2 stitches into the place where you would normally have worked just one stitch. Increasing a stitch in this way can appear anywhere within a row or round: on the first stitch, the end stitch, or at any point across the row or round. However, if you are increasing in this way at the beginning of a row or round, remember that the turning chain may, or may not, count as your first stitch. If it does count as the first stitch of the new row, you would normally miss the stitch at the base of this turning chain. To increase here, work the increasing stitch into the stitch at the base of the turning chain (the stitch usually missed). Similarly, if the turning chain does **NOT** count as a stitch, work 2 stitches into the place where you would normally have just worked the first stitch.

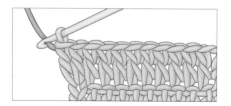

Increasing stitches in this manner retains the appearance of the crochet fabric and, depending on the height of the stitches being worked, this method can be used to increase up to a maximum of about 3 stitches at any one time. Attempting to work more than about 4 stitches into any one base stitch may end up distorting the work. A better effect may be achieved by spreading out the increases over several stitches, or by using another method to increase the stitches.

● *Simple decrease*

A simple decrease of one or two stitches at any point in a row can be worked in two ways.

It is possible to decrease just one stitch by simply missing a stitch of the base row or round. Although this will decrease the required stitch, it may also leave a tiny hole in the work. And, obviously, the more stitches decreased in this way and the taller the stitches are, the larger this 'hole' will be. Sometimes this will be the effect that is required for the item you are making, so check your pattern to ensure this is the correct method to use.

A better way to decrease one or two stitches at any point in a row or round is to work these stitches together, so that they join at the top. This method does not really affect the look of the fabric and will therefore be an ideal choice in most situations.

The abbreviation used to describe this type of decreasing stitch is a combination of the abbreviations used to create the stitch: it will feature the type of stitch to work, the number of stitches it is made up of, and the abbreviation 'tog' to show that it is a decrease. For example, working 3 treble stitches together to leave just one stitch will be abbreviated to 'tr3tog' – 'tr' to show you are working treble stitches, '3' to show you are working a total of 3 trebles, and 'tog' to indicate it is a decrease. The pattern will also tell you where to position each of these stitches.

The stage that completes every crochet stitch is to take the yarn over the hook and draw this new loop through the loops on the hook, leaving just one new working loop on the hook ready to start the next stitch.

With most stitches, there will be only 2 loops left on the hook before the last stage is worked. When working stitches together to make a decrease, each stitch is made up to this point. All the stitches are then completed in one action. At the base of the decrease there are 'legs' (the stems of the stitches) into each stitch of the base row or round, but at the top there is only one stitch.

To work 'tr3tog over next 3 sts', start by working the first treble into the first of these 3 base stitches. Stop just before the

stitch is completed, at the point when there are just 2 loops left on the hook – the original working loop and the loop just drawn through the wrappings.

Now work another treble up to exactly this point again, placing this treble into the second of the base 3 stitches. There are now 3 loops on the hook – the original working loop, the loop left from the previous partly worked treble, and the new loop from this partly worked treble.

Work the third treble of this decreasing stitch in exactly the same way as the second, working this stitch into the third base stitch. There are now 4 loops on the hook – the original working loop and one loop from each of the 3 trebles that have been partly worked.

To complete the tr3tog, take the yarn over the hook and draw this new loop through all the loops on the hook. The lower section of the tr3tog will consist of the lower sections, or 'legs', of 3 separate trebles, but the top section of the tr3tog will consists of just one stitch; thereby, 2 stitches have been decreased.

Make these now!

This cute little baby cardigan combines simple double crochet fabric with a fancy lacy stitch. It would be quite tricky to shape through a lacy stitch like this, so all the shaping appears within the simple double crochet sections, making this garment easy to crochet. The pretty co-ordinating shawl is made just in the lacy stitch. This is straightforward, as there's no shaping at all!

PRETTY IN PINK baby cardigan and shawl are both made in a soft pink shade of 4ply merino wool using a 2.50mm (C2) hook. See pages 112–114 for pattern.

Working stitches together in this way can be adapted to almost any type of stitch and used to decrease quite a few stitches at any one time. The number of stitches decreased is one fewer than those worked into on the row or round below, as there will be one stitch remaining after the decrease has been completed.

It is possible to decrease in this way to create a lacy effect by combining stitches worked together with stitches that are missed. This is particularly useful when shaping through

a lacy or mesh stitch pattern. In the red swatch (left), a tr2tog has been worked over 3 stitches of the previous row to retain the mesh effect. The first partly worked treble, or 'leg', has been worked into a treble of the previous row, the next chain stitch has been missed (thereby decreasing one stitch), and the second 'leg' of the tr2tog has then been worked into the following treble. Although only 2 stitches have been joined, creating

one stitch at the top, as these 2 stitches cover 3 stitches of the row below, a total of 2 stitches has been decreased.

When working stitches together in this way at the beginning of a row or round, where the turning chain counts as the first stitch, care needs to be taken to 'balance' the decreases worked at each end of the row or round, as in the yellow swatch (left). For example, if there are 2 trebles to be decreased at each end of the row by working 3 stitches together, the row needs to end with 'tr3tog over last 3 sts'. To balance this at the beginning of the row, work the turning chain that would normally count as the first stitch but do **NOT** include this in any stitch count (thereby decreasing one stitch). Complete the double decrease by working 'tr2tog over next 2 sts'. Take care when working back across this decrease row to remember whether or not the turning chains are to be counted as stitches or not!

Large increases and decreases

Increasing or decreasing just a few stitches creates a gentle slope at the edge of the crochet. But sometimes you may need to increase or decrease lots of stitches at one time to create a definite 'step' along the edge of the work – such as when shaping an armhole or a neckline. Obviously, these multiple increases or decreases cannot be worked in the same way as smaller shapings.

crochet craft

When working a multiple decrease, take care to check whether the turning chain at the beginning of the previous row counts as a stitch or not. If it does, you must remember to include this in the number of stitches to decrease; otherwise, the shaping will be wrong and any following rows will not work properly.

● *Multiple decreases – end of a row*
To decrease a lot of stitches at the end of a row is simple.

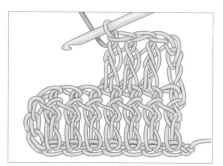

Work across the row until there are the number of stitches left at the end of the row that need to be decreased. Now simply turn the work, leaving these stitches unworked, and begin the new row in the usual way. The stitches left unworked at the end of the row are the decreased stitches and will form the 'step' shaping.

● *Multiple decreases – start of a row*
Decreasing lots of stitches at the beginning of a row can be achieved in one of two ways. The best method to use will be determined by the thickness of the yarn being used and the type of stitch pattern being worked.

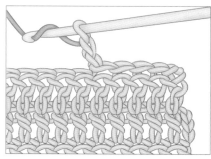

If the yarn is fairly thin and there are not very large quantities of stitches to decrease, start the new (decrease) row by simply slip-stitching across the last few stitches of the previous row until you reach the point at which this new row is to start. If there are 4 stitches to decrease, work one slip stitch into each of the first 4 stitches of the decrease row (the last 4 stitches of the previous row). Now work a slip stitch into the next stitch – this will be the base of the first stitch of the new row.

Work the turning chain at this point, in order to raise the working loop to the required height for this new row of stitches, and check your pattern instructions to find out whether this turning chain counts as the first stitch of the new row or not. If it does count, this last slip stitch and the

turning chain form the first stitch of the new row and the next stitch of this row should be worked into the next stitch of the previous row.

If the turning chain does **NOT** count as your first stitch, then the first new stitch needs to be worked into the stitch at the base of the turning chain. This will be into the same stitch as used for the last slip stitch.

Working a slip stitch adds virtually no height to the work, so decreasing in this way will create a step effect. However, although no real height is added, slip stitches can add bulk to the work.

If you are using a very thick yarn or there is a large number of stitches to decrease, it is often better to break off and rejoin the yarn.

Make these now!

These casual sweaters are worked in a simple textured stitch pattern that combines trebles and double crochet stitches. Due to the nature of the textured stitch, the shaping is worked in a combination of ways so that the overall effect is even. Although the shaping may look complex, the garments remain surprisingly easy to make.

CASUAL COMFORT SWEATERS are made in a yarn that is 75% cotton and 25% microfibre; this has more 'give' than a pure cotton yarn and keeps its shape well. This yarn is slightly heavier than a DK-weight yarn, but is worked on a 4.00mm (G6) hook to create a sturdy, dense fabric. See pages 144–145 for pattern.

At the end of the last row before the decrease row, fasten off and cut the yarn. Turn the work and count across the top of the last row to the point where the new row is to start. If there are 6 stitches to be decreased, the first 6 stitches of the next row need to be left unworked. Rejoin the yarn to the next stitch and work the required turning chain. Working a multiple decrease in this way ensures that no additional bulk is formed by the slip stitches but creates exactly the same effect.

● *Multiple increases at the beginning of a row*

All crochet stitches need a base to be worked on and, when working a large step increase at the beginning of a row, a foundation chain needs to be made first. The new increased stitches of the next row will 'sit' on these chain stitches.

crochet craft

Take care to read the pattern correctly so that you work the correct number of chain – this will be a combination of foundation and turning chains. It is also important to work the first 'real' stitch of this row into the correct chain stitch. Exactly which chain this is will vary depending on whether the turning chain counts as a stitch or not.

Start the increase row by working one chain stitch for each stitch that is to be increased. This will form the foundation chain edge of the step increase. At the end of the foundation chain, work the required extra chain for the turning chain.

Now begin the new row by working the first set of stitches – the increased stitches – into the foundation chain. Once these increased stitches have been worked, continue across the rest of the row in the usual way.

Combinations of shaping

Depending on the type of stitch pattern being worked, the type of yarn being used and the shapes required, often a pattern will use a combination of all these different ways of increasing and decreasing to create the required effect. Make sure you follow the pattern accurately – the way the shaping is given in the pattern has been carefully worked out to create the best result possible.

Often you will find that a pattern explains exactly how to work the first increase or decrease, and then tells you to continue to work any further increases or decreases in this way. Again, take care to follow these instructions. If you alter the way the shaping is worked, you may find the end result is not as it should be!

- *Multiple increases at the end of a row*

In the same way as increased stitches at the beginning of a row need a foundation chain, so do those at the end of a row. But, as the yarn and the working loop are at the opposite end of the row, this foundation chain needs to be worked separately.

Before beginning the increase row, remove the hook from the working loop and slip this loop onto a safety pin. Do **NOT** fasten off or cut the yarn. Using a separate length of yarn, attach this new yarn to the top of the first stitch of the last row, at the opposite end to where the working loop is. Work the required number of chain for each stitch to be increased. Fasten off and cut off this length of yarn.

Return to the beginning of the increase row, slip the working loop (the one that was left on the safety pin) back onto the hook and work across the row until a stitch has been worked into the same stitch as where the yarn was attached for the little length of chain. Now work across the foundation chain for the increase stitches, working one stitch into each chain stitch.

Sometimes, to reduce the bulk, a pattern will start by telling you to make and set aside a short length of chain for a multiple increase that happens later. If this is the case, simply follow the pattern and, when required, pick up this little chain and work across it as specified in the pattern. Once the yarn end has been darned in, the effect created is identical to that achieved by attaching the yarn before making the chain. However, as the yarn is not as firmly attached, the 'join' between the increased and main stitches is not quite as secure and, particularly in the case of tall stitches, a hole can appear later.

Shaping through a fancy stitch pattern

If a stitch pattern is made of groups of stitches that create a lacy or textured pattern, your pattern will usually explain exactly how each row or round needs to be worked to achieve the required shape.

If this is the case, you may find that, rather than simply increasing or decreasing one or two stitches at a time, you will be adding or losing a part of a pattern repeat. This will allow the next few rows or rounds to be worked so that the overall effect remains constant. Take care to follow the pattern instructions carefully so that the stitches of any following rows or rounds are positioned correctly and the original stitch pattern is not distorted.

Joining pieces of crochet

Once the component pieces that will make up your crochet project have been completed, these will need to be joined together to make the final item. If you have spent many hours lovingly making the different sections, it is worth spending time and care at this stage – don't spoil your work now! There are many different ways in which the seams of crocheted sections can be joined. Some are better suited to certain types of crochet than others. The seams can be sewn, or they can be crocheted.

Sewing seams

If a seam is to be joined by sewing it, use a large blunt-pointed needle designed for sewing up knitted items. These are very similar to the needles that are used for tapestry and cross stitch and are widely available. Make sure you choose one that is large enough to easily thread with the yarn you are using.

Using a blunt-pointed needle for the seam means that the fibres forming the yarn are gently eased apart as the needle passes through. A sharp needle can pierce and break the fibres, weakening the yarn and creating unsightly little tufts of fibres along the seam line.

crochet craft

Ideally, the seams should be sewn with the yarn used to make the item. But sometimes this yarn will not be suitable to sew the seams with: it could be too fluffy, too thick, or too textured. If this is the case, sew the seams using a matching shade of a plain yarn instead. Rather than buying a whole ball just for the seams, use a tapestry or embroidery yarn that comes in a short skein.

● *Over-sewing a seam*

This type of seam is probably the best seam to use to join most types of crochet. It adds no bulk to the work and is virtually invisible if worked correctly.

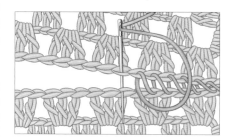

To over-sew a seam, lay the two edges to be joined next to each other. Stitch the seam by carefully over-sewing along the edges, picking up one strand of yarn from each edge and gently pulling the edges together as you sew.

If you are joining the tops of rows to each other, work one seam stitch for every one crochet stitch along the edges. When joining row-end edges, make the size of these seaming stitches the same as those across the crochet rows.

● *Flat seam*

This type of seam creates a similar effect to an over-sewn seam, as it draws the two edges together as it is worked, leaving the stitching virtually invisible. However, as you are stitching through the centre of the edge, this type of seam is really only suitable to use when the crochet fabric is fairly thick and solid.

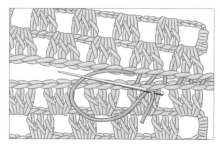

To make a flat seam, lay the two edges to be joined next to each other. Stitch the seam by taking one stitch through one edge, then another stitch through the other edge, creating a ladder-like effect, and gently pulling the edges together as you sew.

Try to keep the stitches small and even, and try not to pull the seaming yarn too tight. This could make the seam pucker and the yarn could snap, causing the seam to come undone.

Make this now!

This cosy wrap cardigan has the whole of its weight supported by the shoulder seams – so these need to be strong! Back-stitching them will give them the strength they need. The back and fronts are worked in one piece to reduce the number of seams that need to be sewn later. But there are sleeve seams to sew, and sleeves to insert into armholes. In order to keep these seams as flat as possible, these have been over-sewn.

LAZY STRIPE WRAP JACKET is made from a unique yarn composed of 70% wool and 30% soybean protein fibre in a standard DK weight. The main body of the jacket is worked using a 4.00mm (G6) hook; the cuff edgings and body edgings are crocheted with a 3.50mm (E4) hook. See pages 142-143 for pattern.

● *Back stitching a seam*

Sewing a seam in this way creates a strong and hard-wearing seam, making it the ideal choice for shoulder seams on large or heavy garments. However, its construction can create bulk on the inside of the work.

To back stitch a seam, hold the two edges to be joined with their right sides together.

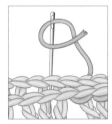

Working as close as possible to the edges, work a line of back stitch along the edges to be joined, taking each stitch through both layers of crochet.

Sometimes an edge along which shaping has been worked will not be totally straight and smooth, as the increases and decreases can cause tiny steps along the edge. If you are joining edges like this, back stitch is the perfect choice as it allows you to straighten off the edge while sewing the seam.

crochet craft

If you leave a long end at the beginning of each section of crochet, this end can be used to sew the seam with. This saves joining in lots of lengths of yarn later and saves time as there are fewer ends to darn in.

Crocheting seams

Joining edges with a line of crochet forms a strong and flexible seam. This type of seam is not as invisible as one that is sewn, but it is often much quicker to do.

If a seam is to be joined with a line of crochet, use the same size crochet hook as was used to make the sections being joined. If more than one size of hook was used when making the crochet sections, choose the hook used for the majority of the work when joining the seams. This will ensure the stitches used for the seam are worked at the same tension as the rest of the item.

● *Slip stitching a seam*
Joining the seam with a line of slip stitches creates a tight and strong seam, pulling the edges together quite closely.

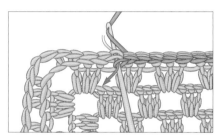

Hold the two edges that are to be joined with their right sides together. Attach the yarn at one end of the seam and make the seam by working a row of slip stitches, inserting the hook through the edges of both pieces to be seamed. Pick up just one strand of yarn from each edge and try not to work the slip stitches too tightly, as this could pucker the seam and distort the item. The seaming stitches should be the same size as those within the work, so the hook should be inserted through the edge at regular intervals to match the size of the main stitches.

crochet craft

If crocheting a seam across the tops of rows, pick up the two closest bars of yarn that make up the little 'V' at the top of each stitch. This will make the seam less visible on the right side of the work.

Once the seam has been completed, fasten off securely. When the two sections are opened out, the resulting seam will be virtually flat. Here, half the seam has been worked in a contrasting colour to show just how visible the slip stitching is. However, when worked in the same yarn, it is not nearly as noticeable.

● *Double crocheting a seam*
This forms a strong and very flexible seam that will have the same amount of stretch, or 'give', as the rest of the work.

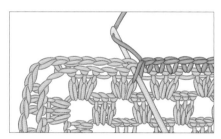

Joining a seam with a row of double crochet is made in exactly the same way as when joining it with a line of slip stitches – except, obviously, you will be working double crochets through the edges, not slip stitches.

A seam joined with a line of double crochet can appear quite bulky, as the double crochet stitches that form the seam create a slight ridge across the work. As the stitches are a little looser, they can show more on the right side of the work.

Often when a seam is joined with a line of double crochet, the two sections to be joined are held with their wrong sides together so that the seam, and the ridge it creates, shows on the outside, with the seam becoming part of the final design. If a seam is being joined in this way across the top of rows, it is best to insert the hook

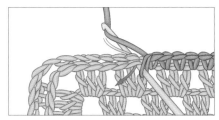

through the two layers under both of the strands that form the 'V'. This ensures both strands are enclosed within the seam.

Working a seam in this way, in a toning or contrasting colour, can be particularly effective. If you decide to do this, take care to work each stitch neatly and evenly spaced along the edge.

If the crocheted seam is to show on the right side of the work, replacing a simple line of double crochet with a row of crab stitch will create a clever corded effect where the sections meet. See page 71 for how to work crab stitch.

● *Flat slip-stitched seam*
A flat seam can be created when joining two edges with crochet by laying the two edges next to each other so that they overlap very slightly.

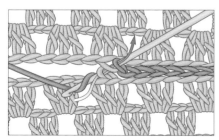

Join the edges by working a row of slip stitches along the seam, inserting the hook from above, picking up one strand from each edge.

A seam joined in this way will appear to have a line of back stitch on one side and a line of chain stitch on the other side.

● *Joining edges with chain bars*

A very pretty effect can be created by joining two edges with little bars of chain stitches. This is particularly useful if the sections being joined are lacy, as this will echo the main body of the work. This method is often used to join lacy motifs.

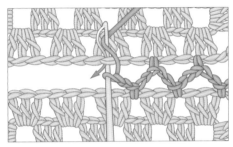

Start by laying the two edges to be joined next to each other and attaching the yarn at one end of the seam on one piece of the crochet. Work a stitch – either a double crochet or a slip stitch – into the point where the yarn has been attached, and then work a few chain stitches. Now work another stitch into the other edge a little way along the edge. Continue in this way, working into each edge alternately and spacing out the stitches worked into the edges with little bars of chain stitches, so that an even line of zig-zagging chains joins the two edges together.

Make this now!

The simple motifs that create this cosy shrug are joined with rows of double crochet. This makes it much quicker to join all the seams and ensures they are as flexible as the rest of the work. Joining the seams with the same colour as used around the edges of the motifs, with their right sides together, makes the seams virtually invisible. However to achieve a more pronounced motif edging, why not break the rules and make a feature of the seams, as shown here?

MULTI-COLOURED MOTIF SHRUG is made in five shades of DK-weight pure wool yarn. The main body of the garment is worked with a 4.00mm (G6) hook, while the edgings are crocheted with a 3.50mm (E4) hook. See pages 140–141 for pattern.

Making crochet motifs

One of the most frequently used elements of crochet is the crocheted motif. These can be lacy or solid, textured or smooth, round or square. In fact, they can be made up of any type of stitch or combination of stitches and appear in any shape at all! Regardless of the final shape of a motif and the type of stitch used to make it, motifs are almost always made in rounds, not rows. The motif will begin at the centre with stitches worked in rounds around this centre point to create the final shape. If the motif is not a simple circle, the height and type of stitches used will be varied to create the corners.

Motif centres

As with any circular piece of crochet, a motif will generally start with a length of chain stitches where the ends are joined with a slip stitch. It is this centre ring that the stitches of the first round are usually worked into.

The starting chain ring of a motif will generally consist of far fewer stitches than those made in the course of the first round. These extra stitches are needed to ensure the motif lays flat and often a small circular hole will be left at the centre of the completed motif.

Sometimes a hole is not wanted at the centre of a motif; there are two ways this hole can be avoided.

Replace the chain ring at the beginning of a motif with one single chain stitch. Work the required number of turning chain needed to raise the hook to the correct height for the stitches of the first round, and then work all the stitches of this round into the first chain stitch, closing the round as specified in the pattern.

Once the first round has been completed, gently pull on the free end of yarn to tighten and close up the first chain stitch, thereby closing the hole. Take care to securely fasten off this end, or it may work loose and the unwanted hole may reappear.

crochet craft

Although a completed motif is worked in rounds, it should be a flat piece of crochet, not cup-shaped. However, sometimes you may find the true shape of the motif does not become completely apparent until after it has been attached – either to another piece of crochet or to more motifs – or pressed.

If the stitches of the first round are simple double crochet stitches, another way to remove the centre hole is by starting with just a simple loop of yarn and working into this loop.

Form the free end of the yarn into a simple loop and insert the hook through the centre of this loop. Take the yarn over the hook and draw this new loop through.

Take the yarn over the hook again and draw this loop through the loop on the hook.

Once more, wrap the yarn around the hook and draw this new loop through the loop on the hook. This completes the first stitch of the first round.

Now make the remaining number of double crochet stitches that are required for the first round, working each stitch into this loop as though it were a chain space and enclosing both strands forming the loop in the stitches.

Once the required number of stitches have been made, gently pull on the free end to close up the slip loop at the centre, and join the ends of the round as specified in pattern instructions.

crochet craft

Instead of making a simple single loop of yarn at the centre of a motif, try wrapping the yarn around a few times. This will create a chunkier ring of stitches at the centre. However, you will still be able to pull up the free end to close the hole.

Make these now!

In order to make these mitts and hat stay cosy and warm, without any 'holes', the stitches at the centres of the motifs here have all been worked into the one chain stitch – but there's no reason why you couldn't work them into a slip loop if you wanted. These motifs are square, but they are worked in rounds. Once the round of stitches that form the contrast circle has been worked, tall and short stitches have been combined on the following round to make the square shape.

CIRCLES AND STRIPES SET is made in a DK-weight tweed yarn that is 50% merino wool, 25% alpaca and 25% viscose/rayon. The contrasting flecks of colour in the tweed give the yarn real depth of colour. Both the hat and the mittens are worked with a 3.00mm (D3) hook. See pages 124–126 for pattern.

Making motifs

Throughout this book (and in many other crochet patterns), you will find the pattern gives you instructions on how to make one basic motif. There will then generally be a paragraph that explains exactly what your motif should look like, with details of what shape it should be and what sort of stitches there are around its outer edge.

Start by making your first motif and then check that your motif matches the description given in the instructions. This allows you to check you have made the motif correctly, and will help you understand how the motifs go together later. Once your first motif is completed, now is the time to check you are working to the correct tension, too.

Joining motifs

The instructions for items that are made up of lots of motifs will tell you how to join them together to form the required shape, or shapes, needed for the completed item. Sometimes this will be a simple strip of motifs, a rectangle or a loop, and sometimes it may be a more complicated shape. You may be joining the motifs as they are made, or you may be joining them all together later. Take time to read through your pattern before you begin so that you understand fully, before you start, exactly when and how the motifs go together.

crochet craft

Although a slip stitch or double crochet stitch are the most commonly used joining stitches, motifs can be joined by working almost any type of stitch; check your pattern to ensure you work the correct type of stitch. If the item you are making is comprised of lots of joined motifs, working the wrong type of joining stitch could completely alter the finished size of the item.

• When to join motifs

If the motifs are to be joined together by seams once they have all been completed, you can make all the motifs you need and then join them in the way your pattern specifies afterwards.

Often motifs are joined to each other while the last round is being worked. Joining motifs in this way creates a very secure join, and often these joins become part of and add to the final design. If motifs are to be joined in this way, your pattern will usually explain this in the paragraph that details the shape and structure of your

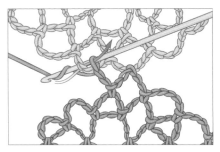

basic motif. Motifs joined while they are being made will usually have chain loops along their edges. These are where they are most likely to be joined to each other.

When motifs are joined at their chain loops, the centre chain stitch of the second, or following, motif is replaced with a stitch worked into the corresponding chain loop of the original motif. Hold the completed motif against the motif being made so that their wrong sides are together, and work the appropriate type of stitch into the corresponding chain loop.

crochet craft

Take time to read the 'tension' section of your chosen pattern before you make the first motif. Sometimes, especially if the motifs are large, you will need to measure the size of the motif before it is completed.

Joining motifs...

To form a strip

Often when a design requires just a simple strip of motifs to be made, you will be told to join the motifs to form a strip of a specific number of motifs.

Start by making the first full motif and fastening off. Now start the second motif, stopping at the beginning of the round where the joins are to be worked. Following the pattern instructions, join this motif to the first one along the relevant edge. Continue in this way, joining each motif to the previous motif as you go along. Take time to check that you are joining them correctly as you make them. Square motifs that are to be joined to form a strip need to be joined along opposite sides of the square, and it can be very easy to accidentally start joining a motif to the previous one in the wrong place.

To form a loop

A simple strip of motifs are often joined together at their ends to create a loop of motifs – as is the case with the hat featured on page 61.

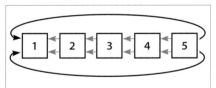

To join the motifs into a loop, start by joining the motifs into a strip, leaving the final motif unworked. While making this last motif, join it to both the appropriate edge of the previous motif and to the appropriate edge of the first motif to form the required loop.

To form a rectangle

Motifs are often joined together in rows to form rectangles and squares that create the main fabric of an item – as is the case with the bedspread on page 65.

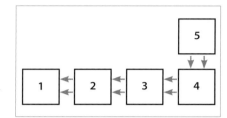

To form the final shape, start by making the first strip of the required number of motifs. Make the first motif of the second row, or strip, joining this motif to one end motif of the existing strip – but joining it along the side of the strip, not at the end.

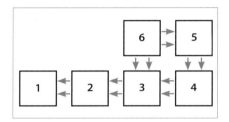

Make the second motif of the second strip, joining it to both the first motif of this strip and the second motif of the first strip. This motif will be joined to other motifs along two adjacent sides. Continue in this way, joining motifs to both the strip being worked and the previous strip, until the required shape is formed.

Following a diagram

Often the way in which the motifs are joined will be shown by a diagram. This can be because the shape required is quite a complicated shape; because the motifs do not simply sit in rows; or because they are worked in different colours.

To make a design where the motifs are joined following a diagram, simply join them together as shown by the diagram. Sometimes you may find that the diagram and written instructions detail extra 'edges' to be joined together to complete the final three-dimensional shape. Read through the pattern before you start to join the motifs so that you are sure which extra edges need to be joined.

Part motifs

Sometimes a design will feature part motifs. These are motifs that are similar to a section of the full basic motif, and will appear in designs where the final desired shape cannot be achieved using only full motifs.

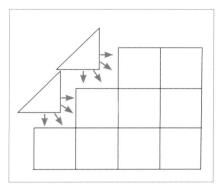

One of the most common places for part motifs to appear is along the edges of a V-neck design made using square motifs: a part (triangular) motif will be needed along the neck edge to obtain the correct shape. If a design requires full and part motifs to be made, start by making and joining all the full motifs. Once these are complete, the part motifs can be made and attached to form the correct shape.

crochet craft

A part motif can be comprised of any part of the full motif: it can be a half or a quarter of a square motif, or it can be a wedge of a circular motif. However, because it is not a full motif, it will usually be worked in rows, rather than rounds. If this is the case, make sure you check the full motif pattern and turn the work where required after the relevant rounds so that the fabric formed by the part motif matches that of the main full motifs.

Layered motifs

Pretty three-dimensional flower effects can be created on motifs by working layers of stitches forming petals that sit neatly on each other. This effect is created by working behind the stitches of the previous round to form the stitches of the new round, leaving those already worked sitting free on the surface.

● *Working into the separate loops*

Unless otherwise stated, the new stitches of a round are usually worked by inserting the hook under both of the bars of yarn that form the 'V' sitting on top of the previous stitches. However, if only one of these strands is worked into, the other strand remains free, allowing a second round to be worked independent of the previous round.

Start by making the centre of the motif up to the point where the first layer of petals is to sit. Now work the round that will form these petals, inserting the hook under the front loop only of the stitches of the previous round.

Now work the next round, inserting the hook through the back loops of the stitches left free in the previous round. This will leave the stitches of the previous petal round sitting on the surface of the work.

● *Working around the stems of stitches*

One way to form a layered effect is to work the round after the petal round by working the stitches of this new round around the stems of the stitches used for the previous round. This is particularly effective if the base round of the petal round consists of chain spaces and fairly tall stitches. The action of pulling out these stems of these stitches causes the petals to fold upwards and adds to the three-dimensional effect they create.

Start by making the centre of the motif (*below left*) up to the point where the first layer of petals has been completed. Layered motifs made in this way will generally place the petal stitches into the chain space between the taller stitches of the previous round.

Now work the next round, working the stitches around the stems of the stitches of the base round used for the petals and taking care to keep the petals at the front of the work.

● *Multi-layered motifs*

Repeat this effect to create layers of petals sitting on top of each other like a real flower. Here, a double crochet circle was turned into a flower by working rounds of petals into the front loops of every other round. To increase the flower effect, the size of the stitches that form the petals increases as the bands of petals move outwards. The first-layer petals are half trebles; the outer-layer ones triple trebles.

Filling motifs

If the motifs being joined are very lacy, the gaps between them can be too large to leave as they are on the finished item. In these situations, filling motifs are used to fill in these spaces.

Obviously, before the filling motifs can be worked, the surrounding full motifs need to be made and joined. Following the pattern instructions, and any diagram, now fill in each relevant hole between motifs with the filling motif. You will often find filling motifs used to complete a fabric made of circular motifs; these filling motifs can add greatly to the look of the finished work.

Make this now!

This stunning heirloom-style bedspread is made of motifs with simple three-dimensional flowers at their centres. Although time-consuming to complete, due to the bedspread's size and the nature of the yarn used, the individual motifs are easy to make – and the final effect is undoubtedly worth the effort. You could make some motifs in a pastel-coloured yarn to create a contrasting cushion cover.

HEIRLOOM BEDSPREAD is made in pure white 4ply cotton to create a vintage look. All the work is done with a 2.50mm (C2) hook. See pages 156–157 for pattern.

Pressing crochet items

Crochet forms a neat fabric that often does not require any pressing at all – to do so would damage the surface texture of the stitches. However, often you will need to press something to even up the stitches, smooth out the fabric and neaten the seamed areas. Whatever reason there is for pressing an item, care needs to be taken with how this is done. The way the item is pressed will depend on the type and composition of the yarn that has been used, and the type of stitches that have been worked.

Pressing

Before you begin to press any item, look at the ball band of the yarn that has been used and follow the directions given there. Although pure wool or cotton yarns can be pressed with a damp cloth and a fairly hot iron, synthetic yarns will be ruined if treated the same way.

● *When to press*

Often it is a good idea to press the crochet sections before they are seamed together. Not only can this make the seaming process easier, as the edges are flat, but it can also allow you to get into areas that would be impossible to reach once the seams are joined – such as the sleeve tops of children's clothes. Once the item has been seamed together, the actual seam lines can be pressed if required.

● *How to press*

To press a piece of crochet, lay it flat on a soft but firm surface. A table covered with a towel and a clean sheet is ideal. Ensure the **wrong** side of the crochet is uppermost (to avoid any chance of damaging the right side of the work) and gently smooth each piece out to the correct shape and size, referring

back to the pattern if necessary. Cover the crochet with a clean pressing cloth (check the ball band to find out whether this should be a dry or a damp cloth) and heat the iron to the correct temperature for the yarn used.

Remember – pressing is very different from ironing! When you iron, you slide the iron backwards and forwards over the fabric. To do this to a piece of crochet could stretch or distort it, possibly causing permanent damage. A pressing action is one where the iron is gently lowered and raised onto different areas of the work. Do NOT push down on the iron; simply let it gently rest on the pressing cloth for a

crochet craft

Regardless of the type of yarn being used, you are safe to use a damp cloth when blocking a piece of crochet, as there is no heat involved at all. It is the steam generated by a hot iron used in conjunction with a damp cloth that damages synthetic fibres.

crochet craft

If a crochet item combines more than one type of yarn, it must be pressed according to the needs of the most delicate yarn within the work. If you don't do this, this area of the work may be irrevocably damaged.

second or two. Depending on the texture of the work, you may not even need the iron to touch the fabric. Pure wool items can be very effectively pressed by holding the iron just above a damp cloth, as the heat of the iron will push the steam through the crochet and do all the pressing for you.

Once the crochet has been pressed, you should leave it to cool and, if relevant, dry naturally **before** removing it from the pressing surface.

Pressing versus blocking

The way in which an item is 'pressed' will vary depending on the character of the crochet. If the surface is quite smooth, without masses of textured stitches, it can be pressed. However, if it is heavily textured, placing an iron on this texture will squash and damage it. For heavily textured items, blocking is a better option.

Items with a smooth surface, such as this motif shrug, should stand up well to pressing, but check the details on the ball band to see if any special care needs to be taken. This shrug was made from pure wool yarn, so, to press it effectively, you could cover it with a damp cloth and hold an iron just over the cloth.

Blocking

If a crochet item has been made using a synthetic yarn, or if it is very heavily textured, blocking it is a much better option than pressing.

To block out an item, start with the same soft but firm surface as if you were pressing it. Lay the crochet section flat on this surface, but with the right side uppermost. If necessary, pin the crochet to the pressing surface around its outer edge, easing it into the correct shape and placing the pins 5 to 10cm (2 to 4in) apart. Cover the crochet with a damp cloth and leave everything to dry naturally. Once totally dry, remove the cloth and any pins and you can complete the item if necessary.

Make this now!

This pretty baby blanket is worked in a yarn that combines pure merino wool with pure cotton so, in theory, it could be pressed with a warm iron over a damp cloth. However, if this were done too fiercely, it could damage the delicate surface texture. To ensure this doesn't happen, press this type of stitch by holding the iron just above a damp cloth and allowing the iron to just push the steam it generates through the work.

THREE-COLOUR BABY BLANKET is made using three shades of a yarn that is 50% merino wool and 50% cotton. The yarn is quite a fine DK weight and is worked using a 3.00mm (D3) hook. See pages 149–150 for pattern.

Borders and edgings

Crochet fabrics can have a tendency to be a little wavy along their edges, so you will often find that a border is added to these edges in order to neaten them and to help the item 'hold' its intended shape. In addition, decorative borders and edgings can be worked to add a little extra detail and interest to a crocheted item. Borders and edgings can also have a practical purpose, for example, to add a buttonband and button loops to a cardigan, or to add ties to hold a garment closed.

To work a border along an edge

Start by attaching the yarn at one end of the edge. Make the required turning chain for the type of stitch to be worked, and then work along the edge, inserting the hook through the edge of the work.

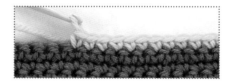

If you are working along the top of a row, insert the hook through the existing stitches in exactly the same way as if making any new row of stitches.

If working along a foundation-chain edge, work each border stitch into the remaining free loops of the foundation chain.

When working along row-end edges, the actual placement of the border stitches will vary greatly depending on the stitch pattern that has been worked within the main section. Experiment to see how best to place the new stitches – work a few stitches and see how they sit on the work. If you are not happy, undo them and try again.

How many stitches to work

Unfortunately, there is no golden rule as to exactly how many stitches you should work along any type of edge – although there are some guidelines.

If you are working with a simple plain crochet fabric, such as a double crochet fabric, working one border stitch for every stitch of the main section should generally create a good border. Along row-end edges, the number of stitches that you will need to work will vary depending on the height of the stitches making up the fabric. Working one double crochet of the border for each row of double crochet on the main fabric works well, as does working two border stitches for every row of trebles.

The only way to ensure the border sits well and does its job properly is to work a small section to check the number of stitches you are making is right. The stitches of a border are usually there to hold the edge in slightly and, as just a few rows of crochet have a tendency to stretch easily, you may find it best to work fewer stitches than you think you will need. Once the border is complete, any tightness can simply be released by very gently easing the edge out to the correct length.

A border that is worked correctly should be slightly shorter than the edge that it sits

along, not longer. If, as you are working the border, it appears to be starting to form a frilly edge, you are most likely working too many stitches. You will either need to start again completely, or change to a smaller size of hook and work the stitches of the border more tightly.

● *Contrast colour borders*

If you are working a border using a contrast colour, it is often a good idea to work the initial row or round with the colour used for the main body of the item. The first row or round of the border can tend to be a little uneven, especially where you are working into row-end edges.

If the contrast colour is introduced for the second row or round of a border, you will find that the line where the two colours meet is much more even and neat than if the whole of the border had been worked in the contrast colour.

● *Working borders in rows or rounds*

If a border is being added once the sections have been joined, it is usually easiest to work it in rounds, rather than rows. However, if there are a few borders to be made and some are to be worked in rows and some in rounds, remember to turn at the end of each round so that the resulting fabric of this border matches that of the borders worked in rows.

Shaping borders

Often a border will fall along a shaped edge, such as around an armhole or a curved neck or hemline. A border should lay flat unless the pattern specifies otherwise. To ensure your border does lay flat around these shaped edges, it may be necessary to increase or decrease a few stitches along the curved edges so that the edge is the correct length.

● *Working a border around a corner*

When a border runs around a corner of a piece of crochet, extra stitches will need to be either made or lost at the actual corner point.

To turn an external corner, such as at the base of a front opening edge, work extra stitches into the actual corner point. If the border is worked in double crochet, work 3 double crochet into the corner point, instead of just one. On the next row or round, you need to work 3 stitches into the corner stitch. The number of extra stitches you need to make to turn the corner will vary depending on the height of the stitches being worked. However, you will always need to work an odd number so that there is a central stitch into which the corner stitches can be worked on the following row or round.

To turn an internal corner, such as one at the base of a V-shaped neckline, stitches need to be decreased at either side of the corner. After the first row or round has been worked, decrease the same number of stitches either side of the actual corner point. Again, the number of stitches to decrease depends on the height of the stitches being worked and the angle of the corner. A border worked in double crochet around a square corner will probably sit nicely if one stitch is decreased at each side of the corner.

Make this now!

This mesh top has neat and narrow double crochet borders around all the edges. Around the lower edge (which is straight) there are the same number of stitches in both rounds of the border. However, both the armhole and neck edges are curved.

As the borders consist of just 2 rounds, they can be shaped either by missing the occasional stitch while working the second round, or by working the first round a little too tightly by spacing the stitches a little too far apart. Once the second round has been added, the edge can be gently eased out to the correct shape.

SUMMER SKY MESH TOP
is made from a crisp 4ply
mercerized cotton in a vibrant
turquoise. The top is worked
with a 2.50mm (C2) hook. See
pages 132–133 for pattern.

Making buttonholes in borders

You will often find that any buttonholes needed for a garment are made while working the borders. These buttonholes can either be parallel to the border rows or rounds, or placed at right angles.

- *Buttonholes placed along a row or round*

To make a buttonhole that sits along a row or round, work along the row to the point where the buttonhole is to be placed. To form the actual buttonhole opening, replace the next few stitches with the equivalent number of chain instead. Miss the required number of stitches in the row, and then complete the row.

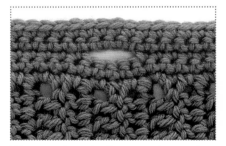

When working back across the stitches, work as many stitches as have been missed into the chain space that forms the buttonhole opening. You can either work these stitches into the chain space, or into the actual chain stitches.

- *Buttonholes placed at right angles*

Buttonholes placed at right angles to the border stitches are best worked in a border worked in rows. If the border is worked in rounds, it will be necessary to turn the work after each round to ensure all the border stitches and rows look the same.

To make this type of buttonhole, work across the row to the point where the buttonhole is to be placed (*above right*). Stop and turn the work, and work back across the stitches. Repeat these short rows until the buttonhole is the required size.

Rejoin the yarn to the last full row at the required point after the first buttonhole placement and work across to where the next buttonhole will be (*above*). Again, turn and now work backwards and forwards in rows on the stitches that sit between the buttonholes.

Continue in this way, working the sections between the buttonholes in separate batches of rows, until all the buttonholes have been completed. Now work one complete row, working across each set of stitches between the buttonholes in turn, and complete the border.

Making button loops

Often a crochet item is fastened with a button loop rather than a buttonhole. Button loops are easy to make while you are working the last row or round of the border.

To make a simple chain button loop, work the border up to the point in the last row or round where the button loop is to fall. Now replace the next few stitches with a length of chain. Miss the next few stitches and complete the row or round. Unlike when making a buttonhole, the number of chain stitches used for a button loop will usually be greater than the number of stitches of the row that are missed, so that the little chain loop will extend slightly from the finished edge. Adjust the number of chain you make so that the button loop snugly fits around the button.

To make a more solid button loop, work the last row or round up to the point where the button loop is to finish, not start. Now turn the work and make the required number of chain for the loop. Miss the required number of stitches for the loop and work a slip stitch into each of the next 2 stitches. Turn the work again and work the same number of double crochet into the chain loop as there were chain stitches, adding one or two extra so the loop forms a neat curve. Now complete the border by working into the remaining stitches of the previous row or round.

Adding ties to a border

Simple ties that are used to fasten the item can be made while working the last row or round of a border. Attaching a tie in this way makes it very secure, as it becomes an integral part of the crochet, and reduces the number of yarn ends to be darned in.

To place a tie within the last row or round of a border, work along the row to the point where the tie is required. Now make the length of chain that will form the base of the tie.

Work a double crochet into the second chain from the hook, and then work back along the length of chain, working one double crochet into each chain.

When all the chain stitches have been worked into, simply complete the row or round, leaving the tie extending free at the edge of the border.

Crab stitch

Crab stitch is a variation of simple double crochet, and is also known as corded or reversed double crochet. It creates a neat edge that looks virtually the same on either side, with tiny knotted bobbles sitting along the edge.

Almost every row or round of crochet is worked starting at the right of the work and progressing along the row or round towards the left. To work a row or round of crab stitch, you simply work double crochet stitches in the opposite direction, starting at the left and working towards the right.

Because you are working back on yourself, and you can find yourself getting a bit tangled up, it can take a while to get the hang of crab stitch. But the effect it creates is well worth the effort of practising until you get it right. It is one of the stitches many people have problems mastering – even experienced crocheters. But it's like learning to ride a bike – you struggle for ages then it suddenly works and there's no looking back!

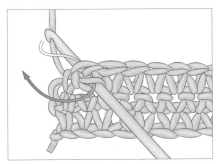

As crab stitch is worked from left to right, instead of right to left, there is no need to turn the work before starting the crab stitch. Make the required one turning chain and then twist the hook forwards and downwards to insert it, from front to back, through the top of the first stitch to be worked into – keep the yarn at the back

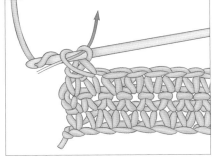

of the work. Take the yarn under the hook at the back of the work and draw this new loop through, so that there are 2 loops on the hook.

Take the yarn around the hook in the usual way and draw this new loop through both the loops on the hook. This completes the first stitch.

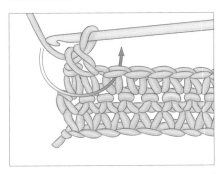

Again, keeping the yarn at the back of the work, twist the hook towards you and downwards and insert it through the next stitch to the right of the one that you just made. Take the yarn under the hook at the back of the work and draw this new loop through the work so that there are, once more, 2 loops left on the hook. Complete the double crochet stitch in the usual fashion, by wrapping the yarn around the hook and drawing this new loop through both loops on the hook. Continue in this way along the row.

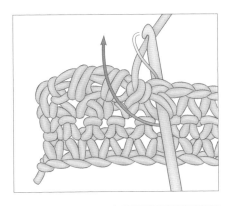

crochet craft

Borders are often worked to a slightly tighter tension than the main sections. Check your pattern to find out whether you should be using the same size crochet hook as for the main areas, or a smaller size hook.

Crochet edgings

Crochet is a great medium to use to make any sort of edging. This could be a simple border to neaten a garment or it could be a fancy lacy edging used to decorate any number of items.

Crocheted edgings can be created either by working directly into an edge, or they can be worked separately and attached afterwards. Edgings can be made in either direction – you can work a few rows on lots of stitches, or you can work lots of rows on a few stitches.

● *Working an edging into an edge*
If an edging is worked directly onto the item, it effectively becomes a fancy border and would be worked accordingly.

● *Attaching a separate edging*
If the edging is made independently of the item and needs to be attached afterwards, the way the edging is seamed onto the item will depend on the effect to be created. Why not try different types of seams (see pages 56–59) to find out which looks best?

Make these now!

This cute baby set has contrast-colour frilly edgings added after the main sections have been completed. Here, the edging stitches have been worked into those of the foundation-chain edge of the main sections so you have a clear guideline as to how many stitches to make. There's no reason why you couldn't adapt this set to suit a baby boy. Simply replace the frilly edging with a simple border of double crochet or crab stitch!

PRECIOUS PASTELS BABY SET is worked using a DK-weight 100% merino wool for both the main part of the garments and the frilly trimmings. The work is done using a 3.50mm (E4) hook. See pages 109–111 for pattern.

● *Working a crochet edging into the edge of a ready-made item*

Often crochet edgings are used to decorate a ready-made item, such as a towel, a pillowcase or a shop-bought sweater. Although often it is best to seam these edgings in place, it is possible to attach them in the same way as if they were being worked into a piece of crochet.

Whether or not you can work the crochet edging directly onto the item depends on whether you can easily get the crochet hook you intend to use through the edge of the item without damaging it. Obviously, in the case of a shop-bought sweater, this should not be too difficult. However, it may be tricky on a woven fabric, especially if it is tightly woven. Before you start, try to push the crochet hook through the fabric somewhere where it will not be visible should any damage be caused – such as within a seam. If the hook goes through fairly easily, you will be able to work the edging. If it is a bit tight, try working the first row or round of the edging using a smaller hook and changing to the correct hook for the following rows or rounds. If the hook passes through quite easily but, once through, a small hole is left in the fabric, don't worry too much – careful pressing or laundering should make the fibres close up again to hide this.

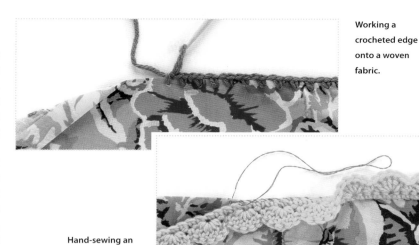

Working a crocheted edge onto a woven fabric.

Hand-sewing an edging into place.

crochet craft

Take care to gently ease the hook through the fabric so that the fibres are pushed apart, not broken. If the fibres break, small holes will appear along the edge, spoiling the final look of the item.

When working an edging onto a woven fabric, there will not be any guidelines as to how often you should place the stitches. If you need to, mark points along the edge before you start; these can either be even sections, between which you will work a certain number of stitches, or they could be the evenly spaced points at which you will pass the hook through the fabric. If you are concerned about pushing the hook through the fabric too often, replace a complete row or round of double crochet

into the edge with a combination of double crochet and chain. On the following row or round, work into these chains to give you the correct number of stitches.

● *Hand-sewing an edging in place*

If a crochet edging is to be attached to a fabric item by hand-sewing it in place, the type of thread that you use to attach it will depend on the type of fabric it is being attached to. If you are attaching a fine crochet edging to a shop-bought knitted item, you may find it possible to attach the edging using the same yarn as was used to make the edging.

If the yarn used for the edging is thicker than that used for the item it is being attached to, it is best to sew it in place using a sewing thread. To attach the edging, hold the edge of the item and the edge of the edging that is to be attached so that their right sides are together. Sew the edging in place by taking tiny over-sewing stitches through both edges, making a back stitch every now and then to secure the thread.

Once the seam has been sewn, fold the edging out away from the item and press the seam carefully. If worked correctly, the stitches that join the two pieces should be virtually invisible. In the example above, the two sections have been sewn together with a contrast-colour thread so that you can see exactly how much the stitches are likely to show. If you are attaching a contrast-colour edging, attach it using a thread that matches the colour of the item, not the edging. The bulk of the edging is likely to swallow up the stitches and the seam will be far less visible.

● *Machine-stitching an edging in place*

If you are going to attach an edging to a very long edge, you may decide to attach it by machine-stitching it in place. Although you may think this will save time, it often doesn't. The crochet will move as you sew and you may well end up with a messy seam that you need to unpick and re-sew. And every time you unpick the stitching, you run the risk of damaging both the edging and the item. It is far better to stitch the edging in place by hand.

Getting the length of the edging right

If an edging is not being worked directly into the main body of the item, it can be tricky to know how long it needs to be. Crocheted edgings have a tendency to 'pull up' once they are attached and when they are laundered. If the edging is too short, your item will be spoilt by the edge it is attached to becoming puckered. To avoid this, your edging needs to start off slightly longer than the edge it will be attached to – adding about 10% to its length should be sufficient. In other words, if the edge is 60cm (24in) long, make your edging about 65–67cm (26–27in) long, depending on the pattern repeat of the edging. When attaching the edging, distribute this slight fullness evenly along the edge, pinning the edging in place at even intervals before sewing it on.

Decorative details

Crochet can be used to create all sorts of little extra embellishments and details, and is ideal for making three-dimensional shapes that give your projects a fabulous finish. Create balls, spirals and leaf-shapes for pretty details and accessories, and cords of various widths and textures for both practical and decorative ties. You can decorate not only crochet projects but also ready-made items. Consider adding a detailed crochet embellishment to a simple knitted bag, or giving a sewn accessory a touch of crocheted interest.

Leaves

Leaf shapes are simple to make in crochet, and they can easily be varied in size to suit their end use.

Start by making a length of chain the length the finished leaf is to be, plus one extra ch. Work a dc into the 2nd ch from hook, and then work along the rest of the ch making sts that gradually get taller then shorter, ending with a dc into the end ch. The finished width of the leaf will be twice the height of these sts used for the first side.

Now work 1 or 2 ch and another dc into this last ch to form the tip of the leaf. Turn the work around and work back along the original length of ch, making sts the same height as used along the first side, ending with a dc into the same ch as used for the first dc of the first side. Fasten off.

If the leaf is to have a stalk, add this stalk length to the starting ch and work along these extra ch in dc before beginning the first side of the leaf. When working back for the second side of the leaf, end this side by working a ss into the ch where the leaf joins its stalk.

Balls

Crochet can be worked to make balls that can be used to form buttons or decorative details.

To make a crochet ball, start by making 2 ch. Now work 6 dc into 2nd ch from hook and join this first round with a ss into the first dc. Turn the work, make 1 ch (as the turning ch) and then work 2 dc into each of the 6 dc of the previous round, closing this round by working a ss into the first dc. Turn the work again, make 1 turning ch and then work 1 dc into each dc of the previous round, closing the round with a ss into the first dc. This completes the lower half of the ball.

Turn the work again, make the turning ch, and then work dc2tog into each pair of dc of the previous round to start to shape in the top half of the ball. Close this round with a ss into the first dc2tog and fasten off, leaving a long end. Tuck the starting yarn end inside the ball and then insert a little toy filling so that it forms a neat, well-rounded ball shape. Thread the yarn end onto a needle and run a line of gathering stitches around the top of the last round. Pull the end up tight and fasten off securely. This completes the ball.

Crochet balls can be made to any size simply by working more or fewer rounds and stitches until the required size is achieved.

Make this now!

Add some crochet leaves to a simple crochet rose to make it more realistic. This rose can be used as a corsage and pinned onto a sweater or a hat. Alternatively, you could make lots of corsages to adorn an evening bag.

THE CORSAGE is made in a luxurious yarn mixture of kid mohair and silk; the red yarn has a touch of lurex in it for an extra glamorous sparkle. The piece is made with a 2.50mm (C2) hook. See page 118 for pattern.

Spirals

Spiralling coils of crochet can be used to form tendrils to decorate an appliquéd floral design, to create a fancy fringe or even on their own to make a narrow boa-style scarf.

To make a simple treble spiral: make a ch the length the finished spiral needs to be plus 3 extra (turning) ch, work 3 tr into the 4th ch from hook, then 3 tr into each ch to end. Fasten off.

As the stitches are worked they will form themselves into a spiral. You can vary the amount of twist in the spiral by increasing or decreasing the number of stitches worked into each chain. The more stitches are worked into each chain, the more the spiral will twist.

crochet craft

To make a much wider, frilly spiral, work a second row of stitches into the first row. Once the base row is complete, turn the work, make the required number of turning chain and then work back along the previous row, working 1–3 sts into each st.

Cords

Crochet can be used to make cords that will work as ties and drawstrings, or to create decorative details.

Make a very simple crochet cord by simply working a length of chain stitches. This is the most basic type of cord, but it can have a tendency to curl up on itself.

A slightly thicker cord can be made in exactly the same way but by using two or more strands of the yarn. If there are lots of colours used for the item the cord is to be attached to, use strands of different colours to create a multi-coloured cord.

Double crochet cord

It is possible to make a thin cord that lays flat without twisting, forming a fine tape-like strip.

Start by making 2 ch and work 1 dc into the 2nd ch from hook. *Insert the hook into this dc, from front to back, under the strand of yarn that runs up the left side of this dc. Take the yarn over the hook and draw through a new loop. Take the yarn over the hook again and draw this new loop through both loops on the hook to finish this new dc. Repeat from * until the cord is the required length, then fasten off.

Tubular cord

Spiralling tubes of double crochet can make firm, chunky cords that are ideal to use for bag handles or where a thick, strong cord is required.

Begin the tubular cord by making the required number of ch (4 or 5 should be sufficient) and join these with a ss to form a ring. Now work 1 ch (as a turning ch) and then work 1 dc into each ch forming the ring. At the end of this round do NOT join the last st to the first st with a ss but simply carry on round and round the ring, making a spiralling tube of 1 dc worked into each dc of the previous round. Once the tube is the required length, complete it by working a ss into the next dc and fastening off.

CORD SLIGHTLY THICKER CORD DOUBLE CROCHET CORD TUBULAR CORD

Using tubular cords

Tubular cords can be made in almost any size, so they are ideal to use as handles for bags. Try threading a purchased piping cord, or several strands of thick yarn, through the centre to stop the crochet stretching and to make sure it stays nice and round in use.

Working with beads

Adding beads to a crochet item can be done either by sewing them in place once the crochet is complete, or by actually working them into the crochet. This second option is the better choice as it means they are firmly secured in position and unlikely to work free and come off. Be aware that if the crochet is quite loose, beads may slip through the work. If this happens, simply ease them back through the crochet so they appear on the correct side.

Threading the beads onto the yarn

If the beads are to be worked into the crochet, they need to be threaded onto the yarn before you begin.

The hole of the beads is often too small to thread straight onto the yarn. Instead, thread the beads onto the yarn by threading a fine needle – one that will pass through the bead – with a length of strong sewing thread. Knot the ends of the sewing thread to form a loop. Check that this knotted length of thread will pass through the centres of the beads.

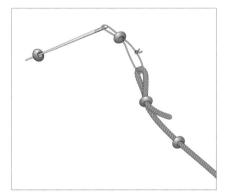

Pass the cut end of the yarn through the loop of the sewing thread. Now slip a bead onto the needle and gently slide it along the thread, and then onto the yarn. Do this slowly so that the thread does not snap and the yarn end remains within the thread loop. Continue in this way until the required number of beads are on the yarn. They will sit on the yarn, ready to be used as and when required. Until they are required, simply slide them along the yarn, away from where you are working.

Working the beads into the crochet

Although beads can be placed virtually anywhere within a piece of crochet, they are most commonly placed on double crochet and chain stitches.

To place a bead on a chain stitch, work up to the point where the beaded chain stitch appears. Now slide one of the beads up the yarn so that it sits next to the hook. Take the yarn over the hook in the usual way, ensuring the bead sits between the hook and the last stitch worked, and draw the new loop through. The bead is securely caught inside the chain stitch.

To place a bead on a double crochet stitch, work up to the point where the beaded double crochet stitch falls. Slide the bead up next to the hook and work the double crochet in the usual way. The bead is trapped between the 2 stitches.

A bead can be caught in any type of stitch in this way. However, as the beads sit on the back of the work, they are best placed on wrong-side rows or rounds.

crochet craft

If you are using a lot of beads within a design, repeatedly sliding all these along the yarn until they are needed can damage the yarn. It is a good idea to thread on some of the beads, use these up and then break the yarn to re-thread it with more beads. If the beads only appear on certain rows or rounds, use one ball of yarn for the unbeaded rows, picking up the yarn from the ball threaded with the beads for the rows where they are needed.

Working with sequins

It is very easy to place sequins within a crochet item – just treat them exactly as though they were beads.

The best type of sequin to use with crochet has its hole placed near one edge. These sequins sit more smoothly on the final crochet fabric.

Make this now!

Antique-effect silver beads decorate the lacy borders of this summer top. As the beads feature only on the borders, there is no need to thread them on to the yarn until you are ready to make these sections. Here, each bead is caught inside a chain stitch.

BEAD-EDGED BEAUTY is made in 4ply cotton. The main body of the garment is worked with a 2.50mm (C2) hook, while the neck edging is crocheted with a 2.00mm (B1) hook. See pages 134–136 for pattern.

● *Sewing sequins in place*

If your sequins have their hole at the centre, it is best to attach them afterwards by sewing them in place, using a matching colour of sewing thread. There are lots of ways to do this.

If you want the sequin to sit flat against the crochet, attach it by making a few straight stitches radiating out from the centre hole. Bring the needle and thread through to the right side of the work where the sequin is to be placed, and

thread the sequin onto the thread. Take the needle back through the fabric at the edge of the sequin. Work another 1 or 2 stitches in this way, positioning the stitches evenly around the edge of the sequin.

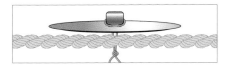

You could also attach the sequin using a tiny bead. Bring the needle and thread through the work where you want to place the sequin. Thread the sequin onto the thread, then thread on the tiny bead. Take

the needle and thread back through the work by passing it back through the centre of the sequin. This will leave the sequin securely attached to the work, with the bead sitting at its centre.

crochet craft

Sequins can twist out of position as they are worked into the crochet. If this happens, simply smooth the sequins back into place afterwards.

Embroidery on crochet

A good way to embellish crochet is to work embroidery on its surface. You will probably find it most effective if the embroidery is worked with a yarn or thread of the same sort of thickness as that used for the crochet. Due to the nature of crochet fabric, it can be tricky to place the embroidery stitches. If you are working on a fabric made up of tall stitches, the holes between the stems of the stitches influence where each stitch can be placed. It is therefore best to work embroidery on a more solid stitch pattern.

Chain stitch

Lines of chain stitch are great for adding design details such as simple lines or swirling curls and spirals.

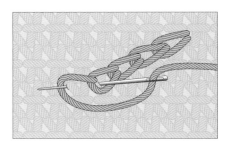

To embroider a line of chain stitch, start by bringing the needle through the fabric at one end of the chain stitch line. Take a stitch through the fabric, inserting the needle at the point where it just came up, and bring it back up further along the line. Loop the thread under the point of the needle and gently pull the needle through the work. Don't pull too tightly, as the resulting chain stitch should be left nice and fat on the surface. Continue along the line in this way. When the last stitch has been made, take the needle back through the work just near where it last came out, securing the last loop in place.

crochet craft

Whatever type of embroidery you work, use a blunt-pointed needle for it. This ensures that the yarn forming the crochet fabric is not damaged, as this type of needle gently pushes apart the fibres, rather than splitting and breaking them.

Chain stitch uses up a lot of thread and, when embroidering it, you can find yourself repeatedly joining in new lengths of thread. One way to avoid this is by crocheting a line of chain stitches through the work instead.

To crochet a line of chain stitch, start with the yarn at the back of the work. Insert the hook through the work at the end of the line of stitching and draw through a loop of yarn. Keeping this loop on the hook, insert the hook back through the work a little further along the line and bring a new loop of yarn through both the work and the loop on the hook. Continue in this way until you reach the other end of the line.

Cut off the yarn at the back of the work and complete the last stitch by pulling the cut end through the final loop. Thread the end onto a needle and complete the last stitch in the same way as if the line had been embroidered.

crochet craft

However you work a line of chain stitch, work the stitches evenly and at the same tension. On the right side you will have a neat, full, rounded stitch and on the other side there will appear to be a line of back stitch.

Blanket stitch

This stitch creates a neat decoration along the edge of a fabric.

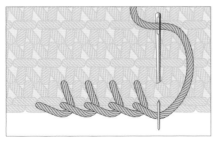

To embroider a line of blanket stitch, start by bringing the thread through the fabric near its edge. Over-sew along the edge, but catch the loop of the previous stitch in the next stitch so that the thread runs from where it comes through, out to the edge of the fabric, where it is caught by the next stitch, and then along the edge of the fabric.

It is possible to create the effect of an embroidered blanket stitch with a row of crochet worked over the edge. Simply work a row of double crochet enclosing the edge: insert the hook through the work a fair distance in from the edge and space the stitches quite widely apart. On one side, you will appear to have blanket stitch, with lots of V-shapes appearing on the other side.

Lazy daisy stitch

A lazy daisy stitch is just one chain stitch worked on its own.

Lazy daisy stitches look like petals or leaves and are an easy way to add floral designs to your work. Make a simple flower by working a group of lazy daisy stitches radiating out from one central point, and try adding a few leaves around the edges. Decorate the centre of your flower by attaching a few beads or sequins or by making a french knot.

Bullion knots

Similar to their crochet counterparts (see page 33), embroidered bullion knots are made up of a wrapped length of thread.

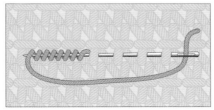

Make a bullion knot in the same way as a french knot, but wrap the thread around the needle a lot more times and make the stitch holding it in place longer.

French knots

French knots can be used to add tiny highlights of colour and texture to the work. However, due to the holey nature of many crochet fabrics, extra care needs to be taken to ensure they sit on the surface, without disappearing down inside the crochet stitches.

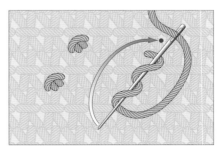

To make a french knot, bring the needle and thread through the work at the required point. Wrap the thread around the needle point 3 or 4 times and, holding this coil of thread in place, take the needle back through the fabric just next to where it came out.

crochet craft

To ensure that the french knot stays on the right side of the crochet, make sure there is sufficient fabric underneath the knot to hold it in place.

Tartan effects

It is possible to create a woven tartan effect in crochet by weaving lengths of chain in and out of a simple crochet mesh. By working the crochet mesh in stripes and using different colours for the lengths of the chains, the check effect created gives the appearance of a tartan fabric. The resulting fabric is surprisingly solid and hard-wearing.

Designing your tartan

You will need to plan your tartan before starting to make it.

Start by deciding on the stripes for the mesh. It is best to use the same colour for both the foundation chain and the first row. Once you are happy with the mesh stripes, make the chains in the same stripe sequence. This will ensure your tartan is even. However, as the 'squares' of the mesh will not be true squares, your design will be slightly elongated.

Making the mesh base

The base through which the chains are woven is a simple treble and chain mesh.

Start by making the foundation chain. This needs to be an even number of stitches plus 4 extra (for the turning chain). Begin the first row by working a treble into the 6th chain from the hook. Continue the row by repeating (1 ch, miss 1 ch, 1 tr into next ch) until the end of the row is reached.

Now turn the work and work back as follows: 4 ch (to count as 1 tr and 1 ch), miss (tr at end of last row and 1 ch), 1 tr into next tr, *1 ch, miss 1 ch, 1 tr into next tr, rep from * to end, working last tr into top of turning ch at beg of previous row, turn.

Continue to build up rows of the mesh in this way, working in stripes as required. Once the required number of rows are completed, fasten off.

Making the weaving chains

To complete the 'tartan', chains are made that are woven in and out of the base mesh.

Using the same size hook as that used to make the base mesh, make a length of chain. The chains are going to be woven up and down the rows of the mesh, not across them – so this is the length you need. However, as some of the length of the chain will be taken up by weaving it in and out of the mesh, these chains need to be slightly longer than the base mesh; adding about 8 to 10% to their length should be sufficient.

If you are not sure you have made the chain lengths quite long enough, fasten off loosely and leave a long end. That way, if they are a little too short, you can undo the fastening off and work a little more chain to get to the correct length.

In the same way as the various rows of the base mesh have been worked in different colours, your lengths of chain also need to be made in different colours.

Make these now!

This cosy muffler scarf and bag are made of woven crochet tartan. The resulting fabric is both warm and hard-wearing – making it ideal for both the scarf and the bag.

TARTAN-STYLE SET is made using three colours of a cosy aran-weight cashmere-blend yarn (57% extra-fine merino, 33% microfibre and 10% cashmere). Both the scarf and the bag are made using a 4.50mm (7) hook. See pages 130–131 for pattern.

Weaving the finished fabric

Once the mesh base and all the chain lengths have been made, you are ready to start weaving the finished tartan fabric.

Start by attaching the end of one length of chain to the foundation-chain edge of the mesh – attach it to one of the 'free' chain stitches, not one that has a treble worked into it. Now carefully thread the chain through the mesh by taking it over the first chain bar and then under the chain bar of the row above.

Continue in this way, taking the chain alternately over and under the chain bars of the mesh, until you reach the final row. Check the fabric lays flat and that the chain is not too loose or too tight and, if necessary, adjust its length. Once you are happy that it fits correctly, fasten off and attach this end of the chain to the chain bar of the last row.

Now attach another length of chain to the next chain bar of the foundation chain of the mesh and weave this in and out of the mesh in the same way – except, for this length, take the chain over the chain bars of the rows where the previous chain length passed under, and vice versa.

Continue in this way until all the chain spaces of the mesh have been filled with woven lengths of chain. Your tartan fabric is now complete.

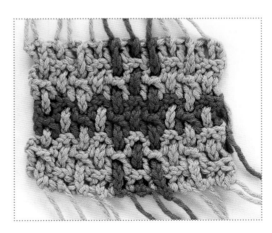

Fringes, tassels and pompons

Fringes, tassles and pompons make great decorative finishes. A fringe is formed by hooking and knotting lengths of yarn through the edges of a piece of crochet. The resulting fringe forms a neat and attractive finish along the edge. Tassels are a good decorative detail to add to the tops of hats or hoods, or to the corners of cushions or throws. Pompons are little fluffy balls of yarn that are often used to decorate scarves and hats.

Making a simple fringe

Start by cutting lots of lengths of yarn. These need to be just over twice the finished length of the fringe. A good way to ensure all the lengths are the same is to wind the yarn around something rigid, like a small book. Once you have sufficient wrappings, cut through the loops to create the strands that will make the fringe.

The knots that form the fringe can be made up of any number of strands of yarn. However, as the strands are folded in half as they are knotted, each strand of yarn will result in two strands in each finished knot.

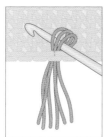

Fold the group of strands of yarn in half, insert a crochet hook through the edge of the work and loop the fold of the fringe strands over the hook.

Carefully pull the folded strands through the work, pulling the loop out so it is quite large.

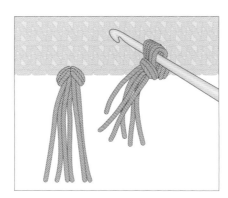

Now pick up all the free ends of the strands with the hook, and gently pull these through the loop you have just pulled through the fabric.

Remove the hook and then gently tighten the knot by pulling on the cut ends of the strands.

Continue to knot lengths of yarn through the edge until you are happy with the effect you have created. The knots can be made up of just one or two strands of yarn and positioned close to each other, or they can consist of lots of strands and be positioned quite far apart. However thick or thin, or close or distant you place the knots, make sure they are even. Space them out evenly along the edge and ensure that each knot contains the same number of strands, cutting more strands if required.

Once the fringe is complete, the cut ends will probably be a little uneven. You can leave them like this, or you can cut them all off straight. If you decide to trim them even, be careful; it's easy to cut the fringe crookedly and for it to slowly become shorter and shorter as you attempt to form a straight line!

crochet craft

Make sure all the knots are placed the same distance below the previous row of knots. You may find it helpful to slip something like a ruler between each row of knots so that this helps you keep the distances correct.

Making a fancy knotted fringe

Fancy effects can be created with a fringe by dividing the strands that form each original knot and knotting these strands together with strands from the next knot.

If you decide to make a fancy knotted fringe, start by making a simple fringe but leaving the ends very long.

Starting at one end, divide the strands of the first knot into two even groups. Divide the strands of the second (next) knot into two equal groups too. Knot together half the strands of the first group with half the strands of the second group, positioning this knot the required distance below the original knots. Continue along the fringe, knotting together half the strands of each original knot with half the strands from the next original knot, until you reach the other edge of the work. At each end there will be a group of unknotted strands left over from each new end-knot.

To work another row of knots, repeat this process of dividing each group of strands and knotting it with strands from the next knot. On this row of knots, use the strands

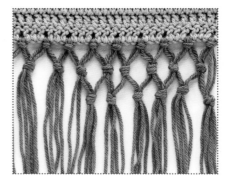

left free at each end on the previous row of knots in the end-knots. Once you are happy with the effect, trim the ends level.

Tassels

Make tassels using the same yarn as used for the item, or choose a contrasting colour or texture to add interest.

To make a simple tassel, wind some yarn round a rigid item roughly the length you want your tassel to be. Wrap the yarn around until you have as many strands as you need. At one folded end, pass a doubled length of yarn under all the strands. Pull this up tight so all the strands are held together securely, and knot the ends together firmly. Leave the ends of these strands quite long.

Very carefully cut through all the strands at the other folded end and remove whatever they were wrapped around. Take care at this point, as the strands are not securely held together.

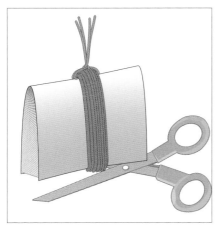

Take another length of yarn and wrap this tightly round all the strands near the folded end. Wrap this length of yarn around all the strands as tightly as you can. Fasten off this length of yarn and darn in the ends.

Pompons

It is possible to buy devices to help you make a pompon, but all you really need is some firm card.

On firm card, draw a circle that is about one and a half to two times the size you want your finished pompon to be. Now draw another circle inside this first circle. The distance between the two circles should be just over half the diameter of your completed pompon. Cut out this ring of card, then cut out a second ring exactly the same size.

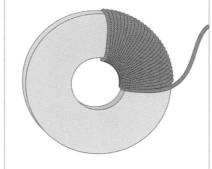

Place the two rings of card together and wrap lengths of yarn around them, passing it through the centre hole, so that there is no card left visible. Carry on wrapping yarn round and round the rings until the centre hole is filled up.

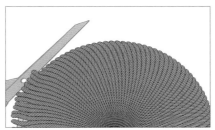

Carefully slip the point of a pair of scissors between the strands of yarn and the two card rings, and cut through all the strands of yarn around the outer edge of the rings.

Slip another length of yarn between the two card rings and tie all the pompon strands together around the middle. Pull the strands together tightly and knot the ends together securely. Leave the ends of this length of yarn quite long for now – it can be used to attach the pompon to the work later.

Very carefully cut through the card rings and remove them. Fluff up the pompon to make a little round ball and, if necessary, trim any ends so that it is even all over.

crochet craft

Pompons don't have to be made using just one colour of yarn. For a multi-coloured pompon, wind the yarn around the rings using several different coloured strands at the same time. This creates a speckled finish to the pompon. Winding one colour around the rings and then the next colour will create a pompon that appears to be striped. Experiment with different ways of wrapping the different colours to see what sorts of fancy effects you can create.

stitch library

We have given a name for each stitch shown in this stitch library for ease of identification. You may recognize some of these stitches and know them by a different name. This is because there is no overall consensus on what stitches 'should' be called, but don't worry: the main point is learning how to create the stitch.

Abbreviations

Crochet patterns use abbreviations as shorthand to describe each stitch, and each type of stitch is abbreviated to a few letters. Many of these abbreviations are the same whatever crochet pattern you follow. Below you will find a list of all the standard abbreviations that are used throughout this book. Some of these abbreviations relate to the actual stitches being worked (such as a treble), and some relate to the way you are working (such as continuing in a certain way).

0	no sts, times or rows to be worked for this size	**inc**	increas(e)(ing)
		mm	millimetres
alt	alternate	**patt**	pattern
beg	beginning	**rem**	remain(ing)
ch	chain	**rep**	repeat
cm	centimetres	**RS**	right side
cont	continue	**sp(s)**	space(s)
dc	double crochet	**ss**	slip stitch
dec	decreas(e)(ing)	**st(s)**	stitch(es)
dtr	double treble	**tr**	treble
foll	following	**ttr**	triple treble
htr	half treble	**WS**	wrong side
in	inches		

Special abbreviations

Some crochet patterns use a special group or combination of crochet stitches to create a particular effect. This group of stitches will be given a name within the pattern, and this name will often be abbreviated as well. You will find the special abbreviation detailed with the pattern it relates to, along with instructions for how this stitch or group of stitches should be worked. Before you begin, take time to read this special abbreviation so you fully understand what stitches to work and how to place them for the design you are making. This is particularly important, as sometimes a special abbreviation on one pattern will appear to be the same as on another pattern, but the actual stitches needed will vary. **For example,** a group of treble stitches is often called a 'cluster'. On one pattern, this cluster may consist of 3 trebles and on another pattern it may consist of 6 trebles – but both patterns will list 'cluster' in the special abbreviations section. Working the wrong type of cluster will mean the crochet fabric will not turn out as it should.

1: Double crochet
Multiple of any number of sts.
Start with any number of ch, plus 1 extra.

Foundation row 1 dc into 2nd ch from hook, 1 dc into each ch to end, turn.
Cont in patt as follows:
Row 1 1 ch (does NOT count as st), 1 dc into each dc to end, turn.
This row forms patt.

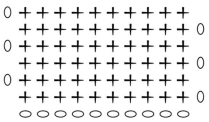

KEY
○ ch
+ dc

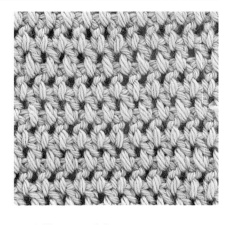

2: Half treble

Multiple of any number of sts.
Start with any number of ch, plus 1 extra.

Foundation row 1 htr into 3rd ch from hook, 1 htr into each ch to end, turn.
Cont in patt as follows:
Row 1 2 ch (counts as first htr), miss htr at base of 2 ch, 1 htr into each htr to end, working last htr into top of 2 ch at beg of previous row, turn.
This row forms patt.

3: Treble

Multiple of any number of sts.
Start with any number of ch, plus 2 extra.

Foundation row 1 tr into 4th ch from hook, 1 tr into each ch to end, turn.
Cont in patt as follows:
Row 1 3 ch (counts as first tr), miss tr at base of 3 ch, 1 tr into each tr to end, working last tr into top of 3 ch at beg of previous row, turn.
This row forms patt.

4: Offset treble

Multiple of any number of sts.
Start with any number of ch, plus 2 extra.

Foundation row 1 tr into 4th ch from hook, 1 tr into each ch to end, turn.
Cont in patt as follows:
Row 1 3 ch (counts as first tr), miss tr at base of 3 ch, *1 tr between tr just missed and next tr, miss 1 tr, rep from * to end, working last tr between first tr of previous row and 3 ch at beg of previous row, turn.
This row forms patt.

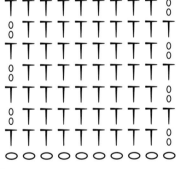

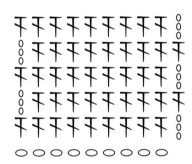

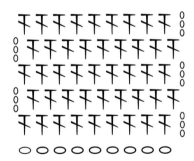

KEY
○ ch
T htr

KEY
○ ch
木 tr

KEY
○ ch
木 tr

Textured stitches

5: Ridged double crochet

Multiple of any number of sts.
Start with any number of ch, plus
1 extra.

Foundation row 1 dc into 2nd ch from
hook, 1 dc into each ch to end, turn.
Cont in patt as follows:

Row 1 1 ch (does NOT count as st), working
into back loops only of sts of previous
row: 1 dc into each dc to end, turn.
This row forms patt.

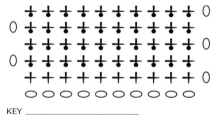

KEY

- ⬭ ch
- + dc
- ⁺ dc into back loop only

6: Mock rib

Multiple of 2 sts plus 1.
Start with an odd number of ch, plus
1 extra.

> **Special abbreviations**
>
> **rftr** work treble in the usual way but
> working around stem of st of
> previous row, inserting hook
> around stem from front to back and
> from right to left.
>
> **rbtr** work treble in the usual way but
> working around stem of st of
> previous row, inserting hook
> around stem from back to front and
> from right to left.

Foundation row 1 htr into 3rd ch from
hook, 1 htr into each ch to end, turn.
Cont in patt as follows:

Row 1 2 ch (counts as first st), miss st at
base of 2 ch, *1 rftr around stem of next
st, 1 rbtr around stem of next st, rep from
* to last st, 1 rftr around 2 ch at beg of
previous row, turn.

Row 2 2 ch (counts as first st), miss st at
base of 2 ch, *1 rbtr around stem of next
st, 1 rftr around stem of next st, rep from
* to last st, 1 rbtr around 2 ch at beg of
previous row, turn.
These 2 rows form patt.

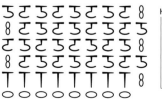

KEY

- ⬭ ch
- ⊤ htr
- ⌇ rftr
- ⌇ rbtr

7: Tweed stitch

Multiple of 2 sts plus 1.
Start with an odd number of ch, plus
1 extra.

Foundation row 1 dc into 2nd ch from
hook, *1 ch, miss 1 ch, 1 dc into next ch,
rep from * to end, turn.
Cont in patt as follows:

Row 1 1 ch (does NOT count as st), 1 dc
into first dc, *1 dc into next ch sp, 1 ch,
miss 1 dc, rep from * to last 2 sts, 1 dc into
last ch sp, 1 dc into last dc, turn.

Row 2 1 ch (does NOT count as st), 1 dc
into first dc, *1 ch, miss 1 dc, 1 dc into
next ch sp, rep from * to end, working
dc at end of last rep into dc at beg of
previous row, turn.
These 2 rows form patt.

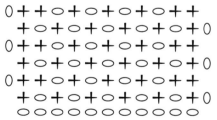

KEY
- ⬭ ch
- + dc

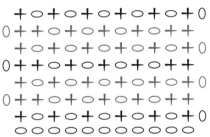

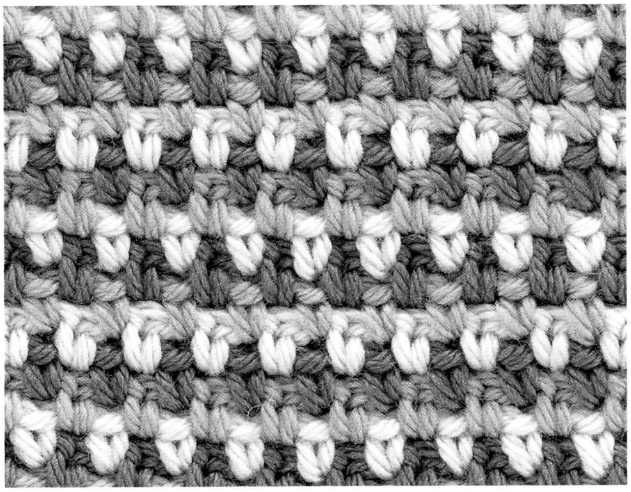

8: Multi-coloured tweed stitch

Multiple of 2 sts plus 1.
Worked in 3 colours.
Start with an odd number of ch, plus 1 extra.

Foundation row Using 1st colour, 1 dc into 2nd ch from hook, *1 ch, miss 1 ch, 1 dc into next ch, rep from * to end, turn.

Cont in patt as follows:

Row 1 Using 2nd colour, 1 ch (does NOT count as st), 1 dc into first dc, *1 dc into next ch sp, 1 ch, miss 1 dc, rep from * to last 2 sts, 1 dc into last ch sp, 1 dc into last dc, turn.

Row 2 Using 3rd colour, 1 ch (does NOT count as st), 1 dc into first dc, *1 ch, miss 1 dc, 1 dc into next ch sp, rep from * to end, working dc at end of last rep into dc at beg of previous row, turn.

Row 3 Using 1st colour, as row 1.

Row 4 Using 2nd colour, as row 2.

Row 5 Using 3rd colour, as row 1.

Row 6 Using 1st colour, as row 2.

These 6 rows form patt.

KEY

�	ch
+	dc
■	1st colour
■	2nd colour
■	3rd colour

9: Griddle stitch

Multiple of 2 sts plus 1.
Start with an odd number of ch, plus 1 extra.

Foundation row (RS) 1 dc into 2nd ch from hook, 1 dc into each ch to end, turn.

Cont in patt as follows:

Row 1 1 ch (does NOT count as st), 1 dc into first dc, *1 tr into next dc, 1 dc into next dc, rep from * to end, turn.

Row 2 1 ch (does NOT count as st), 1 dc into each st to end, turn.

Row 3 1 ch (does NOT count as st), 1 dc into each of first 2 dc, *1 tr into next dc, 1 dc into next dc, rep from * to last dc, 1 dc into last dc, turn.

Row 4 As row 2.

These 4 rows form patt.

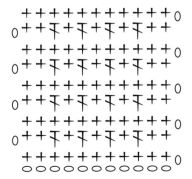

KEY

⌕	ch
+	dc
⊤	tr

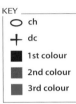
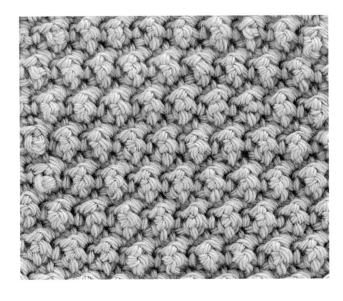

Chevron and wave stitches

10: Treble chevron stitch

Multiple of 8 sts plus 1.
Start with a multiple of 8 ch, plus 4 extra.
Special abbreviation, *see* **box below.**

Foundation row 1 tr into 4th ch from hook, *1 tr into each of next 2 ch, tr2tog over next 3 ch, working first 'leg' into next ch, missing 1 ch and working second 'leg' into next ch, 1 tr into each of next 2 ch**, (1 tr, 1 ch and 1 tr) into next ch, rep from * to end, ending last rep at **, 2 tr into last ch, turn.

Cont in patt as follows:

Row 1 3 ch (counts as first tr), 1 tr into tr at base of 3 ch, *1 tr into each of next 2 tr, tr2tog over next 3 sts, working first 'leg' into next tr, missing tr2tog and working second 'leg' into next tr, 1 tr into each of next 2 tr**, (1 tr, 1 ch and 1 tr) into next ch sp, rep from * to end, ending last rep at **, 2 tr into top of 3 ch at beg of previous row, turn.

This row forms patt.

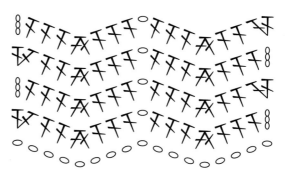

KEY
- O ch
- ⊤ tr
- ⩙ tr2tog

11: Wave stitch

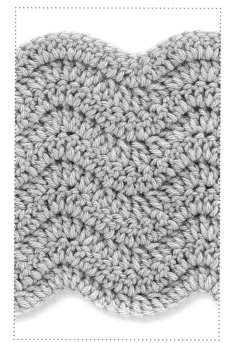

Multiple of 12 sts.
Start with a multiple of 12 ch, plus 2 extra.
Special abbreviation, *see* **box right.**

Foundation row 1 tr into 4th ch from hook, tr2tog over next 2 ch, *2 tr into each of next 4 ch**, (tr2tog over next 2 ch) 4 times, rep from * to end, ending last rep at **, (tr2tog over next 2 ch) twice, turn.

Cont in patt as follows:

Row 1 3 ch (does NOT count as st), miss tr2tog at base of 3 ch, 1 tr into next tr2tog, tr2tog over next 2 tr, *2 tr into

Special abbreviation

tr2tog *yarn over hook and insert hook as indicated, yarn over hook and draw loop through, yarn over hook and draw through 2 loops, rep from * once more, yarn over hook and draw through all 3 loops on hook.

each of next 4 tr**, (tr2tog over next 2 sts) 4 times, rep from * to end, ending last rep at **, (tr2tog over next 2 sts) twice, turn, leaving 3 ch at beg of previous row unworked.

This row forms patt.

KEY
- O ch
- ⊤ tr
- ⩙ tr2tog

12: Double crochet chevron stripes

Multiple of 9 sts plus 1.
Worked in 2 colours.
Start with a multiple of 9 ch, plus 1 extra.

Foundation row (RS) Using 1st colour, 2 dc into 2nd ch from hook, *1 dc into each of next 3 ch, miss 2 ch, 1 dc into each of next 3 ch**, 3 dc into next ch, rep from * to end, ending last rep at **, 2 dc into last ch, turn.

Cont in patt as follows:

Row 1 Using 1st colour, 1 ch (does NOT count as st), 2 dc into first dc, *1 dc into each of next 3 dc, miss 2 dc, 1 dc into each of next 3 dc**, 3 dc into next dc, rep from * to end, ending last rep at **, 2 dc into last dc, turn.
Rows 2 and 3 Using 2nd colour, as row 1.
Row 4 As row 1.
These 4 rows form patt.

KEY
- ⌒ ch
- + dc

13: Wavy stripes

Multiple of 8 sts plus 4.
Worked in 2 colours.
Start with a multiple of 8 ch, plus 5 extra.

Foundation row (RS) Using 1st colour, 1 dc into 2nd ch from hook, 1 dc into each of next 3 ch, *1 tr into each of next 4 ch, 1 dc into each of next 4 ch, rep from * to end, turn.

Cont in patt as follows:

Row 1 Using 2nd colour, 1 ch (does NOT count as st), 1 dc into each st to end, turn.
Row 2 As row 1.
Row 3 Using 1st colour, 3 ch (counts as first tr), miss dc at base of 3 ch, 1 tr into each of next 3 dc, *1 dc into each of next 4 dc, 1 tr into each of next 4 dc, rep from * to end, turn.
Row 4 Using 1st colour, 3 ch (counts as first tr), miss tr at base of 3 ch, 1 tr into each of next 3 tr, *1 dc into each of next 4 dc, 1 tr into each of next 4 tr, rep from * to end, working tr at end of last rep into top of 3 ch at beg of previous row, turn.
Rows 5 and 6 As row 1.
Row 7 Using 1st colour, 1 ch (does NOT count as st), 1 dc into each of first 4 dc, *1 tr into each of next 4 dc, 1 dc into each of next 4 dc, rep from * to end, turn.

Row 8 Using 1st colour, 1 ch (does NOT count as st), 1 dc into each of first 4 dc, *1 tr into each of next 4 tr, 1 dc into each of next 4 dc, rep from * to end, turn.

These 8 rows form patt.

Note: *So that finished work is an even height throughout, end after a 3rd or 7th patt row.*

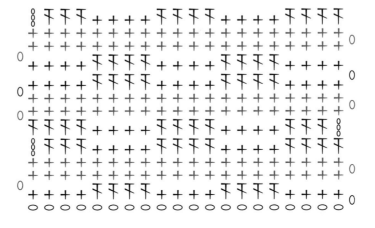

KEY
- ⌒ ch
- + dc
- ⊤ tr

Chevron and wave stitches

14: Alternating waves
Multiple of 6 sts plus 1.
Worked in 2 colours.
Start with a multiple of 6 ch, plus 2 extra.

Foundation row (RS) Using 1st colour, 1 dc into 2nd ch from
hook, *1 htr into next ch, 1 tr into next ch, 1 dtr into next
ch, 1 tr into next ch, 1 htr into next ch, 1 dc into next ch, rep
from * to end, turn.

Cont in patt as follows:

Row 1 Using 2nd colour, 4 ch (counts as first dtr), miss dc at
base of 4 ch, *1 tr into next htr, 1 htr into next tr, 1 dc into
next dtr, 1 htr into next tr, 1 tr into next htr, 1 dtr into next
dc, rep from * to end, turn.

Row 2 Using 2nd colour, 4 ch (counts as first dtr), miss dtr at
base of 4 ch, *1 tr into next tr, 1 htr into next htr, 1 dc into
next dc, 1 htr into next htr, 1 tr into next tr, 1 dtr into next
dtr, rep from * to end, working dtr at end of last rep into top
of 4 ch at beg of previous row, turn.

Row 3 Using 1st colour, 1 ch (does NOT count as st), 1 dc into
dtr at base of 1 ch, *1 htr into next tr, 1 tr into next htr, 1 dtr
into next dc, 1 tr into next htr, 1 htr into next tr, 1 dc into
next dtr, rep from * to end, working dc at end of last rep
into top of 4 ch at beg of previous row, turn.

Row 4 Using 1st colour, 1 ch (does NOT count as st), 1 dc into
first dc, *1 htr into next htr, 1 tr into next tr, 1 dtr into next
dtr, 1 tr into next tr, 1 htr into next htr, 1 dc into next dc, rep
from * to end, turn.

These 4 rows form patt.

Note: *So that finished work is an even height throughout, end
after a 1st or 3rd patt row.*

KEY

◯	ch
+	dc
T	htr
干	tr
丰	dtr

15: Spiked lozenge stitch
Multiple of 4 sts plus 2.
Worked in 2 colours.
Start with a multiple of 4 ch, plus 3 extra.

Foundation row (RS) Using 1st colour, 1 dc into 2nd ch from hook, 1 dc into each ch to end, turn.

Cont in patt as follows:

Row 1 Using 1st colour, 1 ch (does NOT count as st), 1 dc into each dc to end, turn.

Rows 2 and 3 As row 1.

Row 4 Using 2nd colour, 1 ch (does NOT count as st), 1 dc into first dc, *1 dc into next dc, 1 dc into corresponding dc one row below next dc, 1 dc into corresponding dc 2 rows below next dc, 1 dc into corresponding dc 3 rows below next dc, rep from * to last dc, 1 dc into last dc, turn.

Rows 5 to 7 Using 2nd colour, as row 1.

Row 8 Using 1st colour, 1 ch (does NOT count as st), 1 dc into first dc, *1 dc into next dc, 1 dc into corresponding dc one row below next dc, 1 dc into corresponding dc 2 rows below next dc, 1 dc into corresponding dc 3 rows below next dc, rep from * to last dc, 1 dc into last dc, turn.

These 8 rows form patt.

Note: *To keep continuity of fabric, end after a 4th or 8th patt row.*

KEY

○ ch	⌇ dc into corresp. dc 2 rows below next dc
+ dc	
⌇ dc into corresp. dc 1 row below next dc	⌇ dc into corresp. dc 3 rows below next dc

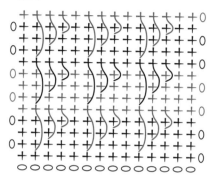

16: Spiked chevron stitch
Multiple of 6 sts plus 1.
Worked in 2 colours.
Start with a multiple of 6 ch, plus 2 extra.

Foundation row (RS) Using 1st colour, 1 dc into 2nd ch from hook, 1 dc into each ch to end, turn.

Cont in patt as follows:

Row 1 Using 1st colour, 1 ch (does NOT count as st), 1 dc into each dc to end, turn.

Rows 2 and 3 As row 1.

Row 4 Using 2nd colour, 1 ch (does NOT count as st), 1 dc into first dc, *1 dc into corresponding dc one row below next dc, 1 dc into corresponding dc 2 rows below next dc, 1 dc into corresponding dc 3 rows below next dc, 1 dc into corresponding dc 2 rows below next dc, 1 dc into corresponding dc one row below next dc, 1 dc into next dc, rep from * to end, turn.

Rows 5 to 7 Using 2nd colour, as row 1.

Row 8 Using 1st colour, 1 ch (does NOT count as st), 1 dc into first dc, *1 dc into corresponding dc one row below next dc, 1 dc into corresponding dc 2 rows below next dc, 1 dc into corresponding dc 3 rows below next dc, 1 dc into corresponding dc 2 rows below next dc, 1 dc into corresponding dc one row below next dc, 1 dc into next dc, rep from * to end, turn.

These 8 rows form patt.

Note: *To keep continuity of fabric, end after a 4th or 8th patt row.*

KEY

○ ch	⌇ dc into corresp. dc 2 rows below next dc
+ dc	
⌇ dc into corresp. dc 1 row below next dc	⌇ dc into corresp. dc 3 rows below next dc

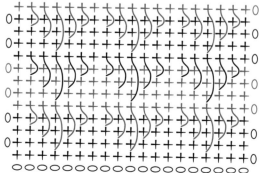

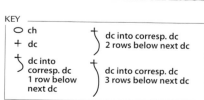

STITCH LIBRARY

projects

Band of bunnies

These cuddly bunnies show just how much the weight of a yarn and the tension you work to can affect the outcome of the overall project. The toys are worked in simple double crochet stitch, with the bunnies' facial features worked in embroidery afterwards.

PROJECT NOTES

MEASUREMENTS

(All measurements include ears)
Miss Pink is 30cm (11¾in) tall
Mr Grey is 26cm (10¼in) tall
Sparkles is 21cm (8¼in) tall
Fluffy is 16cm (6¼in) tall

YARN

Miss Pink: 1 x 50g (1¾oz) ball of aran-weight merino, angora, nylon and metallic fibre in soft pink

Mr Grey: 1 x 50g (1¾oz) ball of DK-weight 50% merino, 50% cotton mix yarn in soft grey

Sparkles: 1 x 50g (1¾oz) ball of 4ply viscose and metallized polyester yarn in rainbow blues and pinks

Fluffy: 1 x 25g (⅞oz) ball of 4ply super kid mohair and silk yarn in cream

HOOKS

Miss Pink: 3.50mm (E4) hook
Mr Grey: 3.00mm (D3) hook
Sparkles: 2.50mm (C2) hook
Fluffy: 1.75mm (5) hook

NOTIONS

ALL BUNNIES:
Washable toy filling
Oddments of embroidery thread for nose and mouth
2 beads for eyes
Length of ribbon

SPECIAL ABBREVIATIONS

dc2tog (insert hook as indicated, yarn over hook and draw loop through) twice, yarn over hook and draw through all 3 loops.

TENSION

Miss Pink: 20 sts and 20 rows to 10cm (4in) measured over double crochet fabric on 3.50mm (E4) hook, or the size required to achieve stated tension.

Mr Grey: 24 sts and 24 rows to 10cm (4in) measured over double crochet fabric on 3.00mm (D3) hook, or the size required to achieve stated tension.

Sparkles: 27 sts and 30 rows to 10cm (4in) measured over double crochet fabric on 2.50mm (C2) hook, or the size required to achieve stated tension.

Fluffy: 35 sts and 33 rows to 10cm (4in) measured over double crochet fabric on 1.75mm (5) hook, or the size required to achieve stated tension.

THE PATTERN

ARMS (make 2)

With appropriate size hook, make 3 ch.

Round 1 (RS) 2 dc into 2nd ch from hook, 4 dc into next ch, then working back along other side of foundation ch work 2 dc into next ch (this is same ch as used for first 2 dc), ss to first dc, turn. 8 sts.

Round 2 1 ch (does NOT count as st), 2 dc into first dc, 1 dc into each of next 2 dc, 2 dc into each of next 2 dc, 1 dc into each of next 2 dc, 2 dc into last dc, ss to first dc, turn. 12 sts.

Round 3 1 ch (does NOT count as st), 1 dc into each st to end, ss to first dc, turn.

Round 4 1 ch (does NOT count as st), 2 dc into first dc, 1 dc into each of next 3 dc, [dc2tog over next 2 dc] twice, 1 dc into each of next 3 dc, 2 dc into last dc, ss to first dc, turn.

Round 5 As round 3.

Round 6 1 ch (does NOT count as st), 1 dc into each of first 4 dc, [dc2tog over next 2 dc] twice, 1 dc into each of last 4 dc, ss to first dc, turn. 10 sts.

Rounds 7 to 14 As round 3.
Fasten off.
Insert toy filling into arms.

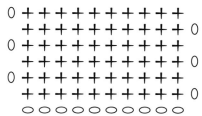

KEY
O ch
+ dc

Here the fluffy yarn obscures the stitch pattern.

The double crochet pattern is clearer here.

LEGS (make 2)

Work as given for arms to end of round 2. 12 sts.

Round 3 1 ch (does NOT count as st), 2 dc into first dc, 1 dc into each of next 4 dc, 2 dc into each of next 2 dc, 1 dc into each of next 4 dc, 2 dc into last dc, ss to first dc, turn. 16 sts.

Round 4 1 ch (does NOT count as st), 2 dc into first dc, 1 dc into each of next 14 dc, 2 dc into last dc, ss to first dc, turn. 18 sts.

Round 5 1 ch (does NOT count as st), 1 dc into each st to end, ss to first dc, turn.

Round 6 As round 5.

Round 7 1 ch (does NOT count as st), 1 dc into each of first 7 dc, [dc2tog over next 2 dc] twice, 1 dc into each of last 7 dc, ss to first dc, turn. 16 sts.

Round 8 1 ch (does NOT count as st), 1 dc into each of first 6 dc, [dc2tog over next 2 dc] twice, 1 dc into each of last 6 dc, ss to first dc, turn. 14 sts.

Round 9 1 ch (does NOT count as st), 1 dc into each of first 5 dc, [dc2tog over next 2 dc] twice, 1 dc into each of last 5 dc, ss to first dc, turn. 12 sts.

Rounds 10 to 13 As round 5.

Round 14 1 ch (does NOT count as st), 1 dc into each of first 5 dc, 2 dc into each of next 2 dc, 1 dc into each of last 5 dc, ss to first dc, turn. 14 sts.

Rounds 15 to 16 As round 5.

Fasten off.

Insert toy filling into legs.

BODY AND HEAD

With RS facing, rejoin yarn to top of last round of one leg by working a ss into 13th dc of last round and then work around top of both legs as follows:

Round 1 (RS) 1 ch (does NOT count as st), 1 dc into st where yarn was rejoined, 1 dc into each of next 13 dc of this leg, starting on 3rd dc of round 16 of other leg, 1 dc into each of the 14 dc of this leg, then ss to first dc, turn. 28 sts.

Round 2 1 ch (does NOT count as st), 1 dc into each of first 6 dc, 2 dc into each of next 2 dc, 1 dc into each of next 5 dc, 2 dc into each of next 2 dc, 1 dc into each of next 5 dc, 2 dc into each of next 2 dc, 1 dc into each of last 6 dc, ss to first dc, turn. 34 sts.

Round 3 1 ch (does NOT count as st), 1 dc into each of first 7 dc, [2 dc into each of next 2 dc, 1 dc into each of next 7 dc] 3 times, ss to first dc, turn. 40 sts.

Round 4 1 ch (does NOT count as st), 1 dc into each of first 8 dc, 2 dc into each of next 2 dc, 1 dc into each of next 20 dc, 2 dc into each of next 2 dc, 1 dc into each of last 8 dc, ss to first dc, turn. 44 sts.

Round 5 1 ch (does NOT count as st), 1 dc into each dc to end, ss to first dc, turn.

Rounds 6 and 7 As round 5.

Round 8 1 ch (does NOT count as st), 1 dc into each of first 20 dc, [dc2tog over next 2 dc] twice, 1 dc into each of last 20 dc, ss to first dc, turn. 42 sts.

Round 9 As round 5.

Round 10 1 ch (does NOT count as st), 1 dc into each of first 8 dc, [dc2tog over next 2 dc] twice, 1 dc into each of next 18 dc, [dc2tog over next 2 dc] twice, 1 dc into each of last 8 dc, ss to first dc, turn. 38 sts.

Round 11 1 ch (does NOT count as st), 1 dc into each of first 17 dc, [dc2tog over next 2 dc] twice, 1 dc into each of last 17 dc, ss to first dc, turn. 36 sts.

Round 12 1 ch (does NOT count as st), 1 dc into each of first 7 dc, [dc2tog over next 2 dc] twice, 1 dc into each of next 14 dc, [dc2tog over next 2 dc] twice, 1 dc into each of last 7 dc, ss to first dc, turn. 32 sts.

Round 13 As round 5.

Round 14 1 ch (does NOT count as st), 1 dc into each of first 6 dc, [dc2tog over next 2 dc] twice, 1 dc into each of next 12 dc, [dc2tog over next 2 dc] twice, 1 dc into each of last 6 dc, ss to first dc, turn. 28 sts.

Round 15 As round 5.

Round 16 1 ch (does NOT count as st), 1 dc into each of first 5 dc, [dc2tog over next 2 dc] twice, 1 dc into each of next 10 dc, [dc2tog over next 2 dc] twice, 1 dc into each of last 5 dc, ss to first dc, turn. 24 sts.

Round 17 1 ch (does NOT count as st), 1 dc into each of first 4 dc, [dc2tog over next 2 dc] twice, 1 dc into each of next 8 dc, [dc2tog over next 2 dc] twice, 1 dc into each of last 4 dc, ss to first dc, turn. 20 sts.

MR GREY

MISS PINK

SPARKLES

FLUFFY

Round 18 1 ch (does NOT count as st), 1 dc into each of first 3 dc, [dc2tog over next 2 dc] twice, 1 dc into each of next 6 dc, [dc2tog over next 2 dc] twice, 1 dc into each of last 3 dc, ss to first dc, turn. 16 sts.
Insert toy filling into body.

● *Join arms*

Round 19 1 ch (does NOT count as st), [dc2tog over next 2 sts] twice, now starting on 8th dc of 14th round of one arm, [dc2tog over next 2 dc] 5 times around top of this arm, now working into body again: [dc2tog over next 2 sts] twice, now starting on 3rd dc of 14th round of other arm, [dc2tog over next 2 dc] 5 times around top of this arm, now working into body again: [dc2tog over next 2 sts] twice, ss to first dc2tog, turn. 18 sts.

Round 20 As round 5.
Insert a little more toy filling into neck.

● *Shape head*

Round 1 (RS) 1 ch (does NOT count as st), 2 dc into first dc, 1 dc into each of next 2 dc, [2 dc into each of next 2 dc, 1 dc into each of next 3 dc] twice, 2 dc into each of next 2 dc, 1 dc into each of next 2 dc, 2 dc into last dc, ss to first dc, turn. 26 sts.

Round 2 1 ch (does NOT count as st), 2 dc into first dc, 1 dc into each of next 4 dc, [2 dc into each of next 2 dc, 1 dc into each of next 5 dc] twice, 2 dc into each of next 2 dc, 1 dc into each of next 4 dc, 2 dc into last dc, ss to first dc, turn. 34 sts.

Round 3 1 ch (does NOT count as st), 1 dc into each of first 7 dc, [2 dc into each of next 2 dc, 1 dc into each of next 7 dc] 3 times, ss to first dc, turn. 40 sts.

Round 4 1 ch (does NOT count as st), 2 dc into first dc, 1 dc into each of next 18 dc, 2 dc into each of next 2 dc, 1 dc into each of next 18 dc, 2 dc into last dc, ss to first dc, turn. 44 sts.

Round 5 1 ch (does NOT count as st), 1 dc into each dc to end, ss to first dc, turn.

Round 6 1 ch (does NOT count as st), 1 dc into each of first 20 dc, [dc2tog over next 2 sts] twice, 1 dc into each of last 20 dc, ss to first dc, turn. 42 sts.

Round 7 1 ch (does NOT count as st), 1 dc into each of first 19 dc, [dc2tog over next 2 sts] twice, 1 dc into each of last 19 dc, ss to first dc, turn. 40 sts.

Round 8 1 ch (does NOT count as st), 1 dc into each of first 18 dc, [dc2tog over next 2 sts] twice, 1 dc into each of last 18 dc, ss to first dc, turn. 38 sts.

Round 9 1 ch (does NOT count as st), dc2tog over first 2 sts, 1 dc into each of next 5 dc, *[dc2tog over next 2 sts] twice, 1 dc into each of next 6 dc, rep from * once more, [dc2tog over next 2 sts] twice, 1 dc into each of next 5 dc, dc2tog over last 2 sts, ss to first dc, turn. 30 sts.

Round 10 1 ch (does NOT count as st), 1 dc into each of first 5 dc, *[dc2tog over next 2 sts] twice, 1 dc into each of next 4 dc, rep from * once more, [dc2tog over next 2 sts] twice, 1 dc into each of last 5 dc, ss to first dc, turn. 24 sts.

Round 11 1 ch (does NOT count as st), dc2tog over first 2 sts, *1 dc into each of next 2 dc, [dc2tog over next 2 sts] twice, rep from * twice more, 1 dc into each of next 2 dc, dc2tog over last 2 sts, ss to first dc, turn. 16 sts.

Insert toy filling into head.

Round 12 1 ch (does NOT count as st), [dc2tog over next 2 sts] 8 times, ss to first dc, turn. 8 sts.

Round 13 1 ch (does NOT count as st), [dc2tog over next 2 sts] 4 times, ss to first dc, turn. 4 sts.

Fasten off.

EARS (make 2)

With appropriate size hook, make 2 ch.

Round 1 (RS) 4 dc into 2nd ch from hook, ss to first dc, turn. 4 sts.

Round 2 1 ch (does NOT count as st), 1 dc into each dc to end, ss to first dc, turn.

Round 3 1 ch (does NOT count as st), 2 dc into each dc to end, ss to first dc, turn. 8 sts.

Round 4 As round 2.

Round 5 1 ch (does NOT count as st), 2 dc into first dc, 1 dc into each of next 2 dc, 2 dc into each of next 2 dc, 1 dc into each of next 2 dc, 2 dc into last dc, ss to first dc, turn. 12 sts.

Round 6 As round 2.

Round 7 1 ch (does NOT count as st), 2 dc into first dc, 1 dc into each of next 4 dc, 2 dc into each of next 2 dc, 1 dc into each of next 4 dc, 2 dc into last dc, ss to first dc, turn. 16 sts.

Rounds 8 to 12 As round 2.

Round 13 1 ch (does NOT count as st), dc2tog over first 2 dc, 1 dc into each of next 4 dc, [dc2tog over next 2 dc] twice, 1 dc into each of next 4 dc, dc2tog over last 2 dc, ss to first dc2tog, turn. 12 sts.

Rounds 14 to 16 As round 2.
Fasten off.

FINISHING

Using photograph (left) as a guide, embroider satin-stitch nose and back-stitch mouth under nose.
Attach beads to form eyes.
Tie ribbon in a bow around neck.

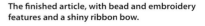

The finished article, with bead and embroidery features and a shiny ribbon bow.

Sunny day stripes

The cheerful colours of this baby sweater and hat are worked in simple rows and rounds of treble crochet. The yarn not being used is simply carried up the edge of the work, which means that there are very few yarn ends for you to darn in when making up.

PROJECT NOTES

MEASUREMENTS
To fit age approximately: 0-3 [3-6: 6-12: 12-18] months

BODY

21 [26:29:34]cm
8¼ [10¼:11½:13¼] in

SLEEVE

13 [14:19:22]cm
(5in [5½:7½:8½]in)

SWEATER:
To fit chest: 41cm (16in) [46cm (18in): 51cm (20in): 56cm (22in)]
Actual size: 45cm (17¾in) [50cm (19½in): 55cm (21½in): 60cm (23½in)]
Full length: 21cm (8¼in) [26cm (10¼in): 29cm (11½in): 34cm (13¼in)]
Sleeve seam: 13cm (5in) [14cm (5½in): 19cm (7½in): 22cm (8½in)]

HAT:
Width around head: 33cm (13in) [35cm (13¾in): 38cm (15in): 40cm (15¾in)]

YARN
All 4ply 100% cotton
SWEATER:
A 2 [2: 2: 3] x 50g (1¾oz) balls in turquoise

B 2 [2: 2: 3] x 50g (1¾oz) balls in lemon yellow
HAT:
A 1 x 50g (1¾oz) ball in turquoise
B 1 x 50g (1¾oz) ball in lemon yellow

HOOK
2.50mm (C2) hook

SPECIAL ABBREVIATIONS
tr2tog *yarn over hook and insert hook as indicated, yarn over hook and draw loop through, yarn over hook and draw through 2 loops, rep from * once more, yarn over hook and draw through all 3 loops on hook.

TENSION
24 sts and 12½ rows to 10cm (4in) measured over treble fabric on 2.50mm (C2) hook, or the size required to achieve stated tension.

THE PATTERN

SWEATER: BACK

With 2.50mm (C2) hook and yarn A, make 55 [61: 67: 73] ch.

Foundation row (RS) 1 dc into 2nd ch from hook, 1 dc into each ch to end, turn. 54 [60: 66: 72] sts.

Next row 1 ch (does NOT count as st), 1 dc into each dc to end, turn.

Rep last row twice more, ending after a WS row.

Join in yarn B and cont in tr fabric as follows:

Next row (RS) 3 ch (counts as first tr), miss st at base of 3 ch, 1 tr into each st to end, turn.

This row forms tr fabric. (*Note: on following rows, last tr will be worked into top of 3 ch at beg of previous row.*)

Cont in tr fabric in stripes as follows:

Using B, work 1 row.
Using A, work 2 rows.
Last 4 rows form striped tr fabric.
Cont in striped tr fabric for a further 8 [12: 14: 18] rows, ending after 2 rows using A [A: B: B] and a WS row.

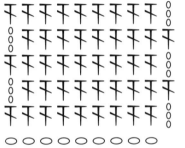

KEY
○ ch
⊤ tr

● *Shape armholes*
Keeping stripes correct, cont as follows:

Next row (RS) Ss across and into 4th st, 3 ch (counts as first tr), miss tr at base of 3 ch (3 sts decreased), 1 tr into each tr to last 3 sts and turn, leaving rem 3 sts unworked (3 sts decreased). 48 [54: 60: 66] sts.

Next row 3 ch (counts as first tr), miss tr at end of previous row, tr2tog over next 2 sts (1 st decreased), 1 tr into each tr to last 3 sts, tr2tog over next 2 sts (1 st decreased), 1 tr into top of 3 ch at beg of previous row, turn.

Working all decreases as set by last row, dec 1 st at each end of next 4 [4: 5: 6] rows. 38 [44: 48: 52] sts.**

Work 4 [6: 7: 8] rows, ending after 2 rows using B [A: A: B] and a WS row.

- *Shape back neck*

Next row Patt 7 sts and turn, leaving rem sts unworked.

Dec 1 st at neck edge of next row.

Place marker at armhole edge of last row – this denotes shoulder point.

Dec 1 st at neck edge of next 4 rows. 2 sts.

Fasten off.

Return to last complete row worked, miss centre 24 [30: 34: 38] sts, rejoin appropriate yarn to next st, 3 ch (counts as first st), patt to end, turn. 7 sts.

Complete to match first side, reversing shaping.

SWEATER: FRONT

Work as given for back to **.

Work 0 [2: 3: 4] rows, ending after 2 rows using B [A: A: B] and a WS row.

- *Shape front neck*

Next row Patt 11 sts and turn, leaving rem sts unworked.

Dec 1 st at neck edge of next 5 rows.

Place marker at armhole edge of last row – this denotes shoulder point.

Dec 1 st at neck edge of next 4 rows. 2 sts. Fasten off.

Return to last complete row worked, miss centre 16 [22: 26: 30] sts, rejoin appropriate yarn to next st, 3 ch (counts as first st), patt to end, turn. 11 sts.

Complete to match first side, reversing shaping.

SWEATER: SLEEVES

With 2.50mm (C2) hook and B [A: A: A], make 30 [32: 34: 36] ch.

Foundation row (RS) 1 dc into 2nd ch from hook, 1 dc into each ch to end, turn. 29 [31: 33: 35] sts.

Next row 1 ch (does NOT count as st), 1 dc into each dc to end, turn.

Rep last row twice more, ending after a WS row.

Join in A [B: B: B] and cont as follows:

Next row (RS) Using A [B: B: B], 3 ch (counts as first tr), miss st at base of 3 ch, 2 tr into next tr (1 st increased), 1 tr into each st to last 2 sts, 2 tr into next tr (1 st increased), 1 tr into last st, turn.

This row sets striped tr fabric as given for back and starts sleeve shaping.

Working all increases as set by last row and keeping striped tr fabric correct, inc 1 st at each end of 2nd [next: next: next] and foll 0 [3: 1: 3] rows, then on foll 4 [4: 8: 9] alt rows. 41 [49: 55: 63] sts.

Cont in striped tr fabric for a further 3 rows, ending after 2 rows using A [A: B: B] and a WS row.

- *Shape top*

Working all shaping in same way as for back armhole, dec 3 sts at each end of next row. 35 [43: 49: 57] sts.

Dec 1 st at each end of next 7 [7: 9: 9] rows, ending after 2 rows using A and a WS row. 21 [29: 31: 39] sts.

Fasten off.

MAKING UP

- *Neck edgings*

With RS facing, 2.50mm (C2) hook and A [B: B: A], rejoin yarn at fasten-off point of right back neck edge, 1 ch (does NOT count as st), work 1 row of dc down right back neck slope, across centre sts, then up left back neck slope to left back fasten-off point, turn.

Next row (WS) 1 ch (does NOT count as st),

The neck edging is added after the main pieces of the sweater have been made.

2 dc into first dc, 1 dc into each dc to last dc, 2 dc into last dc, turn.

Rep last row twice more.

Fasten off.

Work edging along front neck edge in same way.

Lay the back piece over the front so that markers denoting shoulder points match (to create envelope neck) and sew together at armhole edges.

Join side seams. Join sleeve seams. Insert sleeves into armholes, enclosing ends of neck edgings in seams.

HAT

With 2.50mm (C2) hook and A, make 78 [84: 90: 96] ch and join with a ss to form a ring.

Foundation round (RS) 1 ch (does NOT count as st), 1 dc into each ch to end, ss to first dc, turn. 78 [84: 90: 96] sts.

Next round 1 ch (does NOT count as st), 1 dc into each dc to end, ss to first dc, turn.

Rep last round twice more, ending after a WS round.

Join in B and cont in tr fabric as follows:

Next round (RS) 3 ch (counts as first tr), miss st at base of 3 ch, 1 tr into each st to end, ss to top of 3 ch at beg of round, turn.

This round forms tr fabric.

Cont in tr fabric in stripes as follows:

Using B, work 1 round.

Using A, work 2 rounds.

Last 4 rounds form striped tr fabric.

Cont in striped tr fabric for a further 7 rounds, ending after 1 round using A and a RS round.

Keeping stripes correct, shape hat as follows:

Round 1 (WS) 3 ch (counts as first tr), miss st at base of 3 ch, 1 tr into each of next 10 [11: 12: 13] tr, (tr2tog over next 2 tr, 1 tr into each of next 11 [12: 13: 14] tr) 5 times, tr2tog over last 2 tr, ss to top of 3 ch at beg of round, turn. 72 [78: 84: 90] sts.

Round 2 and every foll alt round 3 ch

(counts as first tr), miss st at base of 3 ch, 1 tr into each st to end, ss to top of 3 ch at beg of round, turn.

Round 3 3 ch (counts as first tr), miss st at base of 3 ch, 1 tr into each of next 9 [10: 11: 12] tr, (tr2tog over next 2 tr, 1 tr into each of next 10 [11: 12: 13] tr) 5 times, tr2tog over last 2 tr, ss to top of 3 ch at beg of round, turn. 66 [72: 78: 84] sts.

Round 5 3 ch (counts as first tr), miss st at base of 3 ch, 1 tr into each of next 8 [9: 10: 11] tr, (tr2tog over next 2 tr, 1 tr into each of next 9 [10: 11: 12] tr) 5 times, tr2tog over last 2 tr, ss to top of 3 ch at beg of round, turn. 60 [66: 72: 78] sts.

Round 7 3 ch (counts as first tr), miss st at base of 3 ch, 1 tr into each of next 7 [8: 9: 10] tr, (tr2tog over next 2 tr, 1 tr into each of next 8 [9: 10: 11] tr) 5 times, tr2tog over last 2 tr, ss to top of 3 ch at beg of round, turn. 54 [60: 66: 72] sts.

Round 9 3 ch (counts as first tr), miss st at base of 3 ch, 1 tr into each of next 6 [7: 8: 9] tr, (tr2tog over next 2 tr, 1 tr into each of next 7 [8: 9: 10] tr) 5 times, tr2tog over last 2 tr, ss to top of 3 ch at beg of round, turn. 48 [54: 60: 66] sts.

Round 11 3 ch (counts as first tr), miss st at base of 3 ch, 1 tr into each of next 5 [6: 7: 8] tr, (tr2tog over next 2 tr, 1 tr into each of next 6 [7: 8: 9] tr) 5 times, tr2tog over last 2 tr, ss to top of 3 ch at beg of round, turn. 42 [48: 54: 60] sts.

Round 13 3 ch (counts as first tr), miss st at base of 3 ch, 1 tr into each of next 4 [5: 6: 7] tr, (tr2tog over next 2 tr, 1 tr into each of next 5 [6: 7: 8] tr) 5 times, tr2tog over last 2 tr, ss to top of 3 ch at beg of round, turn. 36 [42: 48: 54] sts.

Cont in this way, dec 6 sts on every foll alt round, until the foll round has been worked:

Next round (RS) 3 ch (counts as first tr), miss st at base of 3 ch, (tr2tog over next 2 tr, 1 tr into next tr) 5 times, tr2tog over last 2 tr, ss to top of 3 ch at beg of round, turn. 12 sts.

Next round As round 2.

Next round 3 ch (does NOT count as st), miss st at base of 3 ch, (tr2tog over next 2 tr) 5 times, 1 tr into last tr, ss to top of first tr2tog at beg of round, turn. 6 sts.

Next round As round 2.

Fasten off.

Using B, make a 10cm (4in) tassel and attach to top of hat.

Precious pastels baby set

This set of matching baby hat, bootees and mittens is worked in variegated yarn with trimmings worked in a matching plain yarn. Toning ribbons create a pretty finishing touch.

PROJECT NOTES

MEASUREMENTS
One size, to fit a newborn baby
BOOTEES:
Length of foot 9cm (3½in)
MITTENS:
Width around hand 10cm (4in)
HAT:
Width around head 32cm (12½in)

YARN
All DK-weight 100% merino wool
M 2 x 50g (1¾oz) balls in variegated pinks
C 1 x 50g (1¾oz) ball in pale pink

HOOK
3.50mm (E4) hook

NOTIONS
2.4m (95in) of 7mm (¼in)-wide ribbon

SPECIAL ABBREVIATIONS
dc2tog (insert hook as indicated, yoh and draw loop through) twice, yoh and draw through all 3 loops
yoh yarn over hook.

TENSION
20 sts and 24 rows to 10cm (4in) measured over pattern on 3.50mm (E4) hook, or the size required to achieve stated tension.

THE PATTERN

BOOTEES

With 3.50mm (E4) hook and yarn M, make 24 ch and join with a ss to form a ring.

Round 1 (RS) 1 ch (does NOT count as st), 1 dc into each ch to end, ss to first dc, turn. 24 sts.

Round 2 1 ch (does NOT count as st), 1 dc into first dc, (1 ch, miss 1 dc, 1 dc into each of next 2 dc) 7 times, 1 ch, miss 1 dc, 1 dc into last dc, ss to first dc, turn.

Round 3 1 ch (does NOT count as st), 1 dc into first dc, (1 dc into next ch sp, 1 dc into

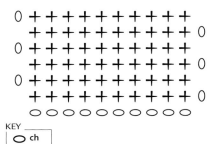

KEY
O ch
+ dc

each of next 2 dc) 7 times, 1 dc into next ch sp, 1 dc into last dc, ss to first dc, turn.

Round 4 1 ch (does NOT count as st), 1 dc into each dc to end, ss to first dc, turn.

● *Shape instep*
Slip working loop onto a safety pin.
With RS facing and separate length of yarn M, miss first 9 dc of next round, rejoin yarn to next dc, 1 ch (does NOT count as st), 1 dc into dc where yarn was rejoined, 1 dc into each of next 5 dc, turn.

Work on this set of 6 sts only for instep.

Next row 1 ch (does NOT count as st), 1 dc into each dc to end, turn.

Rep last row 5 times more.

Next row (WS) 1 ch (does NOT count as st), dc2tog over first 2 dc, 1 dc into each of next 2 dc, dc2tog over last 2 dc. 4 sts.

Fasten off.

Return to working loop left on safety pin, slip this loop back onto hook and cont as follows:

Round 5 (RS) 1 ch (does NOT count as st), 1 dc into each of first dc, 1 dc into each of next 8 row-ends of instep, 1 dc into each of 4 sts across end of instep, 1 dc into each of next 8 row-ends of other side of instep, 1 dc into each of last 9 dc, ss to first dc, turn. 38 sts.

Rounds 6 to 10 As round 4.

● *Shape sole*

Round 11 (RS) 1 ch (does NOT count as st), 1 dc into first dc, dc2tog over next 2 dc, 1 dc into each of next 11 dc, dc2tog over next 2 dc, 1 dc into each of next 6 dc, dc2tog over next 2 dc, 1 dc into each of next 11 dc, dc2tog over next 2 dc, 1 dc into last dc, ss to first dc, turn. 34 sts.

Round 12 1 ch (does NOT count as st), 1 dc into each of first 2 sts, dc2tog over next 2 sts, 1 dc into each of next 10 sts, dc2tog over next 2 sts, 1 dc into each of next 2 sts, dc2tog over next 2 sts, 1 dc into each of next 10 sts, dc2tog over next 2 sts, 1 dc into each of last 2 sts, ss to first dc, turn. 30 sts.

Round 13 1 ch (does NOT count as st), dc2tog over first 2 sts, 1 dc into each of next 9 sts, dc2tog over next 2 sts, 1 dc into each of next 4 sts, dc2tog over next 2 sts, 1 dc into each of next 9 sts, dc2tog over last 2 sts, ss to first dc2tog, turn. 26 sts.

Round 14 1 ch (does NOT count as st), 1 dc into first st, dc2tog over next 2 sts, 1 dc into each of next 8 sts, (dc2tog over next 2 sts) twice, 1 dc into each of next 8 sts, dc2tog over next 2 sts, 1 dc into last st, ss to first dc, turn. 22 sts.

Round 15 1 ch (does NOT count as st), dc2tog over first 2 sts, 1 dc into each of next 7 sts, (dc2tog over next 2 sts) twice, 1 dc into each of next 7 sts, dc2tog over last 2 sts, ss to first dc2tog, turn. 18 sts.

Fold bootee flat with RS facing and join sole seam by working a row of dc through sts of both layers.

Fasten off.

MAKING UP

● *Edging*

With RS facing and C, attach yarn to beg of foundation ch edge, 1 ch (does NOT count as st), 1 dc into each foundation ch around top of bootee, ss to first dc.

Round 1 (RS) 4 ch, 1 ss into same place as ss closing last round, *4 ch, (1 ss, 4 ch and 1 ss) into next dc, rep from * to end, 2 ch, 1 htr into same place as ss at beg of round.

Round 2 1 ch (does NOT count as st), 1 ss into ch sp partly formed by ss at end of previous round, *4 ch, 1 ss into next ch sp, rep from * to end, working last ss into ss at beg of round.

Fasten off.

Cut two 45cm (17¾in) lengths of ribbon and thread each length through holes of round 2 as in photograph. Tie ends in a bow on front of bootees.

MITTENS

With 3.50mm (E4) hook and M, make 20 ch and join with a ss to form a ring.

Round 1 (RS) 1 ch (does NOT count as st), 1 dc into each ch to end, ss to first dc, turn. 20 sts.

Round 2 1 ch (does NOT count as st), 1 dc into first dc, (1 ch, miss 1 dc, 1 dc into next dc, 1 ch, miss 1 dc, 1 dc into each of next 2 dc) 3 times, 1 ch, miss 1 dc, 1 dc into next dc, 1 ch, miss 1 dc, 1 dc into last dc, ss to first dc, turn.

Round 3 1 ch (does NOT count as st), 1 dc into first dc, (1 dc into next ch sp, 1 dc into next dc, 1 dc into next ch sp, 1 dc into each of next 2 dc) 3 times, 1 dc into next ch sp, 1 dc into next dc, 1 dc into next ch sp, 1 dc into last dc, ss to first dc, turn.

Round 4 1 ch (does NOT count as st), 1 dc into each dc to end, ss to first dc, turn.

Rounds 5 to 14 As round 4.

- *Shape top*

Round 15 (RS) 1 ch (does NOT count as st), dc2tog over first 2 dc, 1 dc into each of next 6 dc, (dc2tog over next 2 dc) twice, 1 dc into each of next 6 dc, dc2tog over last 2 dc, ss to first dc2tog, turn. 16 sts.

Round 16 As round 4.

Round 17 1 ch (does NOT count as st), dc2tog over first 2 dc, 1 dc into each of next 4 dc, (dc2tog over next 2 dc) twice, 1 dc into each of next 4 dc, dc2tog over last 2 dc, ss to first dc2tog, turn. 12 sts.

Round 18 1 ch (does NOT count as st), dc2tog over first 2 sts, 1 dc into each of next 2 dc, (dc2tog over next 2 sts) twice, 1 dc into each of next 2 dc, dc2tog over last 2 sts, ss to first dc2tog, turn.

Fold mitten flat with RS facing and join top seam by working a row of dc through sts of both layers.

Fasten off.

MAKING UP

- *Edging*

With RS facing and yarn C, attach yarn to beg of foundation ch edge, 1 ch (does NOT count as st), 1 dc into each foundation ch around lower edge of mitten, ss to first dc.

Work rounds 1 and 2 of edging as given for bootees.

Fasten off.

Cut two 40cm (15¾in) lengths of ribbon and thread each length through holes of round 2 as in photograph. Tie ends in a bow on back of mittens.

HAT

With 3.50mm (E4) hook and yarn M, make 64 ch and join with a ss to form a ring.

Round 1 (RS) 1 ch (does NOT count as st), 1 dc into each ch to end, ss to first dc, turn. 64 sts.

Round 2 1 ch (does NOT count as st), 1 dc into first dc, (1 ch, miss 1 dc, 1 dc into next dc) twice, (1 ch, miss 1 dc, 1 dc into each of next 2 dc, 1 ch, miss 1 dc, 1 dc into next dc) 11 times, 1 ch, miss 1 dc, 1 dc into next dc, 1 ch, miss 1 dc, 1 dc into last dc, ss to first dc, turn.

Round 3 1 ch (does NOT count as st), 1 dc into first dc, (1 dc into next ch sp, 1 dc into next dc) twice, (1 dc into next ch sp, 1 dc into each of next 2 dc, 1 dc into next ch sp, 1 dc into next dc) 11 times, 1 dc into next ch sp, 1 dc into next dc, 1 dc into next ch sp, 1 dc into last dc, ss to first dc, turn.

Round 4 1 ch (does NOT count as st), 1 dc into each dc to end, ss to first dc, turn.

Rounds 5 to 18 As round 4.

Round 19 1 ch (does NOT count as st), (1 dc into each of next 6 dc, dc2tog over next 2 dc) 8 times, ss to first dc, turn. 56 sts.

Rounds 20 to 22 As round 4.

Round 23 1 ch (does NOT count as st), (1 dc into each of next 5 dc, dc2tog over next 2 dc) 8 times, ss to first dc, turn. 48 sts.

Round 24 As round 4.

Round 25 1 ch (does NOT count as st), (1 dc into each of next 4 dc, dc2tog over next 2 dc) 8 times, ss to first dc, turn. 40 sts.

Round 26 As round 4.

Round 27 1 ch (does NOT count as st), (1 dc into each of next 3 dc, dc2tog over next 2 dc) 8 times, ss to first dc, turn. 32 sts.

Round 28 As round 4.

Round 29 1 ch (does NOT count as st), (1 dc into each of next 2 dc, dc2tog over next 2 dc) 8 times, ss to first dc, turn. 24 sts.

Round 30 As round 4.

Round 31 1 ch (does NOT count as st), (1 dc into next dc, dc2tog over next 2 dc) 8 times, ss to first dc, turn. 16 sts.

Round 32 1 ch (does NOT count as st), (dc2tog over next 2 sts) 8 times, ss to first dc, turn. 8 sts.

Round 33 1 ch (does NOT count as st), (dc2tog over next 2 sts) 4 times, ss to first dc, turn. 4 sts.

Fasten off.

MAKING UP

- *Edging*

With RS facing and yarn C, attach yarn to beg of foundation ch edge, 1 ch (does NOT count as st), 1 dc into each foundation ch around lower edge of hat, ss to first dc.

Work rounds 1 and 2 of edging as given for bootees.

Fasten off.

Cut 70cm (27½in) length of ribbon and thread through holes of round 2 as in photograph. Tie ends in a bow at front of hat.

Pretty in pink cardigan and shawl

This fetching baby cardigan combines two stitches to great effect. The upper part is worked in a tightly defined double crochet fabric, while the lower half is worked in a pretty lace stitch for a more flouncy look. This lace stitch is also used for a matching shawl made in the same soft pink yarn.

THE PATTERN

CARDIGAN: YOKE

(Worked in one piece to armholes.)

With 2.50mm (C2) hook, make 112 [124: 136] ch.

Foundation row (RS) 1 dc into 2nd ch from hook, 1 dc into each ch to end, turn. 111 [123: 135] sts.

Cont in dc fabric as follows:

Row 1 1 ch (does NOT count as st), 1 dc into each dc to end, turn.

This row forms dc fabric.

Row 2 (RS) 1 ch (does NOT count as st), 1 dc into each of first 2 dc, 1 ch, miss 1 dc (to make a buttonhole – work 1 dc into this ch sp on next row), 1 dc into each dc to end, turn.

Cont in dc fabric for a further 1 row, ending after a WS row.

● *Shape right front*

Next row (RS) 1 ch (does NOT count as st), 1 dc into each of first 27 [29: 32] dc and turn, leaving rem sts unworked.

Work on this set of 27 [29: 32] sts only for right front.

Next row 1 ch (does NOT count as st), dc2tog over first 2 sts (1 st decreased), 1 dc into each dc to end, turn.

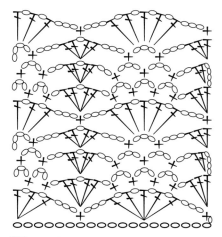

KEY

○ ch
+ dc
T tr

Next row 1 ch (does NOT count as st), 1 dc into each dc to last 2 sts, dc2tog over last 2 sts (1 st decreased), turn.

1st and 2nd sizes only:

Working all decreases as set by last 2 rows, dec 1 st at armhole edge of next and foll 2 alt rows and at same time make a 2nd buttonhole in 3rd [5th] of these rows by replacing last 3 sts of this row with (1 ch, miss 1 dc, 1 dc into each of last 2 dc).

3rd size only:

Working all decreases as set by last 2 rows, dec 1 st at armhole edge of next and foll 3 alt rows and at same time make a 2nd buttonhole in 6th of these rows by replacing first 3 sts of this row with (1 dc into each of first 2 dc, 1 ch, miss 1 dc).

All sizes:

22 [24: 26] sts.

Work 7 [11: 11] rows, making a 3rd buttonhole in 5th [9th: 9th] of these rows by replacing first 3 sts of this row with (1 dc into each of first 2 dc, 1 ch, miss 1 dc) and ending after a RS row.

● *Shape neck*

Next row (WS) 1 ch (does NOT count as st), 1 dc into each of first 16 [17: 19] dc and turn, leaving rem 6 [7: 7] sts unworked.
Dec 1 st at neck edge of next 6 rows, then on foll 1 [1: 2] alt rows. 9 [10: 11] sts.
Work 2 rows, ending after a WS row.
Fasten off.

● *Shape back*

Return to last complete row worked before dividing for right front, miss next 4 [6: 6] dc, rejoin yarn to next dc, 1 ch (does NOT count as st), 1 dc into same dc as where yarn was rejoined, 1 dc into each of next 48 [52: 58] dc and turn, leaving rem sts unworked.
Work on these 49 [53: 59] sts only for back.

Dec 1 st at each end of next 3 rows, then on foll 2 [2: 3] alt rows. 39 [43: 47] sts.
Work 15 [19: 21] rows, ending after a RS row.

● *Shape back neck*

Next row (WS) 1 ch (does NOT count as st), 1 dc into each of first 11 [12: 13] dc and turn, leaving rem sts unworked.
Dec 1 st at neck edge of next 2 rows, ending after a WS row. 9 [10: 11] sts.
Fasten off.

Return to last complete row worked before shaping back neck, miss next 17 [19: 21] dc, rejoin yarn to next dc, 1 ch (does NOT count as st), 1 dc into same dc as where yarn was rejoined, 1 dc into each of dc to end, turn. 11 [12: 13] sts.
Dec 1 st at neck edge of next 2 rows, ending after a WS row. 9 [10: 11] sts.
Fasten off.

● *Shape left front*

Return to last complete row worked before dividing for back and right front, miss next 4 [6: 6] dc, rejoin yarn to next dc, 1 ch (does NOT count as st), 1 dc into same dc as where yarn was rejoined, 1 dc into each dc to end, turn.
Work on this set of 27 [29: 32] sts only for left front.
Dec 1 st at armhole edge of next 3 rows, then on foll 2 [2: 3] alt rows. 22 [24: 26] sts.
Work 7 [11: 11] rows, ending after a RS row.

● *Shape neck*

Next row (WS) Ss along and into 7th [8th: 8th] dc, 1 ch (does NOT count as st), 1 dc into same dc as last ss, 1 dc into each dc to end, turn. 16 [17: 19] sts.
Dec 1 st at neck edge of next 6 rows, then on foll 1 [1: 2] alt rows. 9 [10: 11] sts.
Work 2 rows, ending after a WS row.
Fasten off.

CARDIGAN: SLEEVES

With 2.50mm (C2) hook, make 30 [34: 38] ch.
Work foundation row as given for yoke. 29 [33: 37] sts.

Cont in dc fabric as follows:

Work 1 row, ending after a WS row.
Row 3 (RS) 1 ch (does NOT count as st), 2 dc into first dc (1 st increased), 1 dc into each dc to last dc, 2 dc into last dc (1 st increased), turn.
Working all increases as set by last row, inc 1 st at each end of every foll 6th [6th: 7th] row until there are 39 [45: 51] sts.
Work 7 [9: 9] rows, ending after a WS row.

● *Shape top*

Next row (RS) Ss across and into 3rd [4th: 4th] dc, 1 ch (does NOT count as st), 1 dc into same dc as last ss, 1 dc into each dc to last 2 [3: 3] dc and turn, leaving rem 2 [3: 3] sts unworked. 35 [39: 45] sts.
Dec 1 st at each end of next 12 [14: 16] rows. 11 [11: 13] sts.
Fasten off.

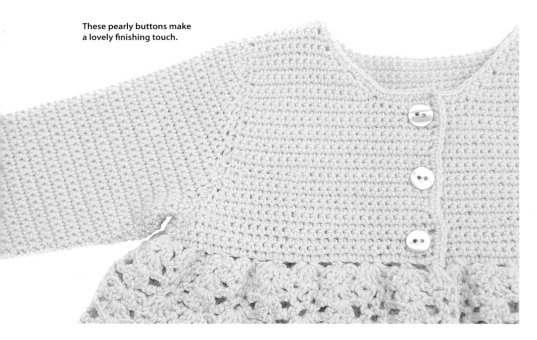

These pearly buttons make a lovely finishing touch.

MAKING UP

Join shoulder seams. Join sleeve seams. Matching centre of top of last row of sleeve to shoulder seam and sleeve seam to centre of sts left unworked at underarm, insert sleeves into armholes.

CARDIGAN: SKIRT

With RS facing and 2.50mm (C2) hook, rejoin yarn at base of left front opening edge, 4 ch (counts as first tr and 1 ch), working into base of each st of first row of bodice, cont as follows: (1 tr, 1 ch and 1 tr) into st at base of 4 ch, *3 ch, miss 2 sts, 1 dc into next st, 3 ch, miss 2 sts, 1 tr into next st, (1 ch, 1 tr into same place as last tr) 4 times*, rep from * to * 7 [8: 9] times more, 3 ch, miss 2 sts, 1 dc into next st, 3 ch, miss 3 [2: 3] sts, 1 tr into next st, (1 ch, 1 tr into same place as last tr) 4 times, 3 ch, miss 3 [2: 3] sts, 1 dc into next st, 3 ch, miss 2 sts, 1 tr into next st, (1 ch, 1 tr into same place as last tr) 4 times, rep from * to * 7 [8: 9] times more, 3 ch, miss 2 sts, 1 dc into next st, 3 ch, miss 2 sts, 1 tr into last st, (1 ch, 1 tr into same place as last tr) twice, turn. 18 [20: 22] patt reps.

Now cont in lace patt as follows:

Row 1 (WS) 3 ch, miss tr at end of previous row, 1 dc into next ch sp, 3 ch, *1 dc into next ch sp, 1 ch, miss (1 tr and 3 ch), (2 tr, 1 ch and 2 tr) into next dc, 1 ch, miss (3 ch and 1 tr)**, (1 dc into next ch sp, 3 ch) 3 times, rep from * to end, ending last rep at **, 1 dc into next ch sp, 3 ch, 1 dc into next ch sp, 1 ch, 1 htr into 3rd of 4 ch at beg of previous row, turn.

Row 2 1 ch (does NOT count as st), 1 dc into htr at end of previous row, 3 ch, miss 1 dc, *1 dc into next ch sp, 2 ch, miss (1 dc, 1 ch and 2 tr), (2 tr, 1 ch and 2 tr) into next ch sp, 2 ch, miss (2 tr, 1 ch and 1 dc)**, (1 dc into next ch sp, 3 ch) twice, rep from * to end, ending last rep at **, 1 dc into next ch sp, 3 ch, 1 dc into last ch sp, turn.

Row 3 4 ch, miss dc at base of 4 ch, *1 dc into next ch sp, 3 ch, miss (1 dc, 2 ch and 2 tr), (2 tr, 1 ch and 2 tr) into next ch sp, 3 ch, miss (2 tr, 2 ch and 1 dc), 1 dc into next ch sp**, 3 ch, rep from * to end, ending last rep at **, 2 ch, 1 htr into dc at beg of previous row, turn.

Row 4 4 ch (counts as first tr and 1 ch), (1 tr, 1 ch and 1 tr) into first ch sp, *3 ch, miss (1 dc, 3 ch and 2 tr), 1 dc into next ch sp, 3 ch, miss (2 tr, 3 ch and 1 dc), 1 tr into next ch sp**, (1 ch, 1 tr into same ch sp as last tr) 4 times, rep from * to end, ending last rep at **, (1 ch, 1 tr into same ch sp as last tr) twice, turn.

These 4 rows form patt.
Work in patt for a further 16 [20: 24] rows.
Fasten off.
Sew on buttons.

SHAWL

With 2.50mm (C2) hook, make 256 ch.

Foundation row (RS) (1 tr, 1 ch and 1 tr) into 4th ch from hook, *3 ch, miss 5 ch, 1 dc into next ch, 3 ch, miss 5 ch, 1 tr into next ch**, (1 ch, 1 tr into same ch as last tr) 4 times, rep from * to end, ending last rep at **, (1 ch, 1 tr into same ch as last tr) twice, turn. 21 patt reps.

Now cont in lace patt as follows:

Row 1 (WS) 3 ch, miss tr at end of previous row, 1 dc into next ch sp, 3 ch, *1 dc into next ch sp, 1 ch, miss (1 tr and 3 ch), (2 tr, 1 ch and 2 tr) into next dc, 1 ch, miss (3 ch and 1 tr)**, (1 dc into next ch sp, 3 ch) 3 times, rep from * to end, ending last rep at **, 1 dc into next ch sp, 3 ch, 1 dc into next ch sp, 1 ch, 1 htr into 3rd of 4 ch at beg of previous row, turn.

Row 2 1 ch (does NOT count as st), 1 dc into htr at end of previous row, 3 ch, miss 1 dc, *1 dc into next ch sp, 2 ch, miss (1 dc, 1 ch and 2 tr), (2 tr, 1 ch and 2 tr) into next ch sp, 2 ch, miss (2 tr, 1 ch and 1 dc)**, (1 dc into next ch sp, 3 ch) twice, rep from * to end, ending last rep at **, 1 dc into next ch sp, 3 ch, 1 dc into last ch sp, turn.

Row 3 4 ch, miss dc at base of 4 ch, *1 dc into next ch sp, 3 ch, miss (1 dc, 2 ch and 2 tr), (2 tr, 1 ch and 2 tr) into next ch sp, 3 ch, miss (2 tr, 2 ch and 1 dc), 1 dc into next ch sp**, 3 ch, rep from * to end, ending last rep at **, 2 ch, 1 htr into dc at beg of previous row, turn.

Row 4 4 ch (counts as first tr and 1 ch), (1 tr, 1 ch and 1 tr) into first ch sp, *3 ch, miss (1 dc, 3 ch and 2 tr), 1 dc into next ch sp, 3 ch, miss (2 tr, 3 ch and 1 dc), 1 tr into next ch sp**, (1 ch, 1 tr into same ch sp as last tr) 4 times, rep from * to end, ending last rep at **, (1 ch, 1 tr into same ch sp as last tr) twice, turn.

These 4 rows form patt.
Work in patt for a further 144 rows.
Fasten off.

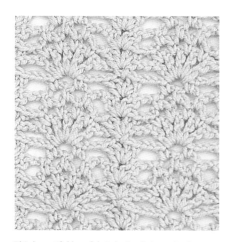

This beautiful lacy fabric is simple to make from double crochet and treble stitches.

Autumn colour coat

This duffle coat is made from a warm, earthy yarn with a wonderful depth of colour that looks like autumn leaves. This textured stitch creates a basketweave effect that makes a robust and cosy fabric, perfect for keeping your little one warm on chilly autumn days – particularly with the addition of the snug hood. See pages 28–31 for more information on relief stitches.

PROJECT NOTES

MEASUREMENTS
To fit age, approx: 1–2 [2–3: 4–5: 5–6] years
To fit chest: 51cm (20in) [56cm (22in): 61cm (24in): 66cm (26in)]
Actual size: 60cm (23½in) [68cm (26¾in): 76cm (30in): 84cm (33in)]
Full length: 49cm (19¼in) [55cm (21½in): 61cm (24in): 67cm (26¼in)]
Sleeve seam: 26cm (10¼in) [30cm (11¾in): 34cm (13¼in): 38cm (15in)]

YARN
14 [15: 16: 17] x 50g (1¾oz) balls of DK-weight 100% wool in variegated reds and browns

HOOK
4.00mm (G6) hook

NOTIONS
4 buttons

SPECIAL ABBREVIATIONS
rbtr work treble in the usual way but working around stem of st of previous row, inserting hook around stem from back to front and from right to left.
rftr work treble in the usual way but working around stem of st of previous row, inserting hook around stem from front to back and from right to left.

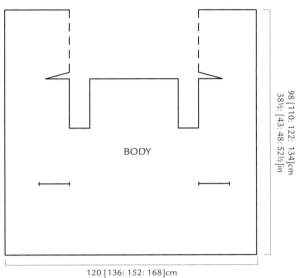

BODY

98 [110: 122: 134]cm
38½ [43: 48: 52½]in

120 [136: 152: 168]cm
47 [53½: 60: 66]in

SLEEVE

26 [30: 34: 38]cm
10¼ [11¾: 13¼: 15]in

TENSION
20 sts and 12½ rows to 10cm (4in) measured over pattern on 4.00mm (G6) hook, or the size required to achieve stated tension.

THE PATTERN

POCKET LININGS (make 2)
With 4.00mm (G6) hook, make 21 ch.
Foundation row (WS) 1 htr into 3rd ch from hook, 1 htr into each ch to end, turn. 20 sts.
Cont in patt as follows:
Row 1 (RS) 2 ch (counts as first st), miss st at base of 2 ch, 1 rbtr around stem of each of next 3 sts, *1 rftr around stem of each of next 4 sts, 1 rbtr around stem of each of next 4 sts, rep from * to end, working last rftr around stem of 2 ch at beg of previous row, turn.

Row 2 2 ch (counts as first st), miss st at base of 2 ch, 1 rftr around stem of each of next 3 sts, *1 rbtr around stem of each of next 4 sts, 1 rftr around stem of each of next 4 sts, rep from * to end, working last rftr around stem of 2 ch at beg of previous row, turn.
Row 3 As row 2.
Row 4 As row 1.
These 4 rows form patt.

Cont in patt for a further 6 rows, ending after 2nd patt row and a WS row.
Fasten off.

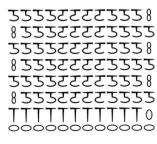

KEY
ch
htr
rbtr
rftr

BODY

(Worked in one piece to armholes.)

With 4.00mm (G6) hook, make 133 [149: 165: 181] ch.

Foundation row (WS) 1 htr into 3rd ch from hook, 1 htr into each ch to end, turn. 132 [148: 164: 180] sts.

Cont in patt as follows:

Row 1 (RS) 2 ch (counts as first st), miss st at base of 2 ch, 1 rftr around stem of each of next 3 sts, *1 rbtr around stem of each of next 4 sts, 1 rftr around stem of each of next 4 sts, rep from * to end, working last rftr around stem of 2 ch at beg of previous row, turn.

Row 2 2 ch (counts as first st), miss st at base of 2 ch, 1 rbtr around stem of each of next 3 sts, *1 rftr around stem of each of next 4 sts, 1 rbtr around stem of each of next 4 sts, rep from * to end, working last rbtr around stem of 2 ch at beg of previous row, turn.

Row 3 As row 2.

Row 4 As row 1.

These 4 rows form patt.

Cont in patt until work measures approx 21cm (8¼in) [23cm (9in): 27cm (10½in): 29cm (11½in)] ending after 4th patt row and a WS row.

● *Place pockets*

Next row (RS) Patt 12 [12: 20: 20] sts, miss next 20 sts and, in their place, patt across 20 sts of first pocket lining, patt to last 32 [32: 40: 40] sts, miss next 20 sts and, in their place, patt across 20 sts of second pocket lining, patt to end, turn.

Cont straight until work measures 34cm (13¼in) [39cm (15¼in): 44cm (17¼in): 49cm (19¼in)] ending after a WS row.

● *Divide for armholes*

Next row (RS) Patt 28 [32: 36: 40] sts and turn, leaving rem sts unworked.

Work on this set of sts only for right front.

Cont straight until work measures 14cm (5½in) [15cm (6in): 16cm (6¼in): 17cm (6½in)] from dividing row, ending after a WS row.

The main bulk of the coat is crocheted in one piece, but the snuggly hood is attached afterwards.

Slip working loop onto a safety pin and set aside this ball of yarn – it will be used for the hood.

Place marker 10 [13: 16: 19] sts in from armhole edge to denote neck point of shoulder seam.

● Shape back

Return to last complete row worked, miss 16 sts (for underarm), rejoin yarn to next st, 2 ch (counts as first st), miss st at base of 2 ch, patt 43 [51: 59: 67] sts and turn.

Work on this set of 44 [52: 60: 68] sts only for back.

Cont straight until work measures 14cm (5½in) [15cm (6in): 16cm (6¼in): 17cm (6½in)] from dividing row, ending after a WS row.

Fasten off, placing markers either side of centre 24 [26: 28: 30] sts to denote back neck.

● Shape left front

Return to last complete row worked, miss 16 sts (for underarm), rejoin yarn to next st, 2 ch (counts as first st), miss st at base of 2 ch, patt to end, turn.

Work on this set of 28 [32: 36: 40] sts only for left front.

Cont straight until work measures 14cm (5½in) [15cm (6in): 16cm (6¼in): 17cm (6½in)] from dividing row, ending after a WS row.

Fasten off, placing marker 10 [13: 16: 19] sts in from armhole edge to denote neck point of shoulder seam.

SLEEVES

With 4.00mm (G6) hook, make 33 [35: 37: 39] ch.

Work foundation row as given for body. 32 [34: 36: 38] sts.

Cont in patt as follows:

Row 1 (RS) 2 ch (counts as first st), miss st at base of 2 ch, 1 rftr around stem of each of next 1 [2: 3: 4] sts, *1 rbtr around stem of each of next 4 sts, 1 rftr around stem of each of next 4 sts, rep from * to last 6 [7: 8: 1] sts, 1 rbtr around stem of each of next 4 [4: 4: 1] sts, 1 rftr around stem of each of next 2 [3: 4: 0] sts, working last st around stem of 2 ch at beg of previous row, turn.

This row sets position of patt as given for body.

Keeping patt correct, cont as follows:

Work 1 row.

Next row 2 ch (counts as first st), work appropriate st (to keep patt correct) around stem of st at base of 2 ch (1 st increased), patt to last st, working 2 sts around stem of 2 ch at beg of previous row, working appropriate sts to keep patt correct (1 st increased), turn.

Working all increases as set by last row, inc 1 st at each end of 2nd and foll 8 [7: 4: 3] alt rows, then on every foll 3rd row until there are 56 [60: 64: 68] sts, taking inc sts into patt.

Cont straight until sleeve measures 29cm (11½in) [33cm (13in): 37cm (14½in): 41cm (16in)] ending after a WS row.

Fasten off, placing markers along row-end edges 4cm (1½in) down from top of last row.

MAKING UP

Join shoulder seams: there will be 18 [19: 20: 21] sts free at neck edge of each front and 24 [26: 28: 30] sts across back neck.

This basketweave effect is simple to create. Choose your buttons carefully to match the yarn.

● Hood

With RS facing and 4.00mm (G6) hook, slip working loop left on safety pin at neck edge of right front back onto hook and, using ball of yarn set to one side with right front, cont as follows:

2 ch (counts as first st), miss st at base of 2 ch, patt next 13 [14: 17: 18] sts of right front, keeping patt correct as set by last set of sts work across rem sts of right front, then back neck, then left front as follows:

(work appropriate 2 sts around stem of next st, patt 1 [2: 1: 2] sts) 7 [5: 7: 5] times, work appropriate 2 sts around stem of next st, patt 2 sts, work appropriate 2 sts around stem of next st, (patt 1 [2: 1: 2] sts, work appropriate 2 sts around stem of next st) 7 [5: 7: 5] times, patt to end, turn. 76 [76: 84: 84] sts.

Cont in patt until hood measures 20cm (7¾in) [21cm (8¼in): 22cm (8½in): 23cm (9in)] from pick-up row, ending after a WS row.

Fold hood in half with RS together and join top seam by working a row of dc across top of last row of patt, working each st through both layers.

Fasten off.

Join sleeve seams below markers. Insert sleeves into armholes, matching sleeve markers to centre of sts missed at underarm and centre of last row of sleeve to shoulder seam.

● Edging

With RS facing and 4.00mm (G6) hook, rejoin yarn to foundation ch edge of body, 1 ch (does NOT count as st), work 1 round of dc evenly around entire hem, front opening and hood edges, working 3 dc into each hem corner point and ending with ss to first dc, do NOT turn.

Now work 1 round of crab st (dc worked from left to right, instead of right to left), ending with ss to first dc.

Fasten off.

Work edging around lower edges of sleeves in same way, rejoining yarn at base of sleeve seams.

Work edging across top of pocket openings in same way.

Sew pocket linings in place on inside. Attach buttons 6 sts in from front opening edge (left front for a girl, or right front for a boy), placing lowest button 20cm (7¾in) up from lower edge, top button 10cm (4in) below hood pick-up row, and rem 2 buttons evenly spaced between. Fasten coat by pushing buttons through fabric along other front opening edge.

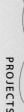

Corsage

A corsage is a lovely accessory easily created in crochet fabric. This corsage has been made in realistic colours, with a scarlet-red yarn for a rose-like flower, but you could make it in more fanciful colours to coordinate it with a favourite outfit.

PROJECT NOTES

MEASUREMENTS
Actual size, across flower: 9cm (3½in)

YARN
A 1 x 25g (⅞oz) ball of 4ply super kid mohair and silk yarn in leaf green

B 1 x 25g (⅞oz) ball of 4ply super kid mohair, silk, polyester and nylon yarn in scarlet

HOOK
2.50mm (C2) crochet hook

NOTIONS
Brooch back

TENSION
One completed leaf measures 5cm (2in) long and 2.5cm (1in) wide, at widest point, on 2.50mm (C2) hook, or the size required to achieve stated tension.

THE PATTERN

LEAVES (make 3)
With 2.50mm (C2) hook and A, make 13 ch.

Round 1 (RS) 1 dc into 2nd ch from hook, *1 htr into next ch, 1 tr into next ch, 1 dtr into each of next 6 ch, 1 tr into next ch, 1 htr into next ch*, 4 dc into last ch, working back along other side of foundation ch, rep from * to * once more, 1 dc into next ch (this is same ch as used for first dc).

Fasten off.

FLOWER

• Petal strip
With 2.50mm (C2) hook and B, make 87 ch.

Row 1 (RS) 1 dc into 2nd ch from hook, 1 dc into each ch to end, turn. 86 sts.

Row 2 1 ch (does NOT count as st), 1 dc into each dc to end, turn.

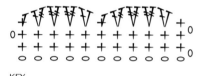

KEY

| ⵔ ch | ✛ dc | ⊤ htr | ⊤ tr | ⊤ dtr |

Row 3 1 ch (does NOT count as st), 1 dc into first dc, *(1 htr and 1 tr) into next dc, 2 dtr into each of next 2 dc, (1 dtr and 1 tr) into next dc, (1 htr and 1 dc) into next dc, rep from * to end, turn. 171 sts, 17 petals.

Row 4 1 ch (does NOT count as st), miss dc at base of 1 ch, *1 dc into next st, 2 tr into each of next 7 sts, 1 dc into next st, 1 ss into next st, rep from * to end.

Fasten off.

• Flower centre
With 2.50mm (C2) hook and B, make 2 ch.

Round 1 5 dc into 2nd ch from hook, ss to first dc.

Now join foundation ch edge of petal strip to flower centre as follows:

1 ch (does NOT count as st), 1 dc into first dc of next round of flower centre inserting hook through first foundation ch of petal strip at same time (to attach petal strip to flower centre), 1 dc into same dc of flower centre inserting hook through next foundation ch of petal strip at same time, *1 dc into next dc of flower centre inserting hook through next foundation ch of petal strip at same time, 1 dc into same dc of flower centre inserting hook through next foundation ch of petal strip at same time, rep from * 41 times more, working around sts of flower centre in a spiral, ss to next dc of flower centre.

Fasten off.

MAKING UP
Do NOT press. Using photograph as a guide, attach leaves to back of flower.

Attach brooch back to back of flower centre.

Glorious glamour scarves

These elegant, feminine scarves demonstrate how one stitch can be transformed depending on the yarn that is used. The stitch texture stands out clearly in the glossy silk yarn and the cashmere-mix, but looks more sturdy and robust in the tweed yarn, while the mohair yarn gives the stitch a wispy, gauzy effect.

PROJECT NOTES

MEASUREMENTS
Actual size 19 x 180cm (7½ x 70¾in)

YARN
CLASSIC VERSION:
4 x 50g (1¾oz) balls of DK-weight merino, microfibre and cashmere mix yarn in lilac

EVENING VERSION:
2 x 25g (⅞oz) balls of 4ply kid mohair yarn in heather

SILK VERSION:
4 x 50g (1¾oz) balls of DK-weight silk yarn in lilac

TWEEDY VERSION:
3 x 50g (1¾oz) balls of DK-weight merino, alpaca, and viscose mix yarn in purple

HOOK
3.50mm (E4) hook

TENSION
19 sts and 13 rows to 10cm (4in) measured over pattern on 3.50mm (E4) hook, or the size required to achieve stated tension.

THE PATTERN

SCARF

With 3.50mm (E4) hook, make 41 ch.

Foundation row (WS) (1 tr, 2 ch and 1 tr) into 8th ch from hook, *3 ch, miss 4 ch, (1 tr, 2 ch and 1 tr) into next ch, rep from * to last 3 ch, 2 ch, miss 2 ch, 1 tr into last ch, turn.

Cont in patt as follows:

Row 1 4 ch (counts as first dtr), miss (tr at base of 4 ch, 2 ch and next tr), *5 dtr into next ch sp**, miss (1 tr, 3 ch and 1 tr), rep from * to end, ending last rep at **, miss (1 tr and 2 ch), 1 dtr into next ch, turn. 37 sts, 7 patt reps.

Row 2 5 ch (counts as first tr and 2 ch), miss last 3 dtr of previous row, *(1 tr, 2 ch and 1

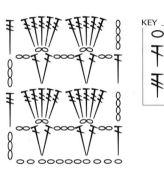

KEY
⭕	ch
🕇	tr
🕇	dtr

tr) into next dtr**, 3 ch, miss 4 dtr, rep from * to end, ending last rep at **, 2 ch, miss 2 dtr, 1 tr into top of 4 ch at beg of previous row, turn.

These 2 rows form patt.

Cont in patt until scarf measures 180cm (70¾in), ending after a 2nd patt row.
Fasten off.

MAKING UP

Press carefully, following the instructions on the ball band.

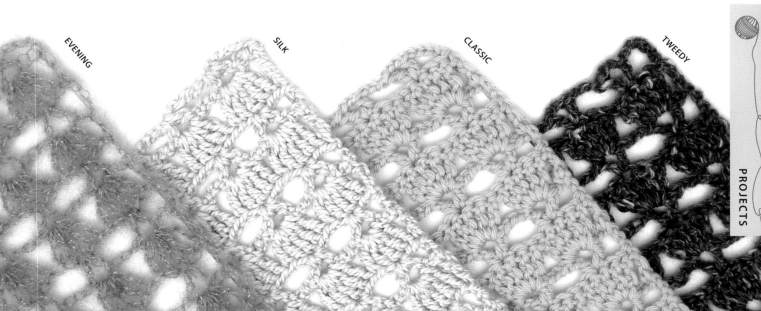

Peruvian-style bag

This stunning bag, which was inspired by traditional Peruvian designs, is worked in simple double crochet, but derives its impact from the strong geometric design and the bold colour changes. See page 43 for more information on working from a chart.

PROJECT NOTES

MEASUREMENTS
Width at widest point 26cm (10¼in)
Depth to opening edge 27cm (10¼in)

YARN
All DK 100% mercerized cotton
A 2 x 50g (1¾oz) balls in dark brown
B 1 x 50g (1¾oz) ball in soft orange
C 1 x 50g (1¾oz) ball in olive

D 1 x 50g (1¾oz) ball in rose
E 2 x 50g (1¾oz) balls in dark purple

HOOK
4.00mm (G6) hook

NOTIONS
Piece of lining fabric 70 x 75cm (27½ x 29½in)

TENSION
20 sts and 20 rows to 10cm (4in) measured over pattern on 4.00mm (G6) hook, or the size required to achieve stated tension.

THE PATTERN

BAG

With 4.00mm (G6) hook and A, make 30 ch.
Changing yarns as required, cont as follows:

Round 1 (RS) Using B, 2 dc into 2nd ch from hook, 1 dc into next ch, (using A 1 dc into each of next 2 ch, using B 1 dc into each of next 2 ch) twice, (using A 1 dc into each of next 2 ch, using C 1 dc into each of next 2 ch) 4 times, using A 1 dc into each of next 2 ch, using B 4 dc into last ch, now working back along other side of foundation ch: using A 1 dc into each of next 2 ch, (using C 1 dc into each of next 2 ch, using A 1 dc into each of next 2 ch) 4 times, (using B 1 dc into each of next 2 ch, using A 1 dc into each of next 2 ch) twice, using B 1 dc into next ch, 2 dc into next ch (this is same ch as used for 2 dc at beg of round), ss to first dc, turn. 62 sts.

This round sets position of chart: on all rounds read chart from right to left for first half of

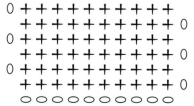

KEY
O ch
+ dc

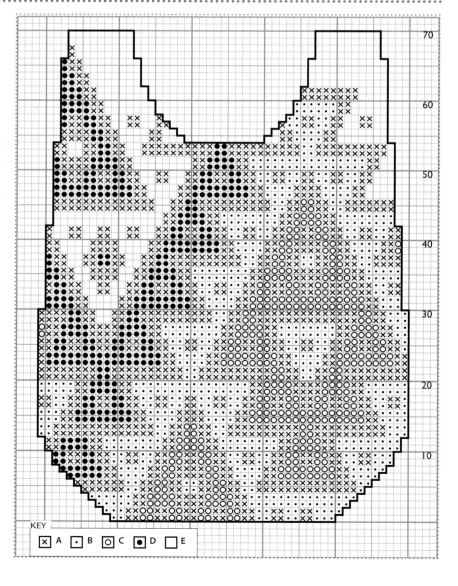

KEY
☒ A   · B   ⊙ C   ● D   ☐ E

sts, then read chart from left to right for second half of sts (to reverse design on other side of bag).

Keeping chart correct as now set and remembering to turn at end of each round, shape bag as follows:

Round 2 1 ch (does NOT count as st), 2 dc into first dc, 1 dc into each of next 29 dc, 2 dc into each of next 2 dc, 1 dc into each of next 29 dc, 2 dc into last dc, ss to first dc, turn. 66 sts.

Round 3 1 ch (does NOT count as st), 2 dc into first dc, 1 dc into each of next 31 dc, 2 dc into each of next 2 dc, 1 dc into each of next 31 dc, 2 dc into last dc, ss to first dc, turn. 70 sts.

Round 4 1 ch (does NOT count as st), 2 dc into first dc, 1 dc into each of next 33 dc, 2 dc into each of next 2 dc, 1 dc into each of next 33 dc, 2 dc into last dc, ss to first dc, turn. 74 sts.

Round 5 1 ch (does NOT count as st), 2 dc into first dc, 1 dc into each of next 35 dc, 2 dc into each of next 2 dc, 1 dc into each of next 35 dc, 2 dc into last dc, ss to first dc, turn. 78 sts.

Round 6 1 ch (does NOT count as st), 2 dc into first dc, 1 dc into each of next 37 dc, 2 dc into each of next 2 dc, 1 dc into each of next 37 dc, 2 dc into last dc, ss to first dc, turn. 82 sts.

Round 7 1 ch (does NOT count as st), 2 dc into first dc, 1 dc into each of next 39 dc, 2 dc into each of next 2 dc, 1 dc into each of next 39 dc, 2 dc into last dc, ss to first dc, turn. 86 sts.

Round 8 1 ch (does NOT count as st), 2 dc into first dc, 1 dc into each of next 41 dc, 2 dc into each of next 2 dc, 1 dc into each of next 41 dc, 2 dc into last dc, ss to first dc, turn. 90 sts.

Round 9 1 ch (does NOT count as st), 2 dc into first dc, 1 dc into each of next 43 dc, 2 dc into each of next 2 dc, 1 dc into each of next 43 dc, 2 dc into last dc, ss to first dc, turn. 94 sts.

The dark brown areas serve to make the vivid colours and bold shapes stand out even more.

Round 10 1 ch (does NOT count as st), 1 dc into each dc to end, ss to first dc, turn.

Round 11 1 ch (does NOT count as st), 2 dc into first dc, 1 dc into each of next 45 dc, 2 dc into each of next 2 dc, 1 dc into each of next 45 dc, 2 dc into last dc, ss to first dc, turn. 98 sts.

Round 12 As round 10.

Round 13 1 ch (does NOT count as st), 2 dc into first dc, 1 dc into each of next 47 dc, 2 dc into each of next 2 dc, 1 dc into each of next 47 dc, 2 dc into last dc, ss to first dc, turn. 102 sts.

Rounds 14 to 30 As round 10.

Round 31 1 ch (does NOT count as st), dc2tog over first 2 dc, 1 dc into each of next 47 dc, (dc2tog over next 2 dc) twice, 1 dc into each of next 47 dc, dc2tog over last 2 dc, ss to first dc, turn. 98 sts.

Rounds 32 to 42 As round 10.

Round 43 1 ch (does NOT count as st), dc2tog over first 2 dc, 1 dc into each of next 45 dc, (dc2tog over next 2 dc) twice, 1 dc into each of next 45 dc, dc2tog over last 2 dc, ss to first dc, turn. 94 sts.

Rounds 44 to 46 As round 10.

● *Divide for sides*

Now working in rows, not rounds, divide for each side of bag as follows:

Row 47 (RS) 1 ch (does NOT count as st), 1 dc into each of next 47 dc and turn, leaving rem sts unworked.

Keeping chart correct as now set (by now reading WS rows in opposite direction to RS rows), work on this set of 47 sts only for first side of bag.

***Row 48** 1 ch (does NOT count as st), 1 dc into each dc to end, turn.

Rows 49 to 54 As row 48.

● *Divide for straps*

Row 55 (RS) 1 ch (does NOT count as st), dc2tog over first 2 dc, 1 dc into each of next 15 dc, dc2tog over next 2 dc and turn, leaving rem sts unworked. 17 sts.

**Row 56 1 ch (does NOT count as st), dc2tog over first 2 dc, 1 dc into each dc to end, turn. 16 sts.

Row 57 1 ch (does NOT count as st), 1 dc into each dc to last 2 sts, dc2tog over last 2 sts, turn. 15 sts.

Rows 58 and 59 As rows 56 and 57. 13 sts.

Row 60 As row 48.

Row 61 As row 57. 12 sts.

Row 62 As row 48.

Row 63 As row 57. 11 sts.

Rows 64 to 66 As row 48.

Row 67 1 ch (does NOT count as st), dc2tog over first 2 dc, 1 dc into each dc to last 2 sts, dc2tog over last 2 sts, turn. 9 sts.

Rows 68 to 70 As row 48.

This completes all 70 rows of chart.

Break off all contrasts and cont using E only.

Rep row 48 until strap measures 45cm (17¾in) from last complete round worked.**

Fasten off.

Return to last complete row worked before shaping first strap, miss next 9 dc, rejoin yarn to next dc, 1 ch (does NOT count as st), dc2tog over dc where yarn was rejoined and next dc, 1 dc into each dc to last 2 dc, dc2tog over last 2 dc, turn. 17 sts.

Complete second strap by working as given for first strap from ** to **.

Join ends of straps by holding them with RS together and working 1 row of dc through sts of last row of both sets of sts.

Fasten off.***

Return to last complete round worked before shaping first side, rejoin yarn to next dc, 1 ch (does NOT count as st), 1 dc into each of next 47 dc, turn.

Keeping chart correct as now set (by now reading WS rows in opposite direction to RS rows), work on this set of 47 sts only for second side of bag.

Work as given for first side of bag from *** to ***.

MAKING UP

Press carefully following the instructions on the ball band.

● *Edging*

With RS facing, using 4.00mm (G6) hook and E, attach yarn to one strap seam, 1 ch (does NOT count as st), work 1 round of dc evenly around opening edge, ending with ss to first dc.

Fasten off.

Work edging around all other strap and opening edges in same way.

Cut 2 pieces of lining fabric same size as crochet piece, adding seam allowance along all edges. Join seams to form same shape as crochet bag. Slip lining inside bag, fold under raw edges and slip stitch folded edge of lining in place around strap and opening edges.

Solomon's knot wrap

This beautiful, airy wrap is a truly special garment that is constructed in a pure silk yarn and a subtle, classy colour that will complement all the outfits in your wardrobe. See page 38 for more information on making Solomon's knots.

PROJECT NOTES

MEASUREMENTS
Actual size 77 x 183cm (30¼ x 72in)

YARN
4 x 50g (1¾oz) balls of DK-weight 100% silk yarn in peach

HOOK
4.00mm (G6) hook

SPECIAL ABBREVIATIONS
LSK longer Solomon's knot worked as follows: lengthen loop on hook to approx 3.5cm (1½in), yoh and draw loop through, 1 dc under back loop of ch.

SSK shorter Solomon's knot worked as follows: lengthen loop on hook to approx 2.5cm (1in), yoh and draw loop through, 1 dc under back loop of ch.

yoh yarn over hook

TENSION
3 patt reps to 12½cm (5in) and 6 rows to 14cm (5½in) measured over pattern on 4.00mm (G6) hook, or the size required to achieve stated tension.

THE PATTERN

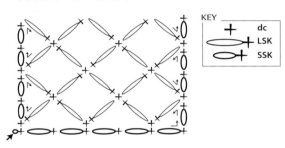

KEY
+ dc
⬭ + LSK
⬭ + SSK

WRAP
With 4.00mm (G6) hook, make 2 ch, 38 SSK, 1 LSK, turn.

Foundation row (RS) 1 dc into dc between 3rd and 4th set of loops, *2 LSK, miss 2 sets of loops, 1 dc into next dc, rep from * to end, working last dc into ch at beg of foundation ch, turn. 18½ patt reps.

Cont in patt as follows:

Row 1 2 SSK, 1 LSK, miss dc at end of previous row, 1 dc into next dc, *2 LSK, miss 2 sets of loops, 1 dc into next dc, rep from * to end, turn.

This row forms patt.

Cont in patt until wrap measures approx 183cm (72in).

Next row 2 SSK, miss dc at end of previous row, 1 dc into next dc, *2 SSK, miss 2 sets of loops, 1 dc into next dc, rep from * to end, turn.

Fasten off.

MAKING UP
Do NOT press.

Solomon's knots make
a very open fabric.

Circles and stripes set

One of the things that makes crochet so versatile is that circular motifs can be combined with linear work. Combine this with colour changes, and you have the opportunity to create some stunning patterns. Here we use simple motifs and bold colour contrasts for a cosy hat-and-mitten set.

PROJECT NOTES

MEASUREMENTS
HAT:
Width around head 50cm (19½in)
MITTENS:
Width around hand 20cm (7¾in)

YARN
All DK-weight merino wool, alpaca and viscose/rayon mix yarn
A 2 x 50g (1¾oz) ball in brick red
B 1 x 50g (1¾oz) ball in gold

HOOK
3.00mm (D3) crochet hook

TENSION
19 sts and 24 rows to 10cm (4in) measured over pattern on 3.00mm (D3) hook, or the size required to achieve stated tension. Basic motif measures 5.5cm (2¼in) square.

THE PATTERN

BASIC MOTIF

With 3.00mm (D3) hook and yarn A, make 2 ch.

Round 1 (RS) 7 dc into 2nd ch from hook, ss to first dc. 7 sts.

Round 2 3 ch (counts as first tr), 2 tr into dc at base of 3 ch, 3 tr into each dc to end, ss to top of 3 ch at beg of round. 21 sts.

Join in yarn B.

Round 3 Using B, 1 ch (does NOT count as st), *1 dc into each of next 2 sts, 2 dc into next st, rep from * 6 times, ss to first dc. 28 sts.

Break off B and cont using A only.

Round 4 4 ch (counts as first dtr), 1 tr into st at base of 4 ch, *1 htr into each of next 2 dc, 1 dc into next dc, 1 htr into each of next 2 dc, (1 tr and 1 dtr) into next dc**, (1 dtr and 1 tr) into next dc, rep from * to end, ending last rep at **, ss to top of 4 ch at beg of round. 36 sts.

Fasten off.

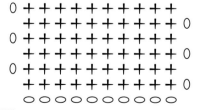

Basic motif is a square, with 9 sts along each side. Corner points fall between the 2 dtr. Using A, join motifs by holding them RS together and working a row of dc along sides to be joined, working each dc through sts of both motifs.

HAT

● **Motif band**
Make and join 9 basic motifs to form a loop.

● **Main section**
With RS facing, 3.00mm (D3) hook and A, attach yarn to one join between motifs around upper edge of motif band and cont as follows:

Round 1 (RS) 1 ch (does NOT count as st), *1 dc into motif joining seam, 1 dc into each of next 9 sts along side of motif, rep from * to end, ss to first dc, turn. 90 sts.

Round 2 Using A, 1 ch (does NOT count as st), 1 dc into each dc to end, ss to first dc, turn.

Join in B.

Round 3 Using B, 1 ch (does NOT count as st), 1 dc into each dc to end, ss to first dc, turn.

Rounds 4 to 6 As round 2.

Round 7 As round 3.

Rounds 8 and 9 As round 2.

Round 10 Using A, 1 ch (does NOT count as st), *1 dc into each of next 8 dc, dc2tog over next 2 dc, rep from * to end, ss to first dc, turn. 81 sts.

Round 11 As round 3.

Rounds 12 and 13 As round 2.

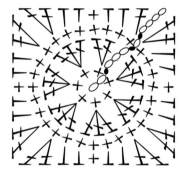

Round 14 Using A, 1 ch (does NOT count as st), *1 dc into each of next 7 dc, dc2tog over next 2 dc, rep from * to end, ss to first dc, turn. 72 sts.

Round 15 As round 3.

Rounds 16 and 17 As round 2.

Round 18 Using A, 1 ch (does NOT count as st), *1 dc into each of next 6 dc, dc2tog over next 2 dc, rep from * to end, ss to first dc, turn. 63 sts.

Round 19 As round 3.

Round 20 As round 2.

Round 21 Using A, 1 ch (does NOT count as st), *dc2tog over next 2 dc, 1 dc into each of next 5 dc, rep from * to end, ss to first dc, turn. 54 sts.

Round 22 As round 2.

Round 23 Using B, 1 ch (does NOT count as st), *dc2tog over next 2 dc, 1 dc into each of next 4 dc, rep from * to end, ss to first dc, turn. 45 sts.

Break off B and cont using A only.

Round 24 As round 2.

Round 25 1 ch (does NOT count as st), *dc2tog over next 2 dc, 1 dc into each of next 3 dc, rep from * to end, ss to first dc, turn. 36 sts.

Round 26 1 ch (does NOT count as st), *1 dc into each of next 2 dc, dc2tog over next 2 dc, rep from * to end, ss to first dc, turn. 27 sts.

Round 27 1 ch (does NOT count as st), *dc2tog over next 2 dc, 1 dc into next dc, rep from * to end, ss to first dc, turn. 18 sts.

Round 28 1 ch (does NOT count as st), *dc2tog over next 2 dc, rep from * to end, ss to first dc, turn. 9 sts.

Round 29 1 ch (does NOT count as st), *dc2tog over next 2 dc, 1 dc into next dc, rep from * to end, do NOT turn. 6 sts.

Round 30 1 dc into each of next 6 dc, do NOT turn.

Rounds 31 to 34 As round 30.

Round 35 (dc2tog over next 2 dc) 3 times. 3 sts.

Fasten off.

● *Lower border*

With RS facing, 3.00mm (D3) hook and A, attach yarn to one join between motifs around lower edge of motif band and cont as follows:

Round 1 (RS) 1 ch (does NOT count as st), *1 dc into joining seam, 1 dc into each of next 9 sts along side of motif, rep from * to end, ss to first dc, turn. 90 sts.

Round 2 1 ch (does NOT count as st), 1 dc into each dc to end, ss to first dc, turn.

Rounds 3 to 5 As round 2 but do NOT turn at end of last round.

Now work 1 round of crab st (dc worked from left to right, instead of right to left) around entire lower edge of hat.

Fasten off.

MAKING UP

Press carefully following the instructions on the ball band.

RIGHT MITTEN

Using 3.00mm (D3) hook and A, make 38 ch and join with a ss to make a ring.

Round 1 (RS) 1 ch (does NOT count as st), 1 dc into each ch to end, ss to first dc, turn. 38 sts.

The thin gold stripes make a lively contrast.

Round 2 Using A, 1 ch (does NOT count as st), 1 dc into each dc to end, ss to first dc, turn.

Rounds 3 and 4 As round 2.

Join in B.

Round 5 Using B, 1 ch (does NOT count as st), 1 dc into each dc to end, ss to first dc, turn.

Rounds 6 to 8 As round 2.

Rounds 9 to 16 As rounds 5 to 8, twice.

Break off B and cont using A only.

● *Shape thumb gusset*

Round 17 1 ch (does NOT count as st), 1 dc into each of first 23 dc, 3 dc into next dc, 1 dc into each of last 14 dc, ss to first dc. 40 sts.

Break off yarn.

● *Shape motif opening*

With WS facing, miss first 35 dc of next round, attach yarn to next dc, 1 ch (does NOT count as st), 1 dc into dc at base of 1 ch, 1 dc into each of first 4 dc of last round, then 1 dc into each of last 25 dc of last round, turn. 30 sts.

Now working in rows, not rounds, cont as follows:

Row 19 1 ch (does NOT count as st), 1 dc into each dc to end, turn.

Row 20 1 ch (does NOT count as st), 1 dc into

each of first 19 dc, 2 dc into next dc, 1 dc into next dc, 2 dc into next dc, 1 dc into each of last 8 dc, turn. 32 sts.

Rows 21 and 22 As row 19.

Row 23 1 ch (does NOT count as st), 1 dc into each of first 8 dc, 2 dc into next dc, 1 dc into each of next 3 dc, 2 dc into next dc, 1 dc into each of last 19 dc, turn. 34 sts.

Rows 24 and 25 As row 19.

Row 26 1 ch (does NOT count as st), 1 dc into each of first 19 dc, 2 dc into next dc, 1 dc into each of next 5 dc, 2 dc into next dc, 1 dc into each of last 8 dc, turn. 36 sts.

Rows 27 and 28 As row 19.

Row 29 1 ch (does NOT count as st), 1 dc into each of first 8 dc, 2 dc into next dc, 1 dc into each of next 7 dc, 2 dc into next dc, 1 dc into each of last 19 dc, turn. 38 sts.

Row 30 As row 19.

Break yarn.

● *Shape thumb*

With RS facing, miss first 8 dc of next row, attach yarn to next dc, 1 ch (does NOT count as st), 1 dc into dc at base of 1 ch, 1 dc into each of next 9 dc, 2 dc into next dc, ss to first dc of this row, turn. 12 sts.

***Now working in rounds, not rows, cont as follows:

Next round 1 ch (does NOT count as st), 1 dc into each dc to end, ss to first dc, turn.

Rep last round 11 times more.

Next round 1 ch (does NOT count as st), (dc2tog over first 2 dc, 1 dc into next dc) 4 times, ss to first dc2tog, turn. 8 sts.

Work 1 round.

Next round 1 ch (does NOT count as st), (dc2tog over next 2 dc) 4 times, ss to first dc2tog. 4 sts.

Fasten off.

Run gathering thread around top of last round. Pull up tight and fasten off securely.***

● *Shape hand*

With RS facing, return to last row worked before shaping thumb, attach yarn to 5th dc at beg of last row, 1 ch (does NOT count as st), 1 dc into dc at base of 1 ch, 1 dc into each of first 4 dc of last row, 10 ch, 1 dc into each of last 8 dc of last row, 1 dc into base of thumb, 1 dc into each of next 14 dc, ss to first dc, turn. 38 sts.

******Next round** 1 ch (does NOT count as st),

1 dc into each dc and ch to end, ss to first dc, turn.

Next round 1 ch (does NOT count as st), 1 dc into each dc to end, ss to first dc, turn.

Rep last round 17 times more, ending after a WS round.

● *Shape top*

Next round (RS) 1 ch (does NOT count as st), dc2tog over first 2 dc, 1 dc into each of next 15 dc, (dc2tog over next 2 dc) twice, 1 dc into each of next 15 dc, dc2tog over last 2 dc, ss to first dc2tog, turn. 34 sts.
Work 1 round.

Next round 1 ch (does NOT count as st), dc2tog over first 2 dc, 1 dc into each of next 13 dc, (dc2tog over next 2 dc) twice, 1 dc into each of next 13 dc, dc2tog over last 2 dc, ss to first dc2tog, turn. 30 sts.
Work 1 round.

Next round 1 ch (does NOT count as st), dc2tog over first 2 dc, 1 dc into each of next 11 dc, (dc2tog over next 2 dc) twice, 1 dc into each of next 11 dc, dc2tog over last 2 dc, ss to first dc2tog, turn. 26 sts.

Next round 1 ch (does NOT count as st), dc2tog over first 2 sts, 1 dc into each of next 10 dc, (dc2tog over next 2 sts) twice, 1 dc into each of next 10 dc, dc2tog over last 2 sts, ss to first dc2tog, turn. 22 sts.

Next round 1 ch (does NOT count as st), dc2tog over first 2 sts, 1 dc into each of next 9 dc, (dc2tog over next 2 sts) twice, 1 dc into each of next 9 dc, dc2tog over last 2 sts, ss to first dc2tog, turn. 18 sts.

Next round 1 ch (does NOT count as st), dc2tog over first 2 sts, 1 dc into each of next 8 dc, (dc2tog over next 2 sts) twice, 1 dc into each of next 8 dc, dc2tog over last 2 sts, ss to first dc2tog, turn. 14 sts.

Fold mitten inside out, then fold flat. Join top seam by working a row of dc across top of last round, working each dc through sts of both layers to close top of mitten.

LEFT MITTEN

Work as given for right mitten to start of thumb gusset shaping.

● *Shape thumb gusset*

Round 17 1 ch (does NOT count as st), 1 dc into each of first 14 dc, 3 dc into next dc, 1 dc into each of last 23 dc, ss to first dc. 40 sts.
Break off yarn.

● *Shape motif opening*

With WS facing, miss first 15 dc of next round, attach yarn to next dc, 1 ch (does NOT count as st), 1 dc into dc at base of 1 ch, 1 dc into each of first 24 dc of last round, then 1 dc into each of last 5 dc of last round, turn. 30 sts.

Now working in rows, not rounds, cont as follows:

Row 19 1 ch (does NOT count as st), 1 dc into each dc to end, turn.

Row 20 1 ch (does NOT count as st), 1 dc into each of first 8 dc, 2 dc into next dc, 1 dc into next dc, 2 dc into next dc, 1 dc into each of last 19 dc, turn. 32 sts.

Rows 21 and 22 As row 19.

Row 23 1 ch (does NOT count as st), 1 dc into

The double crochet fabric is dense and sturdy, making the hat and mittens cosy and warm.

each of first 19 dc, 2 dc into next dc, 1 dc into each of next 3 dc, 2 dc into next dc, 1 dc into each of last 8 dc, turn. 34 sts.

Rows 24 and 25 As row 19.

Row 26 1 ch (does NOT count as st), 1 dc into each of first 8 dc, 2 dc into next dc, 1 dc into each of next 5 dc, 2 dc into next dc, 1 dc into each of last 19 dc, turn. 36 sts.

Rows 27 and 28 As row 19.

Row 29 1 ch (does NOT count as st), 1 dc into each of first 19 dc, 2 dc into next dc, 1 dc into each of next 7 dc, 2 dc into next dc, 1 dc into each of last 8 dc, turn. 38 sts.

Row 30 As row 19.
Break yarn.

- ### *Shape thumb*

With RS facing, miss first 19 dc of next row, attach yarn to next dc, 1 ch (does NOT count as st), 1 dc into dc at base of 1 ch, 1 dc into each of next 9 dc, 2 dc into next dc, ss to first dc of this row, turn. 12 sts.
Work as given for thumb of right mitten from *** to ***.

- ### *Shape hand*

With RS facing, return to last row worked before shaping thumb, attach yarn to 6th dc from end of last row, 1 ch (does NOT count as st), 1 dc into dc at base of 1 ch, 1 dc into each of next 13 dc of last row, 1 dc into base of thumb, 1 dc into each of first 8 dc of last row, 10 ch, 1 dc into each of last 5 dc of last row, ss to first dc, turn. 38 sts.
Complete as given for right mitten from ****.

MAKING UP

Press carefully, following instructions on ball band.

MOTIF

Make one basic motif for each mitten and sew into 'hole' on back of hand.

LOWER EDGING

With RS facing, attach yarn at base of mitten and work 1 round of crab st (dc worked from left to right, instead of right to left) around foundation ch edge, ending with ss to first dc.
Fasten off.

Seaside and shells set

This accessories set of matching hat, belt and bag is made in a mercerized cotton yarn, which, despite the light weight of the yarn and its fineness, is surprisingly hard-wearing. The shade of this yarn is reminiscent of the colour of the ocean, so the fronds of the belt and the straps of the bag were trimmed with shells to continue the seaside theme. You could change the colour theme – lilacs or purples would work well – and use pretty beads to trim the work.

PROJECT NOTES

MEASUREMENTS
BELT: Actual size, excluding fringe: 12 x 163cm (4¾ x 64in)
HAT: Width around head 39cm (15¼in)
BAG: Actual size 24 x 27cm (9½ x 10½in)

YARN
4ply 100% mercerized cotton in ocean blue: 4 x 50g (1¾oz) balls for belt, 2 x 50g (1¾oz) balls for hat, and 3 x 50g (1¾oz) balls for bag

HOOK
2.50mm (C2) hook

NOTIONS
14 beads for belt, 4 for bag

SPECIAL ABBREVIATIONS
beaded ch slide bead up so that it sits on RS of work next to st just worked, yoh and draw loop through leaving bead caught in st.
tr2tog *yoh and insert hook as indicated, yoh and draw loop through, yoh and draw through 2 loops, rep from * once more, yoh and draw through all 3 loops on hook.
yoh yarn over hook.

TENSION
28 sts and 12 rows to 10cm (4in) measured over pattern on 2.50mm (C2) hook, or the size required to achieve stated tension.

THE PATTERN

BELT

With 2.50mm (C2) hook, make 34 ch.

Foundation row (RS) 1 tr into 4th ch from hook, 1 tr into each ch to end, turn. 32 sts.

Next row 3 ch (counts as 1 tr), miss st at base of 3 ch, 1 tr into each tr to end, working last tr into top of 3 ch at beg of previous row, turn.

Rep last row once more.
Cont in patt as follows:

Row 1 (WS) 3 ch (counts as 1 tr), miss st at base of 3 ch, 1 tr into each of next 5 tr, (2 ch, miss 2 tr, 1 tr into next tr) 3 times, 1 tr into each of next 3 tr, (2 ch, miss 2 tr, 1 tr into next tr) 3 times, 1 tr into each of last 5 sts, working last tr into top of 3 ch at beg of previous row, turn.

Row 2 3 ch (counts as 1 tr), miss st at base of

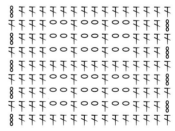

KEY

3 ch, 1 tr into each of next 5 tr, (2 ch, miss 2 ch, 1 tr into next tr) 3 times, 1 tr into each of next 3 tr, (2 ch, miss 2 ch, 1 tr into next tr) 3 times, 1 tr into each of last 5 sts, working last tr into top of 3 ch at beg of previous row, turn.

Row 3 As row 2.

Row 4 3 ch (counts as 1 tr), miss st at base of 3 ch, 1 tr into each of next 5 tr, (2 tr into

next ch sp, 1 tr into next tr) 3 times, 1 tr into each of next 3 tr, (2 tr into next ch sp, 1 tr into next tr) 3 times, 1 tr into each of last 5 sts, working last tr into top of 3 ch at beg of previous row, turn.

Rows 5 to 8 As rows 1 to 4.

Row 9 3 ch (counts as 1 tr), miss st at base of 3 ch, 1 tr into each tr to end, working last tr into top of 3 ch at beg of previous row, turn.

Row 10 As row 9.

These 10 rows form patt.

Cont in patt until belt measures 162cm (63¾in), ending after 10th patt row.

Fasten off.

MAKING UP

● *Edging*

Thread 14 beads onto yarn.

With RS facing, rejoin yarn at one end of foundation ch edge and work one row of crab st (dc worked from left to right, instead of right to left) up entire row-end edge to top of last row, turn, work across 32 sts of last row as follows: *1 dc into first dc, 45 ch, 1 beaded ch, miss beaded ch, 1 dc into each of next 45 ch, 1 dc into each of next 5 dc of last row, 42 ch, 1 beaded ch, miss beaded ch, 1 dc into each of next 42 ch, 1 dc into each of next 5 dc of last row, 39 ch, 1 beaded ch, miss beaded ch, 1 dc into each of next 39 ch, 1 dc into each of next 5 dc of last row, 50 ch, 1 beaded ch, miss beaded ch, 1 dc into each of next 50 ch, 1 dc into each of next 5 dc of last row, 44 ch, 1 beaded ch, miss beaded ch, 1 dc into each of next 44 ch, 1 dc into each of next 5 dc of last row, 36 ch, 1 beaded ch, miss beaded ch, 1 dc into each of next 36 ch, 1 dc into each of next 5 dc of last row, 48 ch, 1 beaded ch, miss beaded ch, 1 dc into each of next 48 ch, 1 dc into last dc of last row*, turn, work one row of crab st (dc worked from left to right, instead of right to left) down entire row-end edge to foundation ch edge, turn, work across foundation ch edge as for top of last row by working from * to *, ss to first dc.

Fasten off.

Press carefully following instructions on ball band.

All three pieces in this set are constructed from a treble and mesh stitch combination.

HAT

With 2.50mm (C2) hook, make 108 ch loosely and join with a ss to form a ring. (Check now that ch will stretch to fit on head.)

Round 1 (RS) 3 ch (counts as first tr), miss st at base of 3 ch, 1 tr into each ch to end, ss to top of 3 ch at beg of round, turn. 108 sts.

Round 2 3 ch (counts as 1 tr), miss st at base of 3 ch, 1 tr into each tr to end, ss to top of 3 ch at beg of round, turn.

Round 3 As round 2.

Round 4 5 ch (counts as 1 tr and 2 ch), miss at base of 3 ch and next 2 tr, *1 tr into each of next 4 tr**, (2 ch, miss 2 tr, 1 tr into next tr) twice, 2 ch, miss 2 tr, rep from * to end, ending last rep at **, 2 ch, miss 2 tr, 1 tr into next tr, 2 ch, miss 2 tr, ss to 3rd of 5 ch at beg of round, turn.

Round 5 5 ch (counts as 1 tr and 2 ch), miss at base of 3 ch and next 2 ch, 1 tr into next tr, *2 ch, miss 2 ch, 1 tr into each of next 4 tr**, (2 ch, miss 2 ch, 1 tr into next tr) twice, rep from * to end, ending last rep at **, 2 ch, miss 2 ch, ss to 3rd of 5 ch at beg of round, turn.

Round 6 5 ch (counts as 1 tr and 2 ch), miss st at base of 3 ch and next 2 ch, *1 tr into each of next 4 tr**, (2 ch, miss 2 ch, 1 tr into next tr) twice, 2 ch, miss 2 ch, rep from * to end, ending last rep at **, 2 ch, miss 2 ch, 1 tr into next tr, 2 ch, miss 2 ch, ss to 3rd of 5 ch at beg of round, turn.

Round 7 3 ch (counts as 1 tr), miss st at base of 3 ch, 2 tr into next ch sp, 1 tr into next tr, *2 tr into next ch sp, 1 tr into each of next 4 tr**, (2 tr into next ch sp, 1 tr into next tr) twice, rep from * to end, ending last rep at **, 2 tr into next ch sp, ss to top of 3 ch at beg of round, turn.

Rounds 8 to 11 As rounds 4 to 7.

Rounds 12 and 13 As round 2.

Round 14 3 ch (counts as 1 tr), miss st at base of 3 ch, 1 tr into each of next 6 tr, *tr2tog over next 2 tr**, 1 tr into each of next 7 tr, rep from * to end, ending last rep at **, ss to top of 3 ch at beg of round, turn. 96 sts.

Round 15 As round 2.

Round 16 3 ch (counts as 1 tr), miss st at base of 3 ch, 1 tr into each of next 5 tr, *tr2tog over next 2 tr**, 1 tr into each of next 6 tr, rep from * to end, ending last rep at **, ss to top of 3 ch at beg of round, turn. 84 sts.

Round 17 As round 2.

Round 18 3 ch (counts as 1 tr), miss st at base of 3 ch, 1 tr into each of next 4 tr, *tr2tog over next 2 tr**, 1 tr into each of next 5 tr, rep from * to end, ending last rep at **, ss to top of 3 ch at beg of round, turn. 72 sts.

Round 19 As round 2.

Round 20 3 ch (counts as 1 tr), miss st at base of 3 ch, 1 tr into each of next 3 tr, *tr2tog over next 2 tr**, 1 tr into each of next 4 tr, rep from * to end, ending last rep at **, ss to top of 3 ch at beg of round, turn. 60 sts.

Round 21 As round 2.

Round 22 3 ch (counts as 1 tr), miss st at base of 3 ch, 1 tr into each of next 2 tr, *tr2tog over next 2 tr**, 1 tr into each of next 3 tr, rep from * to end, ending last rep at **, ss to top of 3 ch at beg of round, turn. 48 sts.

Round 23 3 ch (counts as 1 tr), miss st at base of 3 ch, 1 tr into next tr, *tr2tog over next 2 tr**, 1 tr into each of next 2 tr, rep from * to end, ending last rep at **, ss to top of 3 ch at beg of round, turn. 36 sts.

Round 24 3 ch (counts as 1 tr), miss st at base of 3 ch, *tr2tog over next 2 tr**, 1 tr into next tr, rep from * to end, ending last rep at **, ss to top of 3 ch at beg of round, turn. 24 sts.

Round 25 3 ch (does NOT count as st), miss st at base of 3 ch, 1 tr into next tr, (tr2tog over next 2 tr) 11 times, ss to tr at beg of round, turn. 12 sts.

Round 26 1 ch (does NOT count as st), (dc2tog over next 2 tr) 6 times, ss to dc2tog at beg of round, turn. 6 sts.

Round 27 1 ch (does NOT count as st), (dc2tog over next 2 sts) twice, ss to dc2tog at beg of round. 3 sts.

Fasten off.

MAKING UP

● *Edging*

With RS facing, rejoin yarn to foundation ch edge and work 1 round of crab st (dc worked from left to right, instead of right to left) around entire foundation ch edge, ending with ss to first dc.

Fasten off.

Press following instructions on ball band.

BAG

With 2.50mm (C2) hook, make 132 ch and join with a ss to form a ring.

Round 1 (RS) 3 ch (counts as first tr), miss st at base of 3 ch, 1 tr into each ch to end, ss to top of 3 ch at beg of round, turn. 132 sts.

Round 2 3 ch (counts as 1 tr), miss st at base of 3 ch, 1 tr into each tr to end, ss to top of 3 ch at beg of round, turn.

Round 3 3 ch (counts as 1 tr), miss st at base of 3 ch, 1 tr into next tr, *2 ch, miss 2 tr**, 1 tr into each of next 2 tr, rep from * to end, ending last rep at **, ss to top of 3 ch at beg of round, turn.

Round 4 3 ch (counts as 1 tr), miss st at base of 3 ch, 1 tr into each tr and 2 tr into each ch sp to end, ss to top of 3 ch at beg of round, turn.

Rounds 5 to 7 As round 2.

Now work rounds 4 to 11 as given for hat.

Round 16 As round 2.

Rep last round until bag measures 27cm (10½in).

Fasten off.

MAKING UP

● *Edging*

With RS facing, rejoin yarn to foundation ch edge and work 1 round of crab st (dc worked from left to right, instead of right to left) around entire foundation ch edge, ending with ss to first dc.

Fasten off.

Fold bag flat and join top of last row to form base seam, ensuring patt is evenly placed across bag.

● *Ties* (make 2)

Thread a bead onto yarn.

With 2.50mm (C2) hook, make a ch 130cm (51in) long, 1 beaded ch, miss beaded ch, 1 dc into each ch to end.

Cut yarn leaving a long end and slip working loop onto a safety pin.

Starting at one fold of bag, thread tie through holes of round 3, ending at same folded edge.

Slip working loop back onto hook and thread a bead onto yarn, 1 beaded ch, ss to first ch.

Fasten off.

Knot ends of tie and attach knot to base corner of bag.

Make a second tie in the same way, threading tie through 3rd round from other folded edge.

Press following the instructions on the ball band.

Tartan-style set

Creating a tartan-style effect is surprisingly simple in crochet; this bag and scarf are created from a mesh crochet fabric with lengths of chain woven through it (see pages 80–81 for more information). The three strongly contrasting colours create a bold look, while the cashmere-mix yarn is lusciously soft but robust.

PROJECT NOTES

MEASUREMENTS
SCARF:
Actual size, excluding fringe 19 x 137cm (7½ x 54in)
BAG:
Actual size 28 x 28cm (11 x 11in)

YARN
All aran-weight merino, microfibre and cashmere mix yarn
MC 6 x 50g (1¾oz) balls in grey
A 2 x 50g (1¾oz) balls in red
B 2 x 50g (1¾oz) balls in green

HOOK
4.50mm (7) crochet hook

NOTIONS
FOR BAG:
48cm of 38mm-wide (19in of 1½in-wide) petersham ribbon
Piece of firm card approx 13 x 35cm (5 x 13¾in)

SPECIAL ABBREVIATIONS
dc2tog (insert hook as indicated, yarn over hook and draw loop through)

twice, yarn over hook and draw through all 3 loops.

TENSION
14½ sts and 16 rows to 10cm (4in) measured over double crochet fabric, 17 sts and 7 rows to 10cm (4in) measured over mesh fabric, both on 4.50mm (7) hook, or the size required to achieve stated tension.

THE PATTERN

SCARF

With 4.50mm (7) hook and MC, make 36 ch.
Foundation row (RS) 1 tr into 6th ch from hook, *1 ch, miss 1 ch, 1 tr into next ch, rep from * to end, turn. 33 sts, 16 ch sps.

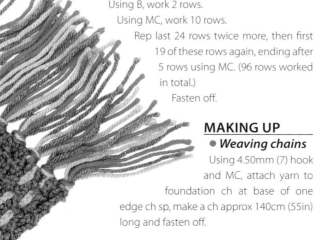

Cont in patt as follows:
Row 1 (WS) 4 ch (counts as 1 tr and 1 ch), miss tr at base of 4 ch and next ch, 1 tr into next tr, *1 ch, miss 1 ch, 1 tr into next tr, rep from * to end, working last tr at end of last rep into 3rd of 4 ch at beg of previous row, turn.
This row forms mesh fabric.
Rep last row 3 times more.
Joining in and breaking off colours as required, cont in mesh fabric in stripes as follows:
Using B, work 2 rows.
Using MC, work 3 rows.
Using A, work 4 rows.
Using MC, work 3 rows.
Using B, work 2 rows.
Using MC, work 10 rows.
Rep last 24 rows twice more, then first 19 of these rows again, ending after 5 rows using MC. (96 rows worked in total.)
Fasten off.

MAKING UP
● **Weaving chains**
Using 4.50mm (7) hook and MC, attach yarn to foundation ch at base of one edge ch sp, make a ch approx 140cm (55in) long and fasten off.

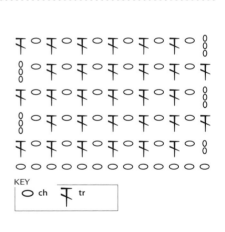

KEY
○ ch   ╤ tr

Weave ch in and out of mesh fabric, taking ch over 1st row, under 2nd row, and so on.
Attach other end of ch to top of last row, adjusting length of ch as required so that fabric lays flat.
Using 4.50mm (7) hook and B, attach yarn to foundation ch at base of next ch sp, make a ch approx 140cm (55in) long and fasten off.
Weave ch in and out of mesh fabric, taking ch under 1st row, over 2nd row, and so on.
Attach other end of ch to top of last row.
Cont in this way, making and weaving chains in and out of mesh, making chains as follows: fill next ch sp with ch using B, next 3 ch sps with ch using MC, next 4 ch sps with ch using A, next 3 ch sps with ch using

MC, next 2 ch sps with ch using B, and last ch sp with ch using MC.

● *Fringe*

Cut 24 lengths of each of MC, A and B, each 26cm (10¼in) long. Using one strand of each colour, knot groups of 3 of these lengths across ends of scarf, positioning 12 knots evenly spaced across each end.

BAG

With 4.50mm (7) hook and MC, make 25 ch.

Round 1 (RS) 2 dc into 2nd ch from hook, 1 dc into each of next 22 ch, 4 dc into last ch, working back along other side of foundation ch: 1 dc into each of next 22 ch, 2 dc into last ch (this is same ch as used for 2 dc at beg of round, ss to first dc, turn. 52 sts.

Round 2 1 ch (does NOT count as st), 2 dc into each of first 2 dc, 1 dc into each of next 22 dc, 2 dc into each of next 4 dc, 1 dc into each of next 22 dc, 2 dc into each of last 2 dc, ss to first dc, turn. 60 sts.

Round 3 1 ch (does NOT count as st), 1 dc into each dc to end, ss to first dc, turn.

Round 4 1 ch (does NOT count as st), *(1 dc into next dc, 2 dc into next dc) twice, 1 dc into each of next 22 dc, (2 dc into next dc, 1 dc into next dc) twice, rep from * once more, ss to first dc, turn. 68 sts.

Round 5 1 ch (does NOT count as st), *1 dc into each of next 3 dc, 2 dc into next dc, 1 dc into each of next 26 dc, 2 dc into next dc, 1 dc into each of next 3 dc, rep from * once more, ss to first dc, turn. 72 sts.

Round 6 1 ch (does NOT count as st), *1 dc into each of next 2 dc, 2 dc into next dc, 1 dc into each of next 3 dc, 2 dc into next dc, 1 dc into each of next 22 dc, 2 dc into next dc, 1 dc into each of next 3 dc, 2 dc into next dc, 1 dc into each of next 2 dc, rep from * once more, ss to first dc, turn. 80 sts.

Round 7 As round 3.

Round 8 1 ch (does NOT count as st), *1 dc into each of next 4 dc, 2 dc into next dc, 1 dc into each of next 3 dc, 2 dc into next dc, 1 dc into each of next 22 dc, 2 dc into next dc, 1 dc into each of next 3 dc, 2 dc into next dc, 1 dc into each of next 4 dc, rep from * once more, ss to first dc, turn. 88 sts.

Round 9 1 ch (does NOT count as st), working into back loops only of sts of previous round: (1 dc into each of next 5 dc, 2 dc into next dc, 1 dc into each of next 5 dc) 8 times, ss to first dc, turn. 96 sts.

This completes base.

Trace outline of base onto firm card and set to one side.

● *Shape sides*

Now cont in mesh fabric for sides as follows:

Round 1 4 ch (counts as 1 tr and 1 ch), miss st at base of 4 ch and next st, *1 tr into next dc, 1 ch, miss 1 dc, rep from * to end, ss to 3rd of 4 ch at beg of round, turn. 48 ch sps.

Round 2 4 ch (counts as 1 tr and 1 ch), miss st at base of 4 ch and next ch, *1 tr into next tr, 1 ch, miss 1 dc, rep from * to end, ss to 3rd of 4 ch at beg of round, turn.

Last round forms mesh fabric.

Rep last row 3 times more.

Joining in and breaking off colours as required, cont in mesh fabric in stripes as follows:

Using B, work 2 rounds.

Using MC, work 3 rounds.

Using A, work 4 rounds.

Using MC, work 3 rounds.

Using B, work 2 rounds.

Using MC, work 2 rounds.

This completes mesh sides of bag.

● *Shape upper band*

Break off contrasts and cont using MC only.

Next round 1 ch (does NOT count as st), (1 dc into next st, dc2tog over next 2 sts) 32 times, ss to first dc, turn. 64 sts.

Next round 1 ch (does NOT count as st), 1 dc into each st to end, ss to first dc, turn.

Rep last round 12 times more.

Fasten off.

MAKING UP

● *Weaving chains*

Mark centre tr on one side of bag.

Using 4.50mm (7) hook and A, attach yarn to dc at base of one ch sp next to this centre tr, make a ch approx 26cm (10¼in) long and fasten off.

Weave ch in and out of mesh fabric, taking ch over 1st round, under 2nd round, and so on.

Attach other end of ch to top of last round of mesh (first round of top band), adjusting length of ch as required so that fabric stays flat.

Using 4.50mm (7) hook and A, attach yarn to dc at base of next ch sp (working away from centre marked tr), make a ch approx 26cm (10¼in) long and fasten off.

Weave ch in and out of mesh fabric, taking ch under 1st round, over 2nd round, and so on.

Attach other end of ch to top of last round of mesh (first round of top band), adjusting length of ch as required so that fabric stays flat.

Cont in this way, making and weaving chains in and out of mesh, working around bag and making chains as follows: fill next 3 ch sps with ch using MC, next 2 ch sps with ch using B, next 10 ch sps with ch using MC, next 2 ch sps with ch using B, next 3 ch sps with ch using MC, next 4 ch sps with ch using A, next 3 ch sps with ch using MC, next 2 ch sps with ch using B, next 10 ch sps with ch using MC, next 2 ch sps with ch using B, next 3 ch sps with ch using MC, and last ch sps with ch using A.

Join ends of petersham ribbon to form a loop of 44cm (17¼in). Fold top band in half to inside and slip stitch in place, enclosing loop of petersham ribbon inside.

● *Handle*

With 4.50mm (7) hook and MC, make 6 ch and join with a ss to form a ring.

Round 1 (RS) 1 ch (does NOT count as st), 1 dc into each dc to end. 6 sts.

Round 2 1 dc into each dc to end.

Rep last round until handle measures 48cm (18¾in), ending last round by working a ss into next dc.

Fasten off.

Using photograph as a guide, sew ends of handle to inside of top band.

Cut out base shape from firm card and slip inside bag.

Summer sky mesh top

This simple vest top, made from a crisp cotton yarn in a simple mesh stitch with an edging of double crochet around the neckline and shoulder straps, is the perfect garment for a gloriously sunny day. The vivid turquoise recalls the deep blue of a cloudless summer sky.

PROJECT NOTES

MEASUREMENTS
To fit bust: 81cm (32in) [86cm (34in): 91cm (36in): 97cm (38in): 102cm (40in): 107cm (42in)]
Actual size: 86cm (33¾in) [90cm (35½in): 96cm (37¾in): 100cm (39¼in): 106cm (41¾in): 110cm (43¼in)]
Full length: 52cm (20½in) [53cm (20¾in): 54cm (21¼in): 55cm (21½in): 56cm (22in): 57cm (22½in)]

YARN
4 [5: 5: 6: 6: 7] x 50g (1¾oz) of 4ply 100% mercerized cotton in turquoise

HOOK
2.50mm (C2) hook

SPECIAL ABBREVIATIONS
tr2tog *yoh and insert hook as indicated, yoh and draw loop through, yoh and draw through 2 loops, rep from * once more, yoh and draw through all 3 loops on hook.
yoh yarn over hook.

TENSION
28 sts and 12 rows to 10cm (4in) measured over pattern on 2.50mm (C2) hook, or the size required to achieve stated tension.

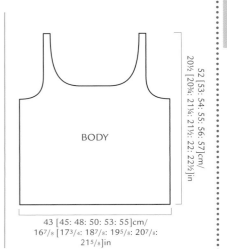

BODY

52 [53: 54: 55: 56: 57]cm/ 20½ [20¾: 21¼: 21½: 22: 22½]in

43 [45: 48: 50: 53: 55]cm/ 16⅞ [17¾: 18⅞: 19⅝: 20⅞: 21⅝]in

THE PATTERN

BODY
(Worked in one piece to armholes.)
With 2.50mm (C2) hook, make 240 [252: 268: 280: 296: 308] ch and join with a ss to form a ring.
Foundation round (RS) 4 ch (counts as first tr and 1 ch), miss first 2 ch, *1 tr into next ch, 1 ch, miss 1 ch, rep from * to end, ss to 3rd of 4th ch at beg of round, turn. 240 [252: 268: 280: 296: 308] sts.

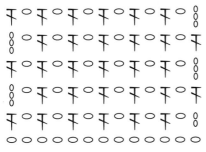

KEY
○ ch
⊤ tr

Cont in patt as follows:
Round 1 (WS) 4 ch (counts as 1 tr and 1 ch), miss st at base of 4 ch and 1 ch, *1 tr into next tr, 1 ch, miss 1 ch, rep from * to end, ss to 3rd of 4th ch at beg of round, turn.
This round forms patt.
Cont in patt until body measures 31cm (12¼in) [32cm (12½in): 32cm (12½in): 33cm (13in): 33cm (13in): 34cm (13¼in)].
Fasten off.

● **Divide for front and back (both alike)**
Now working in rows, not rounds, cont as follows:
With appropriate side of work facing (by remembering to turn at end of last round), miss first 8 [8: 10: 10: 12: 12] sts of next round, rejoin yarn to next tr, 3 ch (does NOT count as st), miss tr at base of 3 ch and 1 ch, 1 tr into next tr, (1 ch, miss 1 ch, 1 tr into next tr) 49 [52: 54: 57: 59: 62] times, 1 ch, miss 1 ch, tr2tog over next 3 sts, working first 'leg' into next tr, missing 1 ch, and working 2nd 'leg' into next tr, turn.
Work on this set of 101 [107: 111: 117: 121:

127] sts only for first side.
***Next row** 3 ch (does NOT count as st), miss tr2tog at base of 3 ch and next ch, 1 tr into next tr (2 sts decreased), *1 ch, miss 1 ch, 1 tr into next tr, rep from * until tr has been worked into tr before last 2 ch sps, 1 ch, miss 1 ch, tr2tog over next 3 sts, working first 'leg' into next tr, missing 1 ch, and working 2nd 'leg' into next tr (2 sts decreased), turn (leaving 3 ch at beg of previous row unworked).
Working all decreases as set by last row, dec 2 sts at each end of next 4 rows. 81 [87: 91: 97: 101: 107] sts.

● **Shape neck**
Next row 3 ch (does NOT count as st), miss tr2tog at base of 3 ch and next ch, 1 tr into next tr (2 sts decreased), (1 ch, miss 1 ch, 1 tr into next tr) 9 [10: 11: 12: 13: 14] times, 1 ch, miss 1 ch, tr2tog over next 3 sts, working first 'leg' into next tr, missing 1 ch, and working 2nd 'leg' into next tr (2 sts decreased), turn, leaving rem sts unworked.
Work on this set of 21 [23: 25: 27: 29: 31] sts only for first shoulder strap.

**Working all decreases as set, dec 2 sts at neck edge of next 6 rows and at same time dec 2 sts at armhole edge of next 2 [3: 3: 4: 4: 5] rows. 5 [5: 7: 7: 9: 9] sts.

Note: When working a row-end edge without shaping, start rows with '4 ch (counts as first tr and 1 ch), miss st at base of 4 ch and next ch, 1 tr into next tr', and end rows with '1 ch, miss 1 ch, 1 tr into 3rd of 4 ch at beg of previous row, turn'.

Cont straight until armhole measures 20cm (7¾in) [20cm (7¾in): 21cm (8¼in): 21cm (8¼in) 22cm (8½in): 22cm (8½in)].

Fasten off.

With appropriate side of work facing, return to last complete row worked before shaping neck, miss next 31 [33: 33: 35: 35: 37] sts, rejoin yarn to next tr, 3 ch (does NOT count as st), miss tr at base of 3 ch and next ch, 1 tr into next tr (2 sts decreased), (1 ch, miss 1 ch, 1 tr into next tr) 9 [10: 11: 12: 13: 14] times, 1 ch, miss 1 ch, tr2tog over next 3 sts, working first 'leg' into next tr, missing 1 ch, and working 2nd 'leg' into next tr (2 sts decreased), turn, leaving rem sts unworked.

Work on this set of 21 [23: 25: 27: 29: 31] sts only for second shoulder strap by working as given for first shoulder strap from **.

With appropriate side of work facing, return to last complete round worked before dividing for front and back, miss next 15 [15: 19: 19: 23: 23] sts, rejoin yarn to next tr, 3 ch (does NOT count as st), miss tr at base of 3 ch and next ch, 1 tr into next tr, (1 ch, miss 1 ch, 1 tr into next tr) 49 [52: 54: 57: 59: 62] times, 1 ch, miss 1 ch, tr2tog over next 3 sts, working first 'leg' into next tr, missing 1 ch, and working 2nd 'leg' into next tr, turn, leaving rem sts unworked (there should be 15 [15: 19: 19: 23: 23] sts unworked between last st used here and first st used for first section).

Work on this set of 101 [107: 111: 117: 121: 127] sts only for second side by working as given for first side from ***.

MAKING UP

Join shoulder seams.

● *Neck edging*

With RS facing and 2.50mm (C2) hook, rejoin yarn at neck edge of left shoulder seam, 1 ch (does NOT count as st), work in dc evenly around entire neck edge, ending with ss to first dc, turn.

Next round 1 ch (does NOT count as st), 1 dc into each dc to end, missing dc as required to ensure edging lays flat and ending with ss to first dc, turn.

The neckline and shoulder strap edgings are worked in double crochet to stabilize the mesh stitch and provide a neat finishing.

Fasten off.

Work edging around armhole edges and lower edge in same way.

Bead-edged beauty

This pretty, lightweight lacy top worked in a fresh-looking crisp cotton yarn is just the garment for a hot summer's day. The sleeves are edged with silvery beads for an extra touch of glamour. See pages 76–77 for more information on working with beads.

PROJECT NOTES

MEASUREMENTS

To fit bust: 81cm (32in) [86cm (34in): 91cm (36in): 97cm (38in): 102cm (40in): 107cm (42in)]

Actual size: 87cm (34¼in) [93cm (36½in): 99cm (39in): 105cm (41¼in): 112cm (44in): 118cm (46½in)]

Full length: 53cm (20¾in) [53cm (20¾in): 55cm (21½in): 59cm (23¼in): 62cm (24½in): 62cm (24½in)]

Sleeve seam: 9cm (3½in) [9cm (3½in): 9cm (3½in): 9cm (3½in): 9cm (3½in): 9cm (3½in)]

YARN

6 [6: 6: 7: 8: 8] x 50g (1¾oz) of 4ply 100% cotton in cream

HOOKS

2.00mm (B1) and 2.50mm (C2) hooks

NOTIONS

288 [300: 330: 342: 372: 384] beads

SPECIAL ABBREVIATIONS

beaded ch slide bead up so that it sits on RS of work next to st just worked, yoh and draw loop through leaving bead caught in st

dtr2tog *(yoh) twice and insert hook as indicated, yoh and draw loop through, (yoh and draw through 2 loops) twice, rep from * once more, yoh and draw through all 3 loops on hook

tr2tog *yoh and insert hook as indicated, yoh and draw loop through, yoh and draw through 2 loops, rep from * once more, yoh and draw through all 3 loops on hook

yoh yarn over hook.

TENSION

26 sts and 13½ rows to 10cm (4in) measured over pattern on 2.50mm (C2) hook, or the size required to achieve stated tension.

BODY

53 [53: 53: 55: 59: 62: 62]cm
20¾ [20¾: 21½: 23¼: 24½: 24½]in

43.5 [46.5: 49.5: 52.5: 56: 59]cm
17¹⁄₈ [18¼: 19½: 20⁵⁄₈: 22: 23¼]in

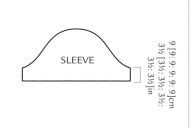

SLEEVE

9 [9: 9: 9: 9: 9]cm
3½ [3½: 3½: 3½: 3½: 3½]in

THE PATTERN

BACK

With 2.50mm (C2) hook, make 114 [122: 130: 138: 146: 154] ch.

Foundation row (WS) 1 dc into 2nd ch from hook, 1 dc into each ch to end, turn. 113 [121: 129: 137: 145: 153] sts.

Cont in patt as follows:

Row 1 (RS) 4 ch (counts as 1 tr and 1 ch), miss first 2 dc, 1 tr into next dc, *1 ch, miss 1 dc, 1 tr into next dc, rep from * to end, turn.

Row 2 1 ch (does NOT count as st), 1 dc into tr at base of 1 ch, *1 dc into next ch sp, 1 dc into next tr, rep from * to end, working dc at end of last rep into 3rd of 4 ch at beg of previous row, turn.

Row 3 3 ch (does NOT count as st), miss first 2 dc, 1 dtr into next dc, *3 ch**, dtr2tog working first 'leg' into same dc as already worked into, missing 3 dc and working

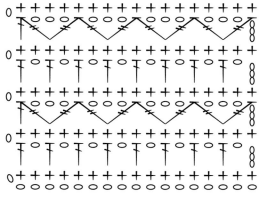

KEY

+	dc
O	ch
⊤	tr
⊥⊤	dtr
⋀	dtr2tog

second 'leg' into next dc, rep from * to end, ending last rep at **, (yoh) twice, insert hook into same dc as already worked into, yoh and draw loop through, (yoh and draw through 2 loops) twice, yoh, miss 1 dc, insert hook into last dc, yoh and draw loop through, yoh and draw through 2 loops, yoh and draw through all 3 loops on hook, turn.

Row 4 1 ch (does NOT count as st), 1 dc into st at base of 1 ch, *3 dc into next ch sp, 1 dc into next dtr2tog, rep from * to end, working dc at end of last rep into top of dtr at beg of previous row, turn.

These 4 rows form patt.

Cont in patt for a further 36 [36: 36: 40: 40: 40] rows, ending after a 4th patt row and a WS row.

● *Shape armholes*

Next row Ss across and into 5th st, 3 ch (does NOT count as st), miss 1 dc, 1 tr into next dc (6 sts decreased), patt to last 8 sts, 1 ch, miss 1 dc, tr2tog working first 'leg' into next dc, missing 1 dc and working second 'leg'

into next dc and turn, leaving rem 6 sts unworked (6 sts decreased). 101 [109: 117: 125: 133: 141] sts.

Next row 1 ch (does NOT count as st), 1 dc into tr2tog at base of 1 ch, patt until dc has been worked into tr at beg of previous and turn, leaving 3 ch at beg of previous row unworked.

Next row 4 ch (does NOT count as st), miss first 4 dc, 1 dtr into next dc (2 sts decreased), 3 ch, patt until second 'leg' of last dtr2tog has been worked into dc at beg of previous row and turn (2 sts decreased). 97 [105: 113: 121: 129: 137] sts.

Next row 1 ch (does NOT count as st), 1 dc into dtr2tog at base of 1 ch, patt until dc has been worked into dtr at beg of previous and turn, leaving 4 ch at beg of previous row unworked.

Next row 3 ch (does NOT count as st), miss first 2 dc, 1 tr into next dc (2 sts decreased), patt to last 4 sts, 1 ch, miss 1 dc, tr2tog working first 'leg' into next dc, missing 1 dc and working second 'leg' into last dc, turn (2 sts decreased). 93 [101: 109: 117: 125: 133] sts.

Rep last 4 rows 0 [1: 1: 2: 2: 3] times more, then first 3 of these rows again. 89 [89: 97: 97: 105: 105] sts.***

Cont in patt for a further 12 [8: 12: 8: 12: 8] rows, ending after a 4th patt row and a WS row.

● *Shape back neck*

Next row (RS) Patt 21 [21: 25: 25: 29: 29] sts, 1 ch, miss 1 dc, tr2tog working first 'leg' into next dc, missing 1 dc and working second 'leg' into last dc and turn, leaving rem sts unworked. 23 [23: 27: 27: 31: 31] sts.

Working shaping in same way as for armhole shaping, work 3 rows, dec 2 sts at neck edge of 2nd of these rows. 21 [21: 25: 25: 29: 29] sts.

Fasten off.

With RS facing, return to last complete row worked, miss centre 39 dc, rejoin yarn to next dc, 3 ch (does NOT count as st), miss 1 dc, 1 tr into next dc, patt to end, turn. 23 [23: 27: 27: 31: 31] sts.

Working shaping in same way as for armhole shaping, work 3 rows, dec 2 sts at neck edge of 2nd of these rows. 21 [21: 25: 25: 29: 29] sts.

Fasten off.

FRONT

Work as for back to ***.

Cont in patt for a further 4 [0: 4: 0: 4: 0] rows, ending after a 4th patt row and a WS row.

● *Shape back neck*

Next row (RS) Patt 25 [25: 29: 29: 33: 33] sts, 1 ch, miss 1 dc, tr2tog working first 'leg' into next dc, missing 1 dc and working second 'leg' into last dc and turn, leaving rem sts unworked. 27 [27: 31: 31: 35: 35] sts.

Working shaping in same way as for armhole shaping, work 7 rows, dec 2 sts at neck edge of 2nd and foll 2 alt rows. 21 [21: 25: 25: 29: 29] sts.

Work 4 rows, ending after a 4th patt row and a WS row.

Fasten off.

With RS facing, return to last complete row worked, miss centre 31 dc, rejoin yarn to next dc, 3 ch (does NOT count as st), miss 1 dc, 1 tr into next dc, patt to end, turn. 27 [27: 31: 31: 35: 35] sts.

Complete second side to match first, reversing shaping.

SLEEVES

With 2.50mm (C2) hook, make 82 [82: 94: 94: 106: 106] ch.

Work foundation row as for back. 81 [81: 93: 93: 105: 105] sts.

Cont in patt as for back as follows:

Work 4 rows, ending after a 4th patt row and a WS row.

● *Shape top*

Working all shaping in same way as for back armhole, dec 6 sts at each end of next row. 69 [69: 81: 81: 93: 93] sts.

Dec 2 sts at each end of 2nd and foll 6 [6: 7: 7: 8: 8] alt rows. 41 [41: 49: 49: 57: 57] sts.

Work 1 row, ending after a WS row.

Fasten off.

MAKING UP

Join shoulder seams.

● *Neck edging*

With RS facing and 2.00mm (B1) hook, rejoin yarn at neck edge of left shoulder seam, 1 ch (does NOT count as st), work in dc evenly around entire neck edge, ending with ss to first dc, turn.

Next round 1 ch (does NOT count as st), 1 dc into each dc to end, missing dc as required to ensure Edging lays flat and ending with ss to first dc, turn.

Rep last round twice more. Fasten off.

Join side seams.

● *Hem edging*

Thread 168 [180: 192: 204: 216: 228] beads onto yarn.

With RS facing and 2.00mm (B1) hook, rejoin yarn at base of left side seam, 1 ch (does NOT count as st), work in dc evenly around entire foundation ch edge, working 1 dc into each foundation ch, missing 1 foundation ch at base of each side seam and ending with ss to first dc, turn. 224 [240: 256: 272: 288: 304] sts.

****Next round** 1 ch (does NOT count as st), 1 dc into each dc to end, ending with ss to first dc, turn.

Next round 1 ch (does NOT count as st), 1 dc into first dc, *5 ch, miss 3 dc, 1 dc into next

The sleeves and the hem are decorated with pretty silver beads.

dc, rep from * to last 3 sts, 2 ch, 1 tr into first dc.

Next round 1 ch (does NOT count as st), (1 dc, 1 beaded ch and 1 dc) into ch sp partly formed by tr at end of last round, *7 ch, (1 dc, 1 beaded ch and 1 dc) into next ch sp, rep from * until last full ch sp has been worked into, 3 ch, 1 dtr into first dc.

Next round 1 ch (does NOT count as st), (1 dc, 1 beaded ch and 1 dc) into ch sp partly formed by dtr at end of last round, *4 ch, 1 beaded ch, 4 ch**, (1 dc, 1 beaded ch and 1 dc) into next ch sp, rep from * to end, ending last rep at **, ss to first dc.

Fasten off.

Join sleeve seams.

● *Sleeve edgings* (both alike)

Thread 60 [60: 69: 69: 78: 78] beads onto yarn.

With RS facing and 2.00mm (B1) hook, rejoin yarn at base of sleeve seam, 1 ch (does NOT count as st), work in dc evenly around foundation ch edge, working 1 dc into each foundation ch, missing 1 foundation ch at base of sleeve seam and ending with ss to first dc, turn. 80 [80: 92: 92: 104: 104] sts.

Complete as given for hem edging from ****.

Insert sleeves into armholes.

Flower-trimmed cardigan

This project shows you just how much you can do with a simple stitch. The body of this versatile cardigan is constructed from simple double crochet and chain in a sturdy denim yarn, while the flowers and leaves add a colourful contrast and detail. Play around with the colours for the embellishments – you could always make them in the same colour as the cardigan if you prefer, or go for a really stunning colour combination.

PROJECT NOTES

MEASUREMENTS

To fit bust: 81cm (32in) [86cm (34in): 91cm (36in): 97cm (38in): 102cm (40in): 107cm (42in)]

Actual size: 86cm (33¾in) [91cm (35¾in): 97cm (38in): 102cm (40in): 107cm (42in): 112cm (44in)]

Full length: 58cm (22¾in) [59cm (23¼in): 60cm (23½in): 61cm (24in): 62cm (24½in): 63cm (24¾in)]

Sleeve seam: 43cm (17in) [43cm (17in): 44cm (17¼in): 44cm (17¼in): 44cm (17¼in): 45cm (17¾in)]

YARN

CARDIGAN:

MC 18 [19: 19: 20: 21: 21] x 50g (1¾oz) balls of DK-weight denim yarn

LEAVES AND FLOWERS:

All 4ply 100% cotton

A 1 x 50g (1¾oz) ball in yellow
B 1 x 50g (1¾oz) ball in maroon
C 1 x 50g (1¾oz) ball in dark red
D 1 x 50g (1¾oz) ball in lime green
E 1 x 50g (1¾oz) ball in leaf green

HOOKS

2.50mm (C2), 3.50mm (E4) and 4.00mm (G6) hooks

NOTIONS

7 buttons

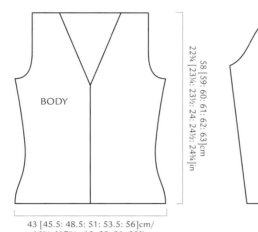

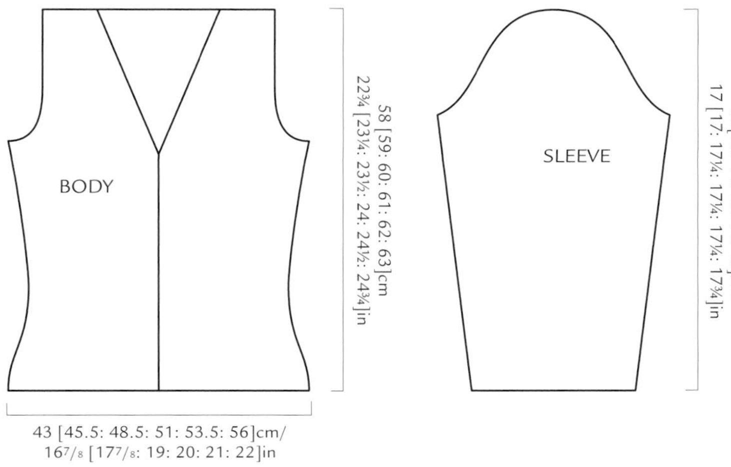

58 [59: 60: 61: 62: 63]cm / 22¾ [23¼: 23½: 24: 24½: 24¾]in

43 [43: 44: 44: 44: 45]cm / 17 [17: 17¼: 17¼: 17¼: 17¾]in

43 [45.5: 48.5: 51: 53.5: 56]cm/ 16⅞ [17⅞: 19: 20: 21: 22]in

SPECIAL ABBREVIATIONS

dtr3tog *(yarn over hook) twice, insert hook as indicated, yarn over hook and draw loop through, (yarn over hook and draw through 2 loops) twice, rep from * twice more, yarn over hook and draw through all 4 loops on hook.

rfdc relief front double crochet: work a dc in the usual way but working around stem of st, inserting hook from front to back and from right to left.

TENSION

Before washing: 21 sts and 18 rows to 10cm (4in) measured over pattern on 4.00mm (G6) hook, or the size required to achieve stated tension.

After washing: 23 sts and 22 rows to 10cm (4in) measured over pattern on 4.00mm (G6) hook, or the size required to achieve stated tension.

NOTE: The yarn used for this project will shrink when washed for the first time. Allowances have been made for this shrinkage.

THE PATTERN

BACK

With 4.00mm (G6) hook and MC, make 100 [106: 112: 118: 124: 130] ch.

Foundation row (RS) 1 dc into 2nd ch from hook, *1 ch, miss 1 ch, 1 dc into next ch, rep from * to end, turn. 99 [105: 111: 117: 123: 129] sts.

Cont in patt as follows:

Row 1 1 ch (does NOT count as st), 1 dc into first dc, *1 dc into next ch sp, 1 ch, miss 1 dc, rep from * to last 2 sts, 1 dc into next ch sp, 1 dc into last dc, turn.

Row 2 1 ch (does NOT count as st), 1 dc into first dc, *1 ch, miss 1 dc, 1 dc into next ch sp, rep from * to last 2 sts, 1 ch, miss 1 dc, 1 dc into last dc, turn.

These 2 rows form patt.

Cont in patt for a further 3 rows, ending after a WS row.

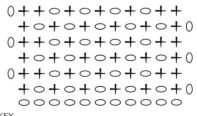

KEY
○ ch
+ dc

Next row (RS) 1 ch (does NOT count as st), dc2tog over first 2 sts (1 st decreased), patt to last 2 sts, dc2tog over last 2 sts (1 st decreased), turn.

Working all decreases as set by last row and keeping patt correct, dec 1 st at each end of 4th and every foll 4th row until 83 [89: 95: 101: 107: 113] sts rem.

Work 9 rows, ending after a WS row.

Next row (RS) 1 ch (does NOT count as st), 2 dc into first dc (1 st increased), patt to last st, 2 dc into last st (1 st increased), turn.

Working all increases as set by last row, inc 1 st at each end of 4th and every foll 4th row until there are 99 [105: 111: 117: 123: 129] sts, taking inc sts into patt.

Cont straight until back measures 46.5cm (18¼in) [47.5cm (18¾in): 47.5cm (18¾in): 49cm (19¼in): 49cm (19¼in): 50cm (19½in)] ending after a WS row.

● *Shape armholes*

Next row (RS) Ss across and into 5th [6th: 6th: 7th: 7th: 8th] st, 1 ch (does NOT count as st), 1 dc into same st as last ss (4 [5: 5: 6: 6: 7] sts decreased), patt to last 5 [6: 6: 7: 7: 8] sts, 1 dc into next st and turn, leaving rem 4 [5: 5: 6: 6: 7] sts unworked (4 [5: 5: 6: 6: 7] sts decreased). 91 [95: 101: 105: 111: 115] sts.

Working all armhole decs in same way as side seam decs, dec 1 st at each end of next 3 [3: 5: 5: 7: 7] rows, then on foll 4 [5: 5: 6: 6: 7] alt rows. 77 [79: 81: 83: 85: 87] sts.

Cont straight until armhole measures 24.5cm (9½in) [24.5cm (9½in): 25.5cm (10in): 25.5cm (10in): 27cm (10½in): 27 cm (10½in)] ending after a WS row.

● *Shape shoulders*

Fasten off.

Place markers either side of centre 39 [41: 41: 43: 43: 43] sts to denote back neck.

LEFT FRONT

With 4.00mm (G6) hook and MC, make 50 [53: 56: 59: 62: 65] ch.

81, 91 and 102cm sizes:

Work foundation row as given for back. 49 [55: 61] sts.

Work in patt as given for back for 5 rows, ending after a WS row.

86, 97 and 107cm sizes:

Foundation row (RS) 1 dc into 2nd ch from hook, *1 ch, miss 1 ch, 1 dc into next ch, rep from * to last ch, 1 dc into last ch, turn. [52: 58: 64] sts.

Cont in patt as follows:

Row 1 1 ch (does NOT count as st), 1 dc into first dc, *1 ch, miss 1 dc, 1 dc into next ch sp, rep from * to last st, 1 dc into last dc, turn.

Row 2 As 1st row.

These 2 rows form patt.

Cont in patt for a further 3 rows, ending after a WS row.

All sizes:

Working all shaping as given for back, dec 1 st at beg of next and every foll 4th row until 41 [44: 47: 50: 53: 56] sts rem.

Work 9 rows, ending after a WS row.

Inc 1 st at beg of next and every foll 4th row until there are 49 [52: 55: 58: 61: 64] sts, taking inc sts into patt.

Cont straight until 4 rows fewer have been worked than on back to start of armhole shaping, ending after a WS row.

● *Shape front slope*

Dec 1 st at end of next and foll alt row. 47 [50: 53: 56: 59: 62] sts.

Work 1 row, ending after a WS row.

● *Shape armhole*

Dec 4 [5: 5: 6: 6: 7] sts at beg and 1 st at end of next row. 42 [44: 47: 49: 52: 54] sts.

Dec 1 st at armhole edge of next 3 [3: 5: 5: 7: 7] rows, then on foll 4 [5: 5: 6: 6: 7] alt rows and at same time dec 1 st at front slope edge on 2nd and every foll alt row. 30 sts.

Dec 1 st at front slope edge only on next and foll 7 [8: 6: 7: 5: 4] alt rows, then on every foll 4th row until 19 [19: 20: 20: 21: 22] sts rem.

Cont straight until left front matches back to shoulder, ending after a WS row.

● *Shape shoulder*

Fasten off.

RIGHT FRONT

With 4.00mm (G6) hook and MC, make 50 [53: 56: 59: 62: 65] ch.

81, 91 and 102cm sizes:

Work foundation row as given for back. 49 [55: 61] sts.

Work in patt as given for back for 5 rows, ending after a WS row.

86, 97 and 107cm sizes:

Foundation row (RS) 1 dc into 2nd ch from hook, 1 dc into next ch, *1 ch, miss 1 ch, 1 dc into next ch, rep from * to end, turn. [52: 58: 64] sts.

Cont in patt as follows:

Row 1 1 ch (does NOT count as st), 1 dc into first dc, *1 ch, miss 1 dc, 1 dc into next ch sp, rep from * to last st, 1 dc into last dc, turn.

Row 2 As row 1.

These 2 rows form patt.

Cont in patt for a further 3 rows, ending after a WS row.

All sizes:

Working all shaping as given for back, dec 1 st at end of next and every foll 4th row until 41 [44: 47: 50: 53: 56] sts rem.

Complete to match left front, reversing shapings.

SLEEVES (make 2)

With 4.00mm (G6) hook and MC, make 54 [54: 56: 58: 58: 60] ch.

Work foundation row as given for back. 53 [53: 55: 57: 57: 59] sts.

Work in patt as given for back for 5 rows, ending after a WS row.

Working all increases as set by back, inc 1 st at each end of next and every foll 6th row to 57 [65: 65: 67: 75: 75] sts, then on every foll 8th row until there are 75 [77: 79: 81: 83: 85] sts, taking inc sts into patt.

Cont straight until sleeve measures 52.5cm (20½in) [52.5cm (20½in): 54cm (21¼in): 54cm (21¼in): 54cm (21¼in): 55cm (21½in)] ending after a WS row.

● *Shape top*

Working all shaping as set by back armholes, dec 4 [5: 5: 6: 6: 7] sts at each end of next row. 67 [67: 69: 69: 71: 71] sts.

Dec 1 st at each end of next 10 rows, then on every foll alt row to 39 sts, then on foll 9 rows, ending after a WS row. 21 sts.

Fasten off.

MAKING UP

Join shoulder seams. Join sleeve seams. Insert sleeves into armholes. Hot machine-wash and tumble-dry cardigan. (Note: garment needs to be washed and shrunk before border is worked, otherwise border will be too long and frilly.) When dry, mark positions for 7 buttonholes along right front opening edge – lowest buttonhole 1.5cm (½in) up from lower edge, top buttonhole just below start of front slope shaping, and rem 5 buttonholes evenly spaced between.

● *Front border*

With RS facing and 3.50mm (E4) hook, rejoin MC at base of right front opening edge, 1 ch (does NOT count as st), work 1 row of dc evenly up right front opening edge, right front slope, across back neck, down left front slope, then down left front opening edge, turn.

Next row 1 ch (does NOT count as st), 1 dc into each dc to end, making buttonholes to correspond with positions marked by replacing (1 dc into each of next 2 dc) with (2 ch, miss 2 dc), turn.

Next row 1 ch (does NOT count as st), 1 dc into each dc to end, working 2 dc into each buttonhole ch sp.

Fasten off.

Hot machine-wash and tumble-dry cardigan again (to shrink border to correct size). Sew on buttons.

SIX-PETAL FLOWERS (make 4)

With 2.50mm (C2) hook and A, make 4 ch and join with a ss to form a ring.

Round 1 5 ch (counts as 1 tr and 2 ch), (1 tr into ring, 2 ch) 5 times, ss to 3rd of 5 ch at beg of round.

Break off A and join in B.

Round 2 4 ch, miss st at base of 4 ch, *dtr3tog into next ch sp, 4 ch, 1 rfdc around stem of next tr**, 4 ch, rep from * to end, ending last rep at **, ss to next ch.

Fasten off.

Make another flower in exactly this way.

Now make another 2 flowers in exactly this way, but using C in place of B.

DOUBLE-LAYER FLOWER

With 2.50mm (C2) hook and A, make 2 ch.

Round 1 5 dc into 2nd ch from hook, ss to first dc. 5 sts.

Round 2 1 ch (does NOT count as st), working into front loops only of sts of previous round: 1 dc into first dc, (3 ch, 1 dc into next dc) 4 times, 3 ch, ss to first dc.

Break off A and join in B.

Round 3 1 ch (does NOT count as st), working into back loops only of sts of round 1: 2 dc into each dc to end, ss to first dc. 10 sts.

Round 4 2 ch (counts as first htr), 1 htr into dc at base of 2 ch, 2 htr into each dc to end, ss to top of 2 ch at beg of round. 20 sts.

Round 5 Working into front loops only of sts of previous round: 3 ch, 1 dtr into st at base of 3 ch, *2 dtr into each of next 2 htr, (1 dtr, 3 ch and 1 ss) into next htr**, (1 ss, 3 ch and 1 dtr) into next htr, rep from * to end, ending last rep at **, ss to st at base of 3 ch at beg of round. 5 petals.

Fasten off.

Round 6 Working into back loops only of sts of round 4: rejoin C to 1 htr at centre of one petal of previous round, 3 ch, 1 ttr into st at base of 3 ch, *2 ttr into each of next 2 htr, (1 ttr, 3 ch and 1 ss) into next htr**, (1 ss, 3 ch and 1 ttr) into next htr, rep from * to end, ending last rep at **, ss to st at base of 3 ch at beg of round.

Fasten off.

FIVE-PETAL FLOWERS (make 2)

With 2.50mm (C2) hook and A, make 6 ch and join with a ss to form a ring.

Round 1 3 ch (count as first tr), 19 tr into ring, ss to top of 3 ch at beg of round.

Break off A and join in B.

Round 2 1 ch (does NOT count as st), 1 dc into st at base of 1 ch, *1 ch, 1 tr into next tr, 2 tr into next tr, 1 tr into next tr, 1 ch, 1 dc into next tr, rep from * to end, replacing dc at end of last rep with ss to first dc. 5 petals.

Fasten off.

Make another flower in exactly this way, but using C in place of B.

LEAVES (make 6)

With 2.50mm (C2) hook and D, make 9 ch.

Row 1 (RS) 1 dc into 2nd ch from hook, 1 dc into each of next 6 ch, 3 dc into last ch, working back along other side of ch: 1 dc into each of next 6 ch, turn.

Working into back loops only of sts of previous row, cont as follows:

Row 2 1 ch (does NOT count as st), 1 dc into each of first 7 dc, 3 dc into next dc, 1 dc into each of next 6 dc, turn.

Rows 3 and 4 As row 2.

Row 5 1 ch (does NOT count as st), 1 dc into each of first 7 dc, 1 ss into next dc.

Fasten off.

Make another 2 leaves in exactly this way.

Now make another 3 leaves in exactly this way, but using E in place of D.

Using photograph above as a guide, arrange flowers and leaves onto front of cardigan and sew in place.

Multi-coloured motif shrug

This simple but boldly colourful shrug works a stylish twist on the traditional 'granny square'; here, the squares are joined together with rows of double crochet to form the garment. This pattern could easily be adapted to create vibrant cushion covers or a colourfully cosy throw. See pages 60–65 for more information on crochet motifs.

PROJECT NOTES

MEASUREMENTS
One size, to fit bust 81–102cm (32–40in)
Width at opening edge 180cm (71in)
Length, laid flat 32cm (12½in)

YARN
All DK-weight 100% wool
A 3 x 50g (1¾oz) balls in purple-red
B 2 x 50g (1¾oz) balls in raspberry
C 2 x 50g (1¾oz) balls in grey-blue
D 2 x 50g (1¾oz) balls in yellow
E 2 x 50g (1¾oz) balls in green

HOOKS
3.50mm (E4) and 4.00mm (G6) hooks

TENSION
Basic motif measures 10cm (4in) square on 4.00mm (G6) hook, or the size required to achieve stated tension.

SHRUG

32cm (12½in)

180cm (71in)

THE PATTERN

BASIC MOTIF

With 4.00mm (G6) hook and first colour, make 4 ch and join with a ss to form a ring.

Round 1 3 ch (counts as first tr), 2 tr into ring, (2 ch, 3 tr into ring) 3 times, 2 ch, ss to top of 3 ch at beg of round.
Break off first colour.

Round 2 Join in 2nd colour to 1-ch sp, 3 ch (counts as first tr), 2 tr into same ch sp, *1 ch, (3 tr, 2 ch and 3 tr) into next ch sp, rep from * twice more, 1 ch, 3 tr into same ch sp as used at beg of round, 2 ch, ss to top of 3 ch at beg of round.
Break off 2nd colour.

Round 3 Join in 3rd colour to one corner 2-ch sp, 3 ch (counts as first tr), 2 tr into same ch sp, *1 ch, 3 tr into next ch sp, 1 ch, (3 tr, 2 ch and 3 tr) into next corner ch sp, rep from * twice more, 1 ch, 3 tr into next ch sp, 1 ch, 3 tr into same ch sp as used at beg of round, 2 ch, ss to top of 3 ch at beg of round.
Break off 3rd colour.

Round 4 Join in A to one corner 2-ch sp, 3 ch (counts as first tr), 2 tr into same ch sp, *(1 ch, 3 tr into next ch sp) twice, 1 ch, (3 tr, 2 ch and 3 tr) into next corner ch sp, rep

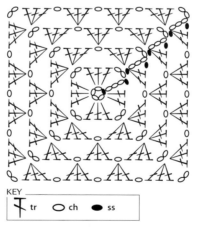

KEY

† tr   ○ ch   ● ss

This is the basic four-round motif.

from * twice more, (1 ch, 3 tr into next ch sp) twice, 1 ch, 3 tr into same ch sp as used at beg of round, 2 ch, ss to top of 3 ch at beg of round.
Fasten off.

Completed basic motif is a square. In each corner there is a 2-ch sp between 2 blocks of 3 tr, and along each side there are a further 2 blocks of 3 tr, separated by a 1-ch sp. (17 sts along each side.)

MOTIF COLOURWAYS
Motifs are worked in 12 different colourways, but all motifs are made using yarn A for round 4. Use yarns for each colourway of motifs as shown in chart below.

SHRUG
Make 63 basic motifs: 6 motifs in each of colourways 1 to 3, and 5 motifs in each of colourways 4 to 12.

Following diagram (*above right*), join motifs to form one large rectangle 9 motifs wide and 7 motifs long. Numbers on diagram relate to colourways of motif. Using yarn A, join motifs by holding them RS together and

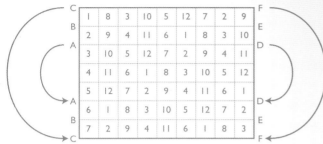

COLOURWAY	1	2	3	4	5	6	7	8	9	10	11	12
1ST COLOUR	B	C	D	E	B	C	D	E	B	C	D	E
2ND COLOUR	C	E	B	C	D	E	C	D	E	D	E	B
3RD COLOUR	D	E	C	D	E	D	E	B	C	E	B	C

working a row of dc along sides to be joined, working each dc through sts of both motifs. Once rectangle is complete, join side seams by joining side motifs as indicated on diagram: join A to A, B to B and so on. Completed joined section will form a bag shape that is 9 motifs wide and 3½ motifs deep. Openings left at the base corners of the bag shape form the armhole openings.

BODY OPENING EDGING

With RS facing, 3.50mm (E4) hook and yarn A, rejoin yarn with a ss into joined corner point indicated by C on diagram, 1 ch (does NOT count as st), work 1 round of dc around entire opening edge, ending with ss to first dc, turn.

Next round 1 ch (does NOT count as st), 1 dc into each dc to end, ss to first dc, turn.

Rep last round twice more.

Fasten off.

ARMHOLE EDGINGS

With RS facing, 3.50mm (E4) hook and yarn A, rejoin yarn with a ss into joined corner point indicated by A (or D) on diagram, 1 ch (does NOT count as st), work 1 round of dc around armhole opening edge, ending with ss to first dc, turn.

Next round 1 ch (does NOT count as st), 1 dc into each dc to end, ss to first dc, turn.

Rep last round twice more.

Fasten off.

MAKING UP

Press following the instructions on the ball band.

The 'sleeves' of this shrug are constructed from a few cunning folds and joins. The edgings are finished off with a band of double crochet.

Lazy stripe wrap jacket

The joy of using variegated yarn is that you can produce striping effects without the need for fiddly yarn changing. Here, the lovely muted tones of the yarn mean the colour changes of this wrap jacket merge subtly into one another. You could use a more vivid palette to produce bolder colour changes.

PROJECT NOTES

MEASUREMENTS
To fit bust: 81–86cm (32–34in) [91–97cm (36–38in): 102–107cm (40–42in)]
Actual size: 108cm (42½in) [117cm (46in): 126cm (49½in)]
Full length: 66cm (26in) [68cm (26¾in): 70cm (27½in)]
Sleeve seam: 43cm (17in) [44cm (17¼in): 45cm (17¾in)]

YARN
18 [20: 22] x 50g (1¾oz) balls of DK-weight wool and soybean protein fibre mix yarn in variegated greys and earth tones

HOOKS
3.50mm (E4) and 4.00mm (G6) hooks

SPECIAL ABBREVIATIONS
rftr relief front treble: work a tr in the usual way but working around stem

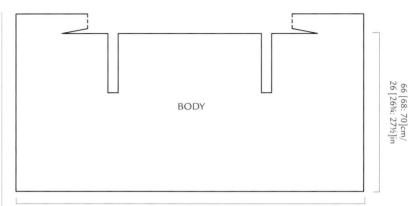

of st, inserting hook from front to back and from right to left.

TENSION
20 sts and 15 rows to 10cm (4in) measured over pattern on 4.00mm (G6) hook, or the size required to achieve stated tension.

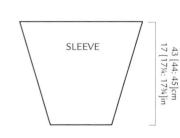

THE PATTERN

BODY
(Worked in one piece to armholes.)
With 4.00mm (G6) hook, make 255 [276: 297] ch.

Foundation row (WS) 1 dc into 2nd ch from hook, 1 dc into each ch to end, turn. 254 [275: 296] sts.

Next row 3 ch (counts as first tr), miss dc at base of 3 ch, *miss next 2 dc, 1 tr into next dc, 1 ch, 1 tr into first of 2 missed dc, rep from * to last dc, 1 tr into last dc, turn.

Cont in patt as follows:

Row 1 (WS) 1 ch (does NOT count as st), 1 dc into each tr and ch sp to end, work last dc into top of 3 ch at beg of last row, turn.

Row 2 3 ch (counts as first tr), miss dc at base of 3 ch, *miss next 2 dc, 1 tr into next dc, 1

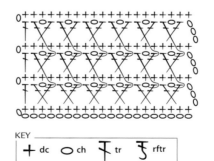

KEY

+ dc	o ch	⊤ tr	⊥ rftr

ch, 1 rftr loosely around stem of tr directly below first missed dc, rep from * to last dc, 1 tr into last dc, turn. 84 [91: 98] patt reps.

These 2 rows form patt.

Cont in patt until body measures 39cm (15¼in) [40cm (15¾in): 41cm (16in)] ending after a WS row.

The soft colours shift and change subtly.

● *Shape right front*

Next row (RS) Patt 67 [73: 79] sts, 1 tr into next dc and turn, leaving rem sts unworked.

Work on this set of 68 [74: 80] sts (22 [24: 26] patt reps) only for right front.

Cont straight in patt until armhole measures 23cm (9in) [24cm (9½in): 25cm (9¾in)] from

dividing row, ending after a WS row.
Fasten off.

Place marker 11 [12: 13] patt reps (34 [37: 40] sts) in from armhole edge to denote neck point.

● Shape back

Return to last complete row worked before dividing for right front, miss next 10 dc, rejoin yarn to next dc, 3 ch (counts as first tr), patt 102 [111: 120] sts, 1 tr into next dc and turn, leaving rem sts unworked.

Work on this set of 104 [113: 122] sts (34 [37: 40] patt reps) only for back.

Cont straight in patt until armhole measures 23cm (9in) [24cm (9½in): 25cm (9¾in)] from dividing row, ending after a WS row.

Fasten off.

Place markers 11 [12: 13] patt reps (34 [37: 40] sts) in from armhole edges to denote back neck. (There should be 12 [13: 14] patt reps between markers.)

● Shape left front

Return to last complete row worked before dividing for back and right front, miss next 10 dc, rejoin yarn to next dc, 3 ch (counts as first tr), patt to end, turn.

Work on this set of 68 [74: 80] sts (22 [24: 26] patt reps) only for left front.

Cont straight in patt until armhole measures 23cm (9in) [24cm (9½in): 25cm (9¾in)] from dividing row, ending after a WS row.

Fasten off.

Place marker 11 [12: 13] patt reps (34 [37: 40] sts) in from armhole edge to denote neck point.

SLEEVES (make 2)

With 4.00mm (G6) hook, make 51 [51: 57] ch.

Work foundation row and next row as given for body. 50 [50: 56] sts.

Now work in patt as given for body for 2 rows, ending with WS facing for next row. 16 [16: 18] patt reps.

Cont in patt, shaping sides as follows:

Row 5 (WS) 1 ch (does NOT count as st), 2 dc into first tr (1 st increased), 1 dc into each tr and ch sp to last st, 2 dc into top of 3 ch at beg of previous row (1 st increased), turn.

Row 6 3 ch (counts as first tr), 1 tr into dc at base of 3 ch (1 st increased), 1 tr into next dc, patt to last 2 sts, 1 tr into next dc, 2 tr into last dc (1 st increased), turn.

Row 7 1 ch (does NOT count as st), 2 dc into first tr (1 st increased), 1 dc into each tr and ch sp to last st, 2 dc into top of 3 ch at beg of previous row (1 st increased), turn.

Row 8 3 ch (counts as first tr), miss dc at base of 3 ch, 1 tr into each of next 3 dc, patt to last 4 sts, 1 tr into each of next 3 dc, 1 tr into last dc, turn. 56 [56: 62] sts, 18 [18: 20] patt reps.

Work 4 rows.

Rep last 8 rows 5 [6: 6] times more, then first 4 of these rows (the inc rows) again. 30 [32: 34] patt reps.

Cont straight until sleeve measures 41cm (16in) [42cm (16½in): 43cm (17in)] ending after a WS row.

Fasten off.

MAKING UP

Join shoulder seams. Join sleeve seams, leaving sleeve seam open for 2 rows at upper edge. Matching centre of top of last row of sleeve to shoulder seam and row-end edges of last 2 rows of sleeve to sts left unworked at underarm, insert sleeves into armholes.

● Collar

With RS facing and 4.00mm (G6) hook, rejoin yarn at top of right front opening edge, 3 ch (counts as first tr), patt next 33 [36: 39] sts of right front, patt 36 [39: 42] sts of back neck, then patt 34 [37: 40] sts of left front, turn. 104 [113: 122] sts, 34 [37: 40] patt reps.

Work in patt for a further 9 rows, ending after a WS row.

Fasten off.

● Cuff edgings (both alike)

With RS facing and 3.50mm (E4) hook, rejoin yarn at base of sleeve seam, 1 ch (does NOT count as st), work 1 round of dc evenly around entire lower edge of sleeve, ss to first dc, turn.

Next round 1 ch (does NOT count as st), 1 dc into each dc to end, ss to first dc, turn.

Rep last round 7 times more, ending after a RS round but do NOT turn at end of last round.

Now work 1 round of crab st (dc worked from left to right, instead of right to left), ending with ss to first dc.

Fasten off.

● Body edging

With RS facing and 3.50mm (E4) hook, rejoin yarn to lower edge directly below base of one armhole, 1 ch (does NOT count as st),

The edging is worked in neat double crochet.

work 1 round of dc evenly around entire lower, front opening and collar edges, working 3 dc into each corner point and ending with ss to first dc, turn.

Next round 1 ch (does NOT count as st), 1 dc into each dc to end, working 3 dc into each corner point and ending with ss to first dc, turn.

Rep last round 7 times more, ending after a RS round but do NOT turn at end of last round.

Now work 1 round of crab st (dc worked from left to right, instead of right to left), ending with ss to first dc.

Fasten off.

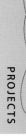

Casual comfort sweaters

The stitch used for this project creates a thick, dense fabric that will keep you warm. The yarn is a mixture of cotton and microfibre, which creates a robust, hard-wearing fabric that will keep its shape better than a pure cotton garment. Here, we've included instructions for both child- and adult-sized sweaters.

PROJECT NOTES

MEASUREMENTS

To fit chest/bust: 56–61cm (22–24in) [66–71cm (26–28in): 76–81cm (30–32in): 86–91cm (34–36in): 97–102cm (38–40in): 107–112cm (42–44in)]

Actual size: 69cm (27in) [80cm (31½in): 91cm (35¾in): 102cm (40in): 113cm (44½in): 124cm (49in)]

Full length: 38cm (15in) [46cm (18in): 54cm (21¼in): 58cm (22¾in): 62cm (24½in): 66cm (26in)]

Sleeve seam: 30cm (11¾in) [38cm (15in): 46cm (18in): 47cm (18½in): 48cm (19in): 49cm (19¼in)]

YARN

6 [8: 9: 11: 13: 14] x 50g (1¾oz) balls of aran-weight 75% cotton, 25% microfibre yarn in either khaki or coral

HOOK

4.00mm (G6) hook

TENSION

18 sts and 15 rows to 10cm (4in) measured over pattern on 4.00mm (G6) hook, or the size required to achieve stated tension.

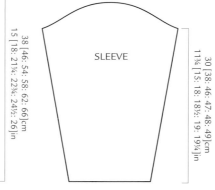

BODY

SLEEVE

34.5 [40: 45.5: 51: 56.5: 62]cm
13½ [15¾: 17⁷/₈: 20: 22¼: 24½]in

38 [46: 54: 58: 62: 66]cm
15 [18: 21¼: 22¾: 24½: 26]in

30 [38: 46: 47: 48: 49]cm
11¾ [15: 18: 18½: 19: 19¼]in

THE PATTERN

BACK

With 4.00mm (G6) hook, make 63 [73: 83: 93: 103: 113] ch.

Foundation row (RS) 1 dc into 2nd ch from hook, *1 tr into next ch, 1 dc into next ch, rep from * to last ch, 1 tr into last ch, turn. 62 [72: 82: 92: 102: 112] sts.

Cont in patt as follows:

Row 1 1 ch (does NOT count as st), 1 dc into first tr, *1 tr into next dc, 1 dc into next tr, rep from * to last dc, 1 tr into last dc, turn. This row forms patt.

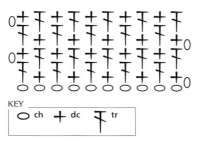

KEY
○ ch   + dc   ⊤ tr

Cont in patt until back measures 23cm (9in) [29cm (11½in): 35cm (13¾in): 37cm (14½in): 39cm (15¼in): 41cm (16in)] ending after a WS row.

● **Shape armholes**

Next row Ss across and into 3rd st, 1 ch (does NOT count as st), 1 dc into same place as last ss (2 sts decreased), patt to last 2 sts and turn, leaving rem 2 sts unworked (2 sts decreased). 58 [68: 78: 88: 98: 108] sts.

Next row Ss across and into 2nd st, 3 ch (count as first tr), miss st at base of 3 ch (1 st decreased), patt to last st and turn, leaving rem st unworked (1 st decreased).

Next row Ss across and into 2nd st, 1 ch (does NOT count as st), 1 dc into tr at base of 1 ch (1 st decreased), patt to last st and turn, leaving rem st unworked (1 st decreased).

Working all shaping as set by last 2 rows, dec 1 st at each end of next 3 [4: 5: 6: 7: 8] rows. 48 [56: 64: 72: 80: 88] sts.**

Cont in patt until armhole measures 15cm

This stitch creates a dense, robust fabric.

(6in) [17cm (6½in): 19cm (7½in): 21cm (8¼in): 23cm (9in): 25cm (9¾in)] ending after a WS row.

(Note: For 1st, 3rd and 5th sizes, rows now start with 3 ch to count as first tr and end with 1 dc worked into top of 3 ch at beg of previous row.)

• Shape shoulders

Fasten off, placing markers either side of centre 24 [26: 28: 30: 32: 34] sts to denote back neck.

FRONT

Work as for back to **.

Cont in patt until armhole measures 5cm (2in) [7cm (2¾in): 7cm (2¾in): 9cm (3½in): 10cm (4in): 12cm (4¾in)] ending after a WS row.

(Note: For 1st, 3rd and 5th sizes, rows now start with 3 ch to count as first tr and end with 1 dc worked into top of 3 ch at beg of previous row.)

• Divide for front opening

Next row (RS) Patt 24 [28: 32: 36: 40: 44] sts and turn. Work on this set of sts only for first side of neck.

Keeping patt correct, cont straight until front matches back to shoulder fasten-off.

• Shape shoulders

Fasten off, placing marker 12 [15: 18: 21: 24: 27] sts in from armhole edge to denote neck point.

With RS facing, rejoin yarn to last complete row worked before dividing for front opening, rejoin yarn to next st and patt to end. 24 [28: 32: 36: 40: 44] sts.

Complete second side to match first.

SLEEVES (make 2)

With 4.00mm (G6) hook, make 37 [39: 43: 45: 49: 51] ch.

Work foundation row as for back. 36 [38: 42: 44: 48: 50] sts.

Cont in patt as for back as follows:

Work 2 [2: 2: 2: 0: 0] rows.

Next row (RS) 3 ch (counts as first tr), 1 dc into tr at base of 3 ch (1 st increased), patt to last st, (1 tr and 1 dc) into last dc (1 st increased), turn. 38 [40: 44: 46: 50: 52] sts.

Next row 3 ch (counts as first tr), miss dc at base of 3 ch, *1 dc into next tr, 1 tr into next dc, rep from * to last st, 1 dc into top of 3 ch at beg of previous row, turn.

Rep last row 2 [2: 2: 2: 0: 0] times more.

Next row (RS) 1 ch (does NOT count as st), (1 dc and 1 tr) into dc at base of 3 ch (1 st increased), patt to last st, (1 dc and 1 tr) into top of 3 ch at beg of previous row (1 st increased), turn. 40 [42: 46: 48: 52: 54] sts.

Work 3 [3: 3: 3: 3: 1] rows.

Working all increases as now set, inc 1 st at each end of next and every foll 4th [4th: 4th:

4th: 4th: 4th] alt row until there are 50 [54: 58: 70: 82: 64] sts, taking inc sts into patt.

1st, 2nd, 3rd, 4th and 6th sizes only:

Inc 1 st at each end of every foll 6th [6th: 6th: 6th: 4th] row until there are 54 [60: 68: 74: 90] sts.

All sizes:

Cont straight until sleeve measures 30cm (11¾in) [38cm (15in): 46cm (18in): 47cm (18½in): 48cm (19in): 49cm (19¼in)], ending after a WS row.

• Shape top

Keeping patt correct and working shaping in same way as for back armhole, dec 2 sts at each end of next 10 [10: 12: 12: 14: 14] rows. 14 [20: 20: 26: 26: 34] sts.

Fasten off.

MAKING UP

Join shoulder seams. Join side seams. Join sleeve seams. Insert sleeves into armholes.

• Collar

With RS facing, rejoin yarn at top of right front opening edge, make the required turning ch, then patt 12 [13: 14: 15: 16: 17] sts of right front, patt across 24 [26: 28: 30: 32: 34] back neck sts keeping patt correct as set by right front sts, then patt across 12 [13: 14: 15: 16: 17] sts of left front, turn. 48 [52: 56: 60: 64: 68] sts.

Work in patt until collar measures 8cm (3in) [8cm (3in): 9cm (3½in): 9cm (3½in): 10cm (4in): 10cm (4in)] from pick-up row.

Fasten off.

• Neck and collar edging

With WS facing, rejoin yarn at base of front opening, 1 ch (does NOT count as st), work in dc up front opening edge, around collar and down other front opening edge, working 3 dc into corner points and ending with ss to first dc.

Fasten off.

Pot pourri sachets

These dainty, picturesque pot pourri sachets are created using filet crochet. This technique features a background grid of mesh stitches that are 'filled in' to create a pattern or picture: here, we've used a heart and a flower shape. See pages 53–55 for more information on filet crochet.

PROJECT NOTES

MEASUREMENTS
Actual size: 18 x 18cm (7 x 7in)

YARN
1 x 50g (1¾oz) ball of 4ply 100% mercerized cotton in either white or red

HOOK
2.50mm (C2) hook

NOTIONS
40 x 20cm (15¾ x 8in) piece of fine white fabric
Pot pourri
160cm of 3mm-wide (63in of ⅛in-wide) ribbon

TENSION
27 sts and 10 rows to 10cm (4in) measured over pattern on 2.50mm (C2) hook, or the size required to achieve stated tension.

SPECIAL NOTE
All sachets are worked in filet mesh. At the sides of each square of chart there is a tr worked into a tr. For open spaces work (2 ch, miss 2 sts), and for solid blocks work either (2 tr into next ch sp) where solid block falls above an open space or (1 tr into each of next 2 tr) where solid block falls above another solid block.

THE PATTERN

SACHET WITH HEART MOTIF

With 2.50mm (C2) hook, make 50 ch.

Foundation row (RS) 1 tr into 8th ch from hook, (2 ch, miss 2 ch, 1 tr into next ch) 14 times, turn. 46 sts, 15 spaces.

Next row 5 ch (counts as 1 tr and 2 ch), miss tr at base of 5 ch and 2 ch, 1 tr into next tr, (2 tr into next ch sp, 1 tr into next tr) 13 times, 2 ch, miss 2 ch, 1 tr into next ch, turn.

Next row 5 ch (counts as 1 tr and 2 ch), miss tr at base of 5 ch and 2 ch, 1 tr into each of next 4 tr, (2 ch, miss 2 tr, 1 tr into next tr) 11 times, 1 tr into each of next 3 tr, 2 ch, miss 2 ch, 1 tr into next ch, turn.

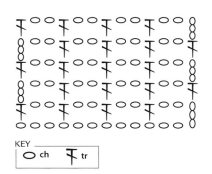

KEY
○ ch   Ŧ tr

These 3 rows set position of filet mesh and chart.

Starting with row 4 of chart A, cont in filet mesh until chart row 17 has been completed.

Chart A

16	×××××××××××××	17	
14	× ×	15	
12	× ××××× ×××× ×	13	
10	× ××××××××× ×	11	
8	× ××××××××× ×	9	
6	× ××××××× ×	7	
4	× ××××× ×	5	
2	× ×	3	
	×××××××××××××	1	

KEY
☐ open space (2ch, miss 2sts)   ☒ solid block (see note)

● Edging

Now work around entire filet panel as follows: 1 ch (does NOT count as st), work 51 dc down first row-end edge (this is 3 dc for each row-end edge), work 45 dc across foundation ch edge (this is 3 dc for each block), work 51 dc up other row-end edge, and work 45 dc across top of last row, ss to first dc. 192 sts.

Next round 1 ch (does NOT count as st), 1 dc into same place as ss at end of previous round, *3 ch, ss to top of dc just worked**, 1 dc into each of next 3 dc, rep from * to end, ending last rep at **, 1 dc into each of last 2 dc, ss to first dc.

Fasten off.

Chart B

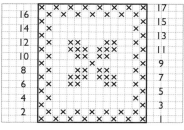

KEY

☐ open space (2ch, miss 2sts) ☒ solid block (see note)

SACHET WITH FLOWER MOTIF

With 2.50mm (C2) hook, make 48 ch.

Foundation row (RS) 1 tr into 4th ch from hook, 1 tr into each of next 2 ch, (2 ch, miss 2 ch, 1 tr into each of next 4 ch) 7 times, turn. 46 sts, 15 squares.

Next row 5 ch (counts as 1 tr and 2 ch), miss 3 tr, 1 tr into next tr, (2 tr into next ch sp, 1 tr into next tr, 2 ch, miss 2 tr, 1 tr into next tr) 7 times, working last tr into top of 3 ch at beg of previous row, turn.

Next row 3 ch (counts as 1 tr), miss tr at base of 3 ch, 1 tr into each of next 4 tr, 2 tr into first ch sp, 1 tr into next tr, (2 ch, miss 2 sts, 1 tr into next tr) 13 times, 2 tr into next ch sp, 1 tr into 3rd of 5 ch at beg of previous row, turn.

These 3 rows set position of filet mesh and chart.

Starting with row 4 of chart B, cont in filet mesh until chart row 17 has been completed.

● *Edging*

Work as given for sachet with heart motif.

MAKING UP

● *Sachet*

From fabric, cut out 2 pieces same size as crochet section, adding seam allowance along all edges. Sew fabric pieces together, leaving a small opening. Turn right-side out, insert pot pourri and close opening. Sew crochet section to front of completed sachet.

● *Trimming*

Cut four 40cm (15¾in) lengths of ribbon and tie each piece in a bow. Using photograph as a guide, attach bows to sachet.

Rose-red heart rug

This gorgeously plush, deep red heart-shaped rug uses a special loop stitch to create its unique texture.

PROJECT NOTES

MEASUREMENTS
Actual size: 106 x 72cm (41¾ x28in)

YARN
19 x 50g (1¾oz) balls of chunky 100% wool in red

HOOK
7.00mm (L11) hook

SPECIAL ABBREVIATIONS
dc2tog (insert hook as indicated, yoh and draw loop through) twice, yoh and draw through all 3 loops
loop 1 insert hook into next st, form loop of yarn around first finger of left hand and draw this loop out to approx 4cm (1¾in), now draw both strands of this looped yarn through st, yoh and draw through all 3 loops on hook
yoh yarn over hook.

TENSION
10 sts and 11½ rows to 10cm (4in) measured over pattern on 7.00mm (L11) hook, or the size required to achieve stated tension.

SPECIAL NOTE
The yarn quantity stated is the amount used for the rug in the photograph. If your loops are longer (or shorter), you may need more (or less) yarn.

THE PATTERN

RUG

With 7.00mm (L11) hook, make 3 ch.

Foundation row (WS) 1 dc into 2nd ch from hook, 1 dc into next ch, turn. 2 sts.

Cont in patt as follows:

Row 1 1 ch (does NOT count as st), 2 dc into first dc, 2 dc into last dc, turn. 4 sts.

Row 2 1 ch (does NOT count as st), (1 dc and loop 1) into first dc, loop 1 into each dc to last st, (loop 1 and 1 dc) into last dc, turn. 6 sts.

Row 3 2 ch, 1 dc into 2nd ch from hook, 2 dc into first dc (2 sts increased), 1 dc into each st to last dc, 2 dc into last dc (1 st increased), turn. 9 sts.

Row 4 2 ch, 1 dc into 2nd ch from hook, (loop 1) twice into first dc (2 sts increased), loop 1 into each dc to last dc, (loop 1 and 1 dc) into last dc, turn. 12 sts.

Rows 5 to 20 As rows 3 and 4, 8 times. 60 sts.

KEY
○ ch
+ dc
⅛ loop 1

Loop stitch: the loops are formed on the front only.

The back of the rug is sturdy double crochet.

Row 21 1 ch (does NOT count as st), 2 dc into first dc (1 st increased), 1 dc into each st to last dc, 2 dc into last dc (1 st increased), turn. 62 sts.

Row 22 1 ch (does NOT count as st), (1 dc and loop 1) into first dc (1 st increased), loop 1 into each dc to last dc, (loop 1 and 1 dc) into last dc (1 st increased), turn. 64 sts.

Rows 23 to 36 As rows 21 and 22, 7 times. 92 sts.

Row 37 1 ch (does NOT count as st), 2 dc into first dc (1 st increased), 1 dc into each st to last dc, 2 dc into last dc (1 st increased), turn. 94 sts.

Row 38 1 ch (does NOT count as st), 1 dc into first dc, loop 1 into each dc to last dc, 1 dc into last dc, turn.

Rows 39 to 48 As rows 37 and 38, 5 times. 104 sts.

Row 49 1 ch (does NOT count as st), 1 dc into first dc, 1 dc into each st to last dc, 1 dc into last dc, turn.

Row 50 1 ch (does NOT count as st), 1 dc into first dc, loop 1 into each dc to last dc, 1 dc into last dc, turn.

Rows 51 to 62 As rows 49 and 50, 6 times.

● *Divide for top*

Row 63 (RS) 1 ch (does NOT count as st), dc2tog over first 2 sts (1 st decreased), 1 dc into each of next 48 sts, dc2tog over next 2 sts and turn, leaving rem sts unworked.

Work on this set of 50 sts only for first side of top shaping.

Row 64 1 ch (does NOT count as st), 1 dc into first dc, loop 1 into each dc to last dc, 1 dc into last dc, turn.

Row 65 1 ch (does NOT count as st), dc2tog over first 2 sts (1 st decreased), 1 dc into each st to last 2 sts, dc2tog over last 2 sts (1 st decreased), turn. 48 sts.

Rows 66 and 67 As rows 64 and 65. 46 sts.

Row 68 As row 64.

Row 69 1 ch (does NOT count as st), dc2tog over first 2 sts (1 st decreased), 1 dc into each st to last 2 sts, dc2tog over last 2 sts (1 st decreased), turn. 44 sts.

Row 70 1 ch (does NOT count as st), dc2tog over first 2 dc (1 st decreased), loop 1 into each dc to last 2 dc, dc2tog over last 2 dc (1 st decreased), turn. 42 sts.

Rows 71 to 74 As rows 69 and 70, twice. 34 sts.

Row 75 1 ch (does NOT count as st), dc2tog over first 2 sts (1 st decreased), 1 dc into each st to last 3 sts, dc2tog over next 2 sts and turn, leaving last st unworked (2 sts decreased). 31 sts.

Row 76 1 ch (does NOT count as st), dc2tog over first 2 dc (1 st decreased), loop 1 into each dc to last 3 dc, dc2tog over next 2 sts and turn, leaving last st unworked. 28 sts.

Rows 77 to 80 As rows 75 and 76, twice. 16 sts.

Fasten off.

Return to last complete row worked before dividing for top, rejoin yarn to next dc and proceed as follows:

Row 63 (RS) 1 ch (does NOT count as st), dc2tog over first 2 sts (this is st where yarn was rejoined and next st) (1 st decreased), 1 dc into each st to last 2 sts, dc2tog over last 2 sts (1 st decreased), turn. 50 sts.

Complete second side of top as for first side by working rows 64 to 80.

Fasten off.

MAKING UP

Do NOT press.

● *Edging*

With RS facing, attach yarn to outer edge of rug, 1 ch (does NOT count as st), work 1 row of dc evenly around entire outer edge, working 3 dc into base corner point and ending with ss to first dc.

Fasten off.

Three-colour baby blanket

This cosy baby blanket is worked in three colours of a merino wool and cotton blend yarn, which combines warmth with resilience. This blanket uses a simple stitch pattern but the pretty combination of soft colours gives it visual interest.

PROJECT NOTES

MEASUREMENTS
Actual size: 68 x 95cm (26¾ x 37½in)

YARN
DK-weight 50% merino, 50% cotton mix yarn

A 5 x 50g(1¾oz) balls in cream
B 4 x 50g (1¾oz) balls in pale pink
C 4 x 50g (1¾oz) balls in pale blue

HOOK
3.00mm (D3) hook

TENSION
21 sts and 16½ rows to 10cm (4in) measured over pattern on 3.00mm (D3) hook, or the size required to achieve stated tension.

THE PATTERN

BLANKET

With 3.00mm (D3) hook and A, make 191 ch.

Foundation row (RS) 1 tr into 4th ch from hook, 1 tr into next ch, *3 ch, miss 3 ch, 1 tr into each of next 3 ch, rep from * to end, turn. 189 sts. Join in B.

Next row Using B, 3 ch, miss 3 tr at end of last row, *(1 tr into next missed foundation ch enclosing ch loop of previous row in st) 3 times**, 3 ch, miss 3 tr, rep from * to end, ending last rep at **, 2 ch, miss 2 tr, ss to top of 3 ch at beg of previous row, turn.

Join in C and cont in patt as follows:

Row 1 (RS) Using C, 3 ch (counts as first tr), miss st at base of 3 ch, (1 tr into next missed tr 2 rows below enclosing ch loop of previous row in st) twice, *3 ch, miss 3 ch, (1 tr into next missed tr 2 rows below enclosing ch loop of previous row in st) 3 times, rep from * to end, working last tr into top of 3 ch at beg of last-but-one row, turn.

Row 2 Using A, 3 ch, miss 3 tr at end of last row, *(1 tr into next missed tr 2 rows below enclosing ch loop of previous row in st) 3 times**, 3 ch, miss 3 tr, rep from * to end, ending last rep at **, 2 ch, miss 2 tr, ss to top of 3 ch at beg of previous row, turn.

Row 3 As row 1 but using B.
Row 4 As row 2 but using C.
Row 5 As row 1 but using A.
Row 6 As row 2 but using B.
These 6 rows form patt.

Cont in patt until work measures approx 63cm (25in), ending after 6th patt row and a WS row.

Break off B and C and cont using A only.

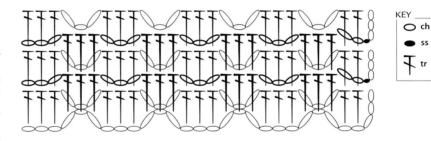

● **Work edging**

Round 1 (RS) 1 ch (does NOT count as st), 1 dc into st 2 rows below at base of 1 ch, (1 dc into next missed tr 2 rows below enclosing ch loop of previous row in st) twice, *1 dc into each of next 3 tr, (1 dc into next missed tr 2 rows below enclosing ch loop of previous row in st) 3 times, rep from * to end, working last dc into top of 3 ch at beg of last-but-one row, 2 dc into same place as last dc, now work down first row-end edge as follows: 1 dc into each row-end edge to foundation ch edge, now work across foundation ch edge as follows: 3 dc into first foundation ch, 1 dc into each foundation ch to last foundation ch, 3 dc into last foundation ch, now work up other row-end edge as follows: 1 dc into each row-end edge until dc has been worked into last row-end edge, 2 dc into same place as dc at beg of round, ss to first dc, turn.

Join in B.

Round 2 Using B, 1 ch (does NOT count as st), 1 dc into each dc to end, working 3 dc into each corner point and ending with ss to first dc, turn.

Break off B.

KEY
○ ch
● ss
⊤ tr

Three pastel shades create a pretty colour effect.

Using A, rep round 2 once more.

Join in C.

Using C, rep round 2 once more.

Break off C and cont using A only.

Rep round 2 once more but do NOT turn at end of round.

Now work 1 round of crab st (dc worked from left to right, instead of right to left) around entire outer edge, ending with ss to first dc.

Fasten off.

MAKING UP

Press carefully following instructions on the ball band.

Rainbow ribbon throw

The yarns used for this vibrantly colourful throw create a lush and velvety texture. These are chunky yarns that will work up satisfyingly quickly. The bold strips of colour are simply made from blocks of treble crochet.

PROJECT NOTES

MEASUREMENTS

Actual size: 150 x 150cm (59 x 59in)

YARNS

A 5 x 100g (3½oz) hanks of chunky-weight 90% merino, 10% nylon ribbon yarn in variegated turquoises

B 5 x 100g (3½oz) hanks of chunky-weight 90% merino, 10% nylon ribbon yarn in turquoise, pink and yellow

C 5 x 100g (3½oz) hanks of chunky-weight 50% wool, 50% cotton tweed yarn in variegated hot pinks

D 5 x 100g (3½oz) hanks of chunky-weight 50% cotton, 40% rayon, 10% nylon ribbon yarn in variegated greens and blues

HOOK

6.00mm (J10) hook

TENSION

11 sts and 7 rows to 10cm (4in) measured over pattern on 6.00mm (J10) hook, or the size required to achieve stated tension.

THE PATTERN

FIRST STRIP

With 6.00mm (J10) hook and yarn A, make 57 ch.

Foundation row (RS) 1 tr into 4th ch from hook, 1 tr into each ch to end, turn. 55 sts.

Cont in patt as follows:

Row 1 3 ch (counts as first tr), 1 tr between last 2 tr of previous row, *miss 1 tr, 1 tr between tr just missed and next tr, rep from * until tr has been worked between first tr and 3 ch at beg of previous row, turn.

This row forms patt.

Cont in patt until work measures 40cm (15¾in).

Break off yarn A and join in yarn B.

The colour changes create stunning effects.

Cont in patt until work measures 56cm (22in).

Break off B and join in C.

Cont in patt until work measures 64cm (25in).

Break off C and join in D.

Cont in patt until work measures 96cm (37¾in).

Break off D and join in A.

Cont in patt until work measures 102cm (40in).

Break off A and join in B.

Cont in patt until work measures 108cm (42½in).

Break off B and join in A.

Cont in patt until work measures 114cm (44¾in).

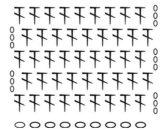

KEY

○ ch

⊤ tr

Break off A and join in B.

Cont in patt until work measures 150cm (59in).

Fasten off.

SECOND STRIP

With 6.00mm (J10) hook and B, make 57 ch.

Work foundation row as given for first strip. 55 sts.

Cont in patt as given for first strip as follows:

Cont in patt until work measures 10cm (4in).

Break off B and join in C.

Cont in patt until work measures 44cm (17¼in).

Break off C and join in D.

Cont in patt until work measures 60cm (23½in).

Break off D and join in A.

Cont in patt until work measures 80cm (31½in).

Break off A and join in B.

Cont in patt until work measures 90cm (35½in).

Break off B and join in C.

Cont in patt until work measures 130cm (51in).

Break off C and join in D.

Cont in patt until work measures 150cm (59in).

Fasten off.

THIRD STRIP

With 6.00mm (J10) hook and A, make 57 ch.

Work foundation row as given for first strip. 55 sts.

Cont in patt as given for first strip as follows:

Cont in patt until work measures 20cm (7¾in).

Break off A and join in B.

Cont in patt until work measures 24cm (9½in).

Break off B and join in D.

Cont in patt until work measures 28cm (11in).

Break off D and join in B.

Cont in patt until work measures 50cm (19½in).

Break off B and join in C.

Cont in patt until work measures 72cm (28¼in).

Break off C and join in D.

Cont in patt until work measures 110cm (43¼in).

Break off D and join in A.

Cont in patt until work measures 120cm (47¼in).

Break off A and join in B.

Cont in patt until work measures 140cm (55in).

Break off B and join in A.

Cont in patt until work measures 150cm (59in).

Fasten off.

MAKING UP

Press carefully, following instructions on the ball band.

Join strips together along row-end edges, placing second strip in centre and matching foundation ch edges.

Picture-perfect cushion covers

Crochet can be used to create shapes and motifs through combinations of stitches; here, the lush texture of double crochet fabric creates the perfect backdrop for motifs of bobbles and trellises, or panels of dainty flowers. The yarn is a sturdy cotton, so it will withstand household wear and will also be easy to launder.

PROJECT NOTES

MEASUREMENTS
Actual size: 45 x 45cm (17¾ x 17¾in)

YARN
All DK-weight 100% cotton
TRELLIS CUSHION COVER:
10 x 50g (1¾oz) balls in either gold or soft green
FLOWER PANEL CUSHION COVER:
10 x 50g (1¾oz) balls in either plum or taupe

HOOK
3.50mm (E4) hook

NOTIONS
5 buttons
46cm (18in) square cushion pad

SPECIAL ABBREVIATIONS
dc3tog (insert hook as indicated, yoh and draw loop through) 3 times, yoh and draw through all 4 loops on hook.
dtr3tog *(yoh) twice, insert hook as indicated, yoh and draw loop through, (yoh and draw through 2 loops) twice, rep from * twice more, yoh and draw through all 4 loops on hook.
rbtr relief back treble: work a tr in the usual way but working around stem of st, inserting hook from back to front and from right to left.
rftr relief front treble: work a tr in the usual way but working around stem of st, inserting hook from front to back and from right to left; yoh = yarn over hook.
tr3tog (yoh and insert hook as indicated, yoh and draw loop through, yoh and draw through 2 loops) 3 times, yoh and draw through all 4 loops on hook.
ttr triple treble; dc2tog = (insert hook as indicated, yoh and draw loop through) twice, yoh and draw through all 3 loops on hook.

TENSION
17 sts and 20 rows to 10cm (4in) measured over double crochet fabric on 3.50mm (E4) hook, or the size required to achieve stated tension.

THE PATTERN

TRELLIS CUSHION COVER: FRONT

With 3.50mm (E4) hook, make 79 ch.
Foundation row (WS) 1 dc into 2nd ch from hook, 1 dc into each ch to end, turn. 78 sts.
Next row 1 ch (does NOT count as st), 1 dc into each dc to end, turn.
Next row 1 ch (does NOT count as st), 1 dc

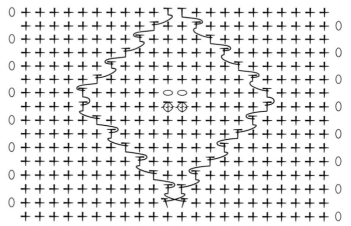

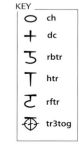

KEY

O	ch
+	dc
⌐ⱼ	rbtr
T	htr
Ɩ	rftr
⊕	tr3tog

into each of first 10 dc, *1 htr into each of next 2 dc**, 1 dc into each of next 12 dc, rep from * to end, ending last rep at **, 1 dc into each of last 10 dc, turn.
Now work in patt as follows:
Row 1 (RS) Row 1 (RS) 1 ch (does NOT count as st), 1 dc into each of first 10 dc, *miss 1 st, 1 rbtr around stem of next st, 1 rftr around stem of missed st**, 1 dc into each of next

12 dc, rep from *to end, ending last rep at**, 1 dc into each of last 10 dc, turn.
Row 2 1 ch (does NOT count as st), 1 dc into each of first 9 dc, *miss 1 st, 1 rbtr around stem of next st, 1 dc into missed st, miss 1 st, 1 dc into next st, 1 rbtr around stem of missed st**, 1 dc into each of next 10 dc, rep from * to end, ending last rep at **, 1 dc into each of last 9 dc, turn.

152

Row 3 1 ch (does NOT count as st), 1 dc into each of first 8 dc, *miss 1 st, 1 rftr around stem of next st, 1 dc into missed st, 1 dc into each of next 2 dc, miss 1 st, 1 dc into next st, 1 rftr around stem of missed st**, 1 dc into each of next 8 dc, rep from * to end, ending last rep at **, 1 dc into each of last 8 dc, turn.

Row 4 1 ch (does NOT count as st), 1 dc into each of first 7 dc, *miss 1 st, 1 rbtr around stem of next st, 1 dc into missed st, 1 dc into each of next 4 dc, miss 1 st, 1 dc into next st, 1 rbtr around stem of missed st**, 1 dc into each of next 6 dc, rep from * to end, ending last rep at **, 1 dc into each of last 7 dc, turn.

Row 5 1 ch (does NOT count as st), 1 dc into each of first 6 dc, *miss 1 st, 1 rftr around stem of next st, 1 dc into missed st, 1 dc into each of next 6 dc, miss 1 st, 1 dc into next st, 1 rftr around stem of missed st**, 1 dc into each of next 4 dc, rep from * to end, ending last rep at **, 1 dc into each of last 6 dc, turn.

Row 6 1 ch (does NOT count as st), 1 dc into each of first 5 dc, *miss 1 st, 1 rbtr around stem of next st, 1 dc into missed st, 1 dc into each of next 8 dc, miss 1 st, 1 dc into next st, 1 rbtr around stem of missed st**, 1 dc into each of next 2 dc, rep from * to end, ending last rep at **, 1 dc into each of last 5 dc, turn.

Row 7 1 ch (does NOT count as st), 1 dc into each of first 4 dc, *miss 1 st, 1 rftr around stem of next st, 1 dc into missed st, 1 dc into each of next 4 dc, (tr3tog into next dc) twice, 1 dc into each of next 4 dc, miss 1 st, 1 dc into next st, 1 rftr around stem of missed st**, rep from * to end, ending last rep at **, 1 dc into each of last 4 dc, turn.

Row 8 1 ch (does NOT count as st), 1 dc into each of first 4 dc, 1 rbtr around stem of next st, *1 dc into each of next 5 dc, 2 ch, miss 2 sts, 1 dc into each of next 5 dc**, miss 1 st, 1 rbtr around stem of next st, 1 rbtr around stem of missed st, rep from * to end, ending last rep at **, 1 rbtr around stem of next st, 1 dc into each of last 4 dc, turn.

Row 9 1 ch (does NOT count as st), 1 dc into each of first 4 dc, *miss 1 st, 1 dc into next st, 1 rftr around stem of missed st, 1 dc into each of next 4 dc, 1 dc into each of next 2 tr3tog into next dc (leaving 2 ch of previous row unworked on WS of work), 1 dc into each of next 4 dc, miss 1 st, 1 rftr around stem of next st, 1 dc into missed st**, rep from * to end, ending last rep at **, 1 dc into each of last 4 dc, turn.

Row 10 1 ch (does NOT count as st), 1 dc into each of first 5 dc, *miss 1 st, 1 dc into next st, 1 rbtr around stem of missed st, 1 dc into each of next 8 dc, miss 1 st, 1 rbtr around stem of next st, 1 dc into missed st**, 1 dc into each of next 2 dc, rep from * to end, ending last rep at **, 1 dc into each of last 5 dc, turn.

Row 11 1 ch (does NOT count as st), 1 dc into each of first 6 dc, *miss 1 st, 1 dc into next st, 1 rftr around stem of missed st, 1 dc into each of next 6 dc, miss 1 st, 1 rftr around stem of next st, 1 dc into missed st**, 1 dc into each of next 4 dc, rep from * to end, ending last rep at **, 1 dc into each of last 6 dc, turn.

Row 12 1 ch (does NOT count as st), 1 dc into each of first 7 dc, *miss 1 st, 1 dc into next st, 1 rbtr around stem of missed st, 1 dc into each of next 4 dc, miss 1 st, 1 rbtr around stem of next st, 1 dc into missed st**, 1 dc into each of next 6 dc, rep from * to end, ending last rep at **, 1 dc into each of last 7 dc, turn.

Row 13 1 ch (does NOT count as st), 1 dc into each of first 8 dc, *miss 1 st, 1 rftr around stem of next st, 1 dc into missed st, 1 dc into each of next 2 dc, miss 1 st, 1 dc into next st, 1 rftr around stem of missed st**, 1 dc into each of next 8 dc, rep from * to end, ending last rep at **, 1 dc into each of last 8 dc, turn.

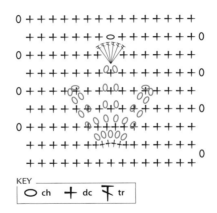

KEY

◯ ch	✛ dc	⊤ tr

Row 14 1 ch (does NOT count as st), 1 dc into each of first 9 dc, *miss 1 st, 1 dc into next st, 1 rbtr around stem of missed st, miss 1 st, 1 rbtr around stem of next st, 1 dc into missed st**, 1 dc into each of next 10 dc, rep from * to end, ending last rep at **, 1 dc into each of last 9 dc, turn.

These 14 rows form patt.

Rep last 14 rows 5 times more, then 1st row again.

Next row 1 ch (does NOT count as st), 1 dc into each st to end, turn.

Rep last row twice more.

Fasten off.

LOWER BACK

With 3.50mm (E4) hook, make 79 ch.

Foundation row (RS) 1 dc into 2nd ch from hook, 1 dc into each ch to end, turn. 78 sts.

Next row 1 ch (does NOT count as st), 1 dc into each dc to end, turn.

This row forms dc fabric.

Cont in dc fabric until lower back measures 25cm (9¾in).

Fasten off.

UPPER BACK

Work as given for lower back until 5 rows fewer have been worked than on lower back to fasten-off point.

Next row 1 ch (does NOT count as st), 1 dc into each of first 10 dc, *2 ch, miss 2 dc (to make a buttonhole), 1 dc into each of next 12 dc, rep from * 3 times more, 2 ch, miss 2 dc (to make 5th buttonhole), 1 dc into each of last 10 dc, turn.

Next row 1 ch (does NOT count as st), 1 dc into each of first 10 dc, *2 dc into next ch sp, 1 dc into each of next 12 dc, rep from * 3 times more, 2 dc into next ch sp, 1 dc into each of last 10 dc, turn.

Work 3 rows.

Fasten off.

FLOWER PANEL CUSHION COVER: CENTRE FRONT PANEL

With 3.50mm (E4) hook, make 56 ch.

Foundation row (RS) 1 dc into 2nd ch from hook, (1 dc into next ch, 1 htr into next ch) 3 times, 1 dc into each of next 41 ch, (1 htr into next ch, 1 dc into next ch) 3 times, 1 dc into last ch, turn. 55 sts.

Now work in patt as follows:

Row 1 (WS) 1 ch (does not count as st), 1 dc into first st, (1 dc into next dc, 1 rbtr around stem of next st) 3 times, 1 dc into each of next 41 dc, (1 rbtr around stem of next st, 1 dc into next dc) 3 times, 1 dc into last dc, turn.

Row 2 1 ch (does not count as st), 1 dc into first st, (1 dc into next dc, 1 rftr around stem of next st) 3 times, 1 dc into each of next 41 dc, (1 rftr around stem of next st, 1 dc into next dc) 3 times, 1 dc into last dc, turn.

Rows 3 and 4 As rows 1 and 2.

Row 5 1 ch (does not count as st), 1 dc into first st, (1 dc into next dc, 1 rbtr around stem of next st) 3 times, 1 dc into each of next 20 dc, (1 dc, 10 ch, 1 dc, 10 ch, 1 dc, 10 ch and 1 dc) into next dc, 1 dc into each of next 20 dc, (1 rbtr around stem of next st, 1 dc into next dc) 3 times, 1 dc into last dc, turn.

Row 6 1 ch (does not count as st), 1 dc into first st, (1 dc into next dc, 1 rftr around stem of next st) 3 times, 1 dc into each of next 20 dc, miss (1 dc and 10 ch), keeping the three 10-ch loops at front (RS) of work dc2tog over next 2 dc missing the 10 ch between them, miss (next 10 ch and 1 dc), 1 dc into each of next 20 dc, (1 rftr around stem of next st, 1 dc into next dc) 3 times, 1 dc into last dc, turn.

Row 7 As row 1.

Row 8 1 ch (does not count as st), 1 dc into first st, (1 dc into next dc, 1 rftr around stem of next st) 3 times, 1 dc into each of next 17 dc, 1 dc into next dc picking up first 10-ch loop of 5th row and enclosing this loop in st, 1 dc into each of next 5 dc, 1 dc into next dc picking up third 10-ch loop of 5th row and enclosing this loop in st, 1 dc into each of next 17 dc, (1 rftr around stem of next st, 1 dc into next dc) 3 times, 1 dc into last dc, turn.

Row 9 As row 1.

Row 10 1 ch (does not count as st), 1 dc into first st, (1 dc into next dc, 1 rftr around stem of next st) 3 times, 1 dc into each of next 20 dc, 6 tr into next dc picking up centre 10-ch loop of 5th row and enclosing this loop in sts, 1 dc into each of next 20 dc, (1 rftr around stem of next st, 1 dc into next dc) 3 times, 1 dc into last dc, turn.

Row 11 1 ch (does not count as st), 1 dc into first st, (1 dc into next dc, 1 rbtr around stem of next st) 3 times, 1 dc into each of next 20 dc, 1 ch, miss 6 tr, 1 dc into each of next 20 dc, (1 rbtr around stem of next st, 1 dc into next dc) 3 times, 1 dc into last dc, turn.

Row 12 1 ch (does not count as st), 1 dc into first st, (1 dc into next dc, 1 rftr around stem of next st) 3 times, 1 dc into each of next 20 dc, 1 dc into next ch sp, 1 dc into each of next 20 dc, (1 rftr around stem of next st, 1 dc into next dc) 3 times, 1 dc into last dc, turn.

Rows 13 to 16 As rows 1 and 2 twice.

Row 17 1 ch (does not count as st), 1 dc into first st, (1 dc into next dc, 1 rbtr around stem of next st) 3 times, 1 dc into each of next 8 dc, (1 dc, 10 ch, 1 dc, 10 ch, 1 dc, 10 ch and 1 dc) into next dc, 1 dc into each of next 23 dc, (1 dc, 10 ch, 1 dc, 10 ch, 1 dc, 10 ch and 1 dc) into next dc, 1 dc into each of next 8 dc, (1 rbtr around stem of next st, 1 dc into next dc) 3 times, 1 dc into last dc, turn.

Row 18 1 ch (does not count as st), 1 dc into first st, (1 dc into next dc, 1 rftr around stem of next st) 3 times, 1 dc into each of next 8 dc, *miss (1 dc and 10 ch), keeping the three 10-ch loops at front (RS) of work dc2tog over next 2 dc missing the 10 ch between them, miss (next 10 ch and 1 dc)*, 1 dc into each of next 23 dc, rep from * to * once more, 1 dc into each of next 8 dc, (1 rftr around stem of next st, 1 dc into next dc) 3 times, 1 dc into last dc, turn.

Row 19 As row 1.

Row 20 1 ch (does not count as st), 1 dc into first st, (1 dc into next dc, 1 rftr around stem of next st) 3 times, 1 dc into each of next 5 dc, *1 dc into next dc picking up first 10-ch loop of 17th row and enclosing this loop in st, 1 dc into each of next 5 dc, 1 dc into next dc picking up third 10-ch loop of 17th row and enclosing this loop in st*, 1 dc into each of next 17 dc, rep from * to * once more, 1 dc into each of next 5 dc, (1 rftr around stem of next st, 1 dc into next dc) 3 times, 1 dc into last dc, turn.

Row 21 As row 1.

Row 22 1 ch (does not count as st), 1 dc into first st, (1 dc into next dc, 1 rftr around stem of next st) 3 times, 1 dc into each of next 8 dc, *6 tr into next dc picking up centre 10-ch loop of 17th row and enclosing this loop in sts*, 1 dc into each of next 23 dc, rep from * to * once more, 1 dc into each of next 8 dc, (1 rftr around stem of next st, 1 dc into next dc) 3 times, 1 dc into last dc, turn.

Row 23 1 ch (does not count as st), 1 dc into first st, (1 dc into next dc, 1 rbtr around stem of next st) 3 times, 1 dc into each of next 8 dc, 1 ch, miss 6 tr, 1 dc into each of next 23 dc, 1 ch, miss 6 tr, 1 dc into each of next 8 dc, (1 rbtr around stem of next st, 1 dc into next dc) 3 times, 1 dc into last dc, turn.

Row 24 1 ch (does not count as st), 1 dc into first st, (1 dc into next dc, 1 rftr around stem of next st) 3 times, 1 dc into each of next 8 dc, 1 dc into next ch sp, 1 dc into each of next 23 dc, 1 dc into next ch sp, 1 dc into each of next 8 dc, (1 rftr around stem of next st, 1 dc into next dc) 3 times, 1 dc into last dc, turn.

These 24 rows form patt.
Rep rows 1 to 24 twice more, then rows 1 to 16 again.

Next row As row 1.
Next row As row 2 but do NOT turn at end of row.
Do NOT fasten off.

SIDE FRONT PANELS (both alike)

With RS facing and 3.50mm (E4) hook, work down row-end edge of centre front panel as follows:

1 ch (does NOT count as st), 79 dc evenly down row-end edge to foundation ch edge (this is approx 13 dc for every 15 row-ends plus one extra), turn.

Row 1 (WS) 1 ch (does NOT count as st), 1 dc into each dc to end, turn. 79 sts.

Rows 2 to 7 As row 1.

Row 8 1 ch (does NOT count as st), 1 dc into each of first 7 dc, miss first 3 dc of 4th row, 1

Five buttons close the cushion at the back.

ttr into next dc of 4th row, *miss 3 dc of 4th row, dtr3tog into next dc of 4th row, miss 3 dc of 4th row, 1 ttr into next dc of 4th row, miss 1 dc of 7th row**, 1 dc into each of next 7 dc of 7th row, 1 ttr into dc of 4th row used for last ttr, rep from * to end, ending last rep at **, 1 dc into each of last 7 dc of 7th row, turn.

Row 9 1 ch (does NOT count as st), 1 dc into each of first 7 dc, *dc3tog over next 3 sts, 1 dc into each of next 7 dc, rep from * to end, turn.

Rows 10 to 14 As row 1.
Fasten off.

With RS facing and 3.5mm (E4) hook, attach yarn at rem free end of foundation ch edge of centre front panel and work up other row-end edge of centre front panel as follows:

1 ch (does NOT count as st), 79 dc evenly down row-end edge to foundation ch edge (this is approx 13 dc for every 15 row-ends plus one extra), turn.

Complete as for first side front panel.

LOWER AND UPPER BACK

Work as given for lower and upper back of Trellis cushion cover.

MAKING UP (both cushions)

Press carefully following instructions on ball band. Lay upper back over lower back so that fasten-off edges overlap by 5cm (2in) and sew together along side edges. Sew front to backs along all 4 edges. Sew on buttons.

Heirloom bedspread

This project is one that requires time and dedication. This bedspread is an heirloom piece that will take a long time to create with the fine cotton yarn, but will be treasured for a lifetime. You could work a smaller number of motifs to make, for example, a christening blanket for a precious baby. See pages 60–65 for more information on working motifs.

THE PATTERN

BASIC MOTIF

With 2.50mm (C2) hook, make 6 ch and join with a ss to form a ring.

Round 1 1 ch (does NOT count as st), 16 dc into ring, ss to first dc. 16 sts.

Round 2 5 ch (counts as 1 tr and 2 ch), miss first 2 dc, *1 tr into next dc, 2 ch, miss 1 dc, rep from * to end, ss to 3rd of 5 ch at beg of round. 8 ch sps.

Round 3 (1 ss, 1 ch, 5 tr, 1 ch and 1 ss) into each ch sp to end. 8 petals.

Round 4 1 ch (does NOT count as st), working behind petals of previous round: 1 dc around stem of first 'tr' of 2nd round, *5 ch, 1 dc around stem of next tr of 2nd round, rep from * 6 times more, 2 ch, 1 tr into first dc. 8 ch sps.

Round 5 5 ch (counts as 1 tr and 2 ch), 1 tr into ch sp partly formed by tr at end of previous round, *3 ch**, (1 tr, 2 ch and 1 tr) into next ch sp, rep from * to end, ending last rep at **, ss to 3rd of 5 ch at beg of round. 16 ch sps.

Round 6 Ss into first ch sp, 5 ch (counts as 1 tr and 2 ch), 1 tr into same ch sp, *2 ch, (3 tr into next ch sp, 1 tr into next tr) twice, 3 tr into next ch sp, 2 ch**, (1 tr, 2 ch and 1 tr) into next ch sp, rep from * to end, ending last rep at **, ss to 3rd of 5 ch at beg of round.

Round 7 Ss into first ch sp, 6 ch (counts as 1 tr and 3 ch), 1 tr into same ch sp*, 2 ch, 1 tr into next ch sp, 2 ch, 1 tr into each of next 11 tr, 2 ch, 1 tr into next ch sp, 2 ch**, (1 tr, 3 ch and 1 tr) into next ch sp, rep from * to end, ending last rep at **, ss to 3rd of 6 ch at beg of round.

Round 8 Ss into centre of first ch sp, 3 ch (counts as first tr), 2 tr into same ch sp, *(2 ch, 1 tr into next ch sp) twice, 2 ch, miss 1 tr, 1 tr into each of next 9 tr, (2 ch, 1 tr into next ch sp) twice, 2 ch**, (3 tr, 3 ch and 3 tr) into next ch sp, rep from * to end, ending last rep at **, 3 tr into same ch sp as used at

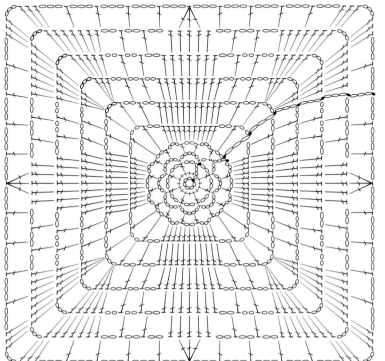

KEY
○ ch
+ dc
● ss
⊤ tr
⋔ tr3 tog

overlay panels

beg of round, 1 ch, 1 htr into top of 3 ch at beg of round.

Round 9 3 ch (counts as first tr), 1 tr into ch sp partly formed by htr at end of previous round, *1 tr into each of next 3 tr, 2 ch, miss 1 ch sp, (1 tr into next ch sp, 2 ch) twice, miss 1 tr, 1 tr into each of next 7 tr, (2 ch, 1 tr into next ch sp) twice, 2 ch, miss 1 ch sp, 1 tr into each of next 3 tr**, (2 tr, 3 ch and 2 tr) into next ch sp, rep from * to end, ending last rep at **, 2 tr into same ch sp as used at beg of round, 1 ch, 1 htr into top of 3 ch at beg of round.

Round 10 3 ch (counts as first tr), 1 tr into ch sp partly formed by htr at end of previous round, *1 tr into each of next 5 tr, 2 ch, miss 1 ch sp, (1 tr into next ch sp, 2 ch) twice, miss 1 tr, 1 tr into each of next 5 tr, (2 ch, 1 tr into next ch sp) twice, 2 ch, miss 1 ch sp, 1 tr into each of next 5 tr**, (2 tr, 3 ch and 2 tr) into next ch sp, rep from * to end, ending last rep at **, 2 tr into same ch sp as used at beg of round, 1 ch, 1 htr into top of 3 ch at beg of round.

Round 11 3 ch (counts as 1 tr), 2 tr into ch sp partly formed by htr at end of previous round, *3 ch, miss 3 tr, 1 tr into next tr, 3 ch, miss 2 tr, 1 tr into next tr, (3 ch, 1 tr into next tr) twice, 3 ch, miss 1 tr, tr3tog over next 3 tr, miss 1 tr, (3 ch, 1 tr into next tr) 3 times, 3 ch, miss 2 tr, 1 tr into next tr, 3 ch**, (3 tr, 3 ch and 3 tr) into next ch sp, rep from * to end, ending last rep at **, 3 tr into same ch sp as used at beg of round, 3 ch, ss to top of 3 ch at beg of round.
Fasten off.

Completed basic motif is a square.
In each corner there is a 3-ch sp between 2 blocks of 3 tr, and along each side there are a further ten 3-ch sps. Join motifs while working

The basic motif (shown in darker colour for clarity).

round 11 by replacing each (3 ch) with (1 ch, 1 dc into corresponding ch sp of adjacent motif, 1 ch).

MAKING UP
● *Single bedspread*
Make and join 165 basic motifs to form one large rectangle 11 motifs wide and 15 motifs long.

● *Double bedspread*
Make and join 225 basic motifs to form one large square 15 motifs wide and 15 motifs long.

● *Edging*
With RS facing and 2.50mm (C2) hook, rejoin yarn with a ss into a ch sp around outer edge and cont as follows:

Round 1 (RS) 6 ch (counts as 1 tr and 3 ch), *1 tr into next ch sp (or corner joining point of motifs), 3 ch, rep from * to end, working (3 tr, 3 ch and 3 tr) into each corner ch sp, and replacing (3 ch) at end of last rep with (1 ch, 1 htr into 3rd of 6 ch at beg of round.

Round 2 6 ch (counts as 1 tr and 3 ch), miss ch sp partly formed by htr at end of previous round, *1 tr into next ch sp, 3 ch, rep from * to end, working (3 tr, 3 ch and 3 tr) into

each corner ch sp and ending with ss to 3rd of 6 ch at beg of round.

Round 3 3 ch (counts as 1 tr), miss st at base of 3 ch, 3 tr into first ch sp, *1 tr into next tr, 3 tr into next ch sp, rep from * to end, working across corner (3 tr, 3 ch and 3 tr) as (1 tr into each of next 3 tr, 3 tr, 1 ch and 3 tr into corner ch sp, 1 tr into each of next 3 tr) and ending with ss to top of 3 ch at beg of round.
Fasten off.

Press carefully following instructions on ball band and taking care not to crush flowers at centres of motifs.

Edging detail (shown in darker colour for clarity).

Yarn details

The actual yarns and colours used to crochet the projects on pages 104–157 are given below. If you have difficulty locating the yarns, see the suppliers list on the opposite page. Yarn manufacturers frequently discontinue certain shades of yarn within a yarn range, or discontinue a yarn range altogether. The information given here will allow you to source a suitable substitute yarn.

Page 104
Band of bunnies
Miss Pink: 1 x 50g (1¾oz) ball of Rowan RYC Soft Lux (64% extra fine merino, 10% angora, 24% nylon, 2% metallic fibre, 125m/137yd per ball) in Powder (002)
Mr Grey: 1 x 50g (1¾oz) ball of Rowan Wool Cotton (50% merino wool, 50% cotton, 113m/123yd per ball) in Clear (941)
Sparkles: 1 x 50g (1¾oz) ball of Twilleys Goldfingering (80% viscose, 20% metallized polyester, 200m/218yd per ball) in Pastel Rainbow (11)
Fluffy: 1 x 25g (⅞oz) ball of Rowan Kidsilk Haze (70% super kid mohair, 30% silk, 210m/229yd per ball) in Cream (634)

Page 107
Sunny day stripes
Two shades of Rowan 4 ply Cotton (100% cotton, 170m/186yd per ball):
Sweater: A 2 [2: 2: 3] x 50g (1¾oz) balls of Aegean (129); B 2 [2: 2: 3] x 50g (1¾oz) balls of Honeydew (140)
Hat: A 1 x 50g (1¾oz) ball of Aegean (129); B 1 x 50g (1¾oz) ball of Honeydew (140)

Page 109
Precious pastels baby set
Two shades of Jaeger Baby Merino DK (100% merino wool, 120m/131yd per ball):
M 2 x 50g (1¾oz) balls of Petal (212)
C 1 x 50g (1¾oz) ball of Mallow (221)

Page 112
Pretty in pink cardigan and shawl
Rowan 4 ply Soft (100% merino wool, 175m/191yd per ball) in Fairy (395): 3 [4: 4] x 50g (1¾oz) balls for baby cardigan; 11 x 50g (1¾oz) balls for shawl

Page 115
Autumn colour coat
14 [15: 16: 17] x 50g (1¾oz) balls of Twilleys Freedom Spirit (100% wool, 120m/131yd per ball) in Fire (502)

Page 118
Corsage
A 1 x 25g (⅞oz) ball of Rowan Kidsilk Haze (70% super kid mohair, 30% silk, 210m/229yd per ball) in Elegance (577)

B 1 x 25g (⅞oz) ball of Rowan Kidsilk Night (67% super kid mohair, 18% silk, 10% polyester, 5% nylon, 208m/227yd per ball) in Dazzle (609)

Page 119
Glorious glamour scarves
Classic version: 4 x 50g (1¾oz) balls of Rowan RYC Cashsoft DK (57% extra fine merino, 33% microfibre, 10% cashmere, 130m/142yd per ball) in Bella Donna (502)
Evening version: 2 x 25g (⅞oz) balls of Rowan Kidsilk Night (67% super kid mohair, 18% silk, 10% polyester, 5% nylon, 208m/227yd per ball) in Fountain (612)
Silk version: 4 x 50g (1¾oz) balls of Jaeger Pure Silk DK (100% silk, 125m/137yd per ball) in Dawn (002)
Tweedy version: 3 x 50g (1¾oz) balls of Rowan Felted Tweed (50% merino wool, 25% alpaca, 25% viscose, 175m/191yd per ball) in Sigh (148)

Page 120
Peruvian-style bag
Five shades of Jaeger Aqua (100% mercerized cotton, 106m/116yd per ball):
A 2 x 50g (1¾oz) balls of Cocoa (336)
B 1 x 50g (1¾oz) ball of Pumpkin (335)
C 1 x 50g (1¾oz) ball of Olive (334)
D 1 x 50g (1¾oz) ball of Rose (333)
E 2 x 50g (1¾oz) balls of Salvia (329)

Page 123
Solomon's knot wrap
4 x 50g (1¾oz) balls of Jaeger Pure Silk DK (100% silk, 125m/137yd per ball) in Cameo (008)

Page 124
Circles and stripes set
Two shades of Rowan Felted Tweed (50% merino wool, 25% alpaca, 25% viscose/nylon, 175m/191yd per ball):
A 2 x 50g (1¾oz) balls of Rage (150)
B 1 x 50g (1¾oz) ball of Pickle (155)

Page 127
Seaside and shells set
Jaeger Siena (100% mercerized cotton, 140m/153yd per ball) in Ocean (430): 4 x 50g (1¾oz) balls for belt, 2 x 50g (1¾oz) balls for hat, 3 x 50g (1¾oz) balls for bag

Page 130
Tartan-style set
Three shades of Rowan RYC Cashsoft Aran (57% extra fine merino, 33% microfibre, 10% cashmere, 87m/95yd per ball):
MC 6 x 50g (1¾oz) balls of Thunder (014)
A 2 x 50g (1¾oz) balls of Poppy (010)
B 2 x 50g (1¾oz) balls of Bud (006)

Page 132
Summer sky mesh top
4 [5: 5: 6: 6: 7] x 50g (1¾oz) balls of Jaeger Siena (100% mercerized cotton, 140m/153yd per ball) in Borage (424)

Page 134
Bead-edged beauty
6 [6: 6: 7: 8: 8] x 50g (1¾oz) balls of Rowan 4 ply Cotton (100% cotton, 170m/186yd per ball) in Cream (153)

Page 137
Flower-trimmed cardigan
Cardigan:
18 [19: 19: 20: 21: 21] x 50g (1¾oz) balls of Rowan Denim (100% cotton, 93m/102yd per ball) in Memphis (229)

Leaves and flowers: five shades of Rowan Cotton Glace (100% cotton, 115m/126yd per ball):
A 1 x 50g (1¾oz) ball of Buttercup (825)
B 1 x 50g (1¾oz) ball of Damson (823)
C 1 x 50g (1¾oz) ball of Blood Orange (445)
D 1 x 50g (1¾oz) ball of Shoot (814)
E 1 x 50g (1¾oz) ball of Ivy (812)

Page 140
Multi-coloured motif shrug
Five shades of Rowan Pure Wool DK (100% superwash wool, 125m/137yd per ball):
A 3 x 50g (1¾oz) balls of Pomegranate (029)
B 2 x 50g (1¾oz) balls of Raspberry (028)
C 2 x 50g (1¾oz) balls of Cypress (007)
D 2 x 50g (1¾oz) balls of Gilt (032)
E 2 x 50g (1¾oz) balls of Avocado (019)

Page 142
Lazy stripe wrap jacket
18 [20: 22] x 50g (1¾oz) balls of Rowan Tapestry (70% wool, 30% soybean protein fibre, 120m/131yd per ball) in Moorland (175)

Page 144
Casual comfort sweaters
6 [8: 9: 11: 13: 14] x 50g (1¾oz) balls Rowan Calmer (75% cotton, 25% microfibre, 160m/175yd per ball) in either Khaki (474) or Coral (476)

Page 146
Pot pourri sachets
1 x 50g (1¾oz) ball of Jaeger Siena (100% mercerized cotton, 140m/153yd per ball) in either White (401) or Chilli (425)

Page 147
Rose-red heart rug
19 x 50g (1¾oz) balls of Twilleys Freedom Wool (100% wool, 50m/54yd per ball) in Red (403)

Page 149
Three-colour baby blanket
Three shades of Rowan Wool Cotton (50% merino wool, 50% cotton, 113m/123 yd per ball):
A 5 x 50g (1¾oz) balls of Antique (900)
B 4 x 50g (1¾oz) balls of Tender (951)
C 4 x 50g (1¾oz) balls of Clear (941)

Page 150
Rainbow ribbon throw
A 5 x 100g (3½oz) hanks of Colinette Tagliatelle (90% merino wool, 10% nylon, 145m/158yd per hank) in Lagoon (138)
B 5 x 100g (3½oz) hanks of Colinette Tagliatelle (90% merino wool, 10% nylon, 145m/158yd per hank) in Jamboree (134)
C 5 x 100g (3½oz) hanks of Colinette Prism (50% wool, 50% cotton, 120m/131yd per hank) in Rio (140)
D 5 x 100g (3½oz) hanks of Colinette Giotto (50% cotton, 40% rayon, 10% nylon, 144m/157yd per hank) in Neptune (139)

Page 152
Picture-perfect cushion covers
Four shades of Twilleys Freedom Cotton DK (100% cotton, 85m/92yd per ball):
Trellis cushion cover: 10 x 50g (1¾oz) balls of either Faded Gold (7) or Soft Green (11)
Flower panel cushion cover: 10 x 50g (1¾oz) balls of either Light Plum (12) or Taupe (6)

Page 156
Heirloom bedspread
77 x 50g (1¾oz) balls of Rowan Cotton Glace (100% cotton, 115m/126yd per ball) in Bleached (726) for single bedspread; 106 x 50g balls (1¾oz) for double bedspread

Yarn suppliers

US
Jaeger
Westminster Fibres Inc.
4 Townsend West
Suite 8, Nashua
NH 03063
Tel: (603) 886 5041
www.westminsterfibers.com

Rowan and RYC
Rowan USA
4 Townsend West
Suite 8, Nashua
NH 03063
Tel: (603) 886 5041
www.westminsterfibers.com

UK
Colinette Yarns
Units 2–5
Banwy Industrial Estate
Llanfair Caereinion
Powys
SY21 0SG
Tel: 01938 552141
www.colinette.com

Jaeger Handknits
Green Lane Mill
Holmfirth
West Yorks
HD9 2DX
Tel: 01484 680050

Rowan and RYC
Green Lane Mill
Holmfirth
West Yorks
HD9 2DX
Tel: 01484 681881
www.knitrowan.com
www.ryclassic.com

Twilleys of Stamford
Roman Mill
Little Casterton Road
Stamford
Lincs
PE9 1BG
Tel: 01780 752661
www.twilleys.co.uk

Acknowledgments

Many thanks to Christine Roberts, Mrs Palmer, Ann Casey and Caroline Ashman for their many hours spent crocheting.

Thanks also to Ann Hinchliffe and Kate Buller at Rowan, to Jenny Thorpe at Twilleys, and Colinette Sansbury at Colinette Yarns.

The publishers would like to thank the models, Sharryn McGall and Emma Dyas, and thanks also to our young models – Joel, Kiera and Bryony. *Make-up by Sharryn McGall at www.sharryn.co.uk*

Thanks also to Joyce Mason at Spin A Yarn for help with yarns and equipment on pp7–10. Visit her website at www.spinayarndevon.co.uk

Index

A...
abbreviations 50, 84

B...
babies
 hat, bootee and mitten set 72, 109–11, 158
 pink cardigan and shawl 45, 112–14, 158
 striped sweater and hat 41, 107–9, 158
 three-colour blanket 67, 149–50, 159
bags 23, 43, 80–1, 120–2, 128–9, 130–1, 158
 handles 75
balls 74, 83
bamboo stitch 95
bars 55, 59
beads, working with 76–7, 136
bedspread, heirloom 65, 156–7, 159
belt, seaside and shells 23, 127–8, 158
blanket stitch 79
blocking 66, 67
bobbles 19, 26
borders 68–73
boxed flowers stitch 94
branched stitches 36–7
bullion knots 79
bullion stitches 33
bunnies 25, 104–6, 158
buttonholes 70
buttons 7, 52, 74

C...
cardigans 15, 57, 137–9, 142–3, 158
chain 16, 18, 19, 48, 75, 78
charts 42–3, 55, 63
chevron stitch 88–9, 90, 91
clones knot 33
clusters 19, 26
coat, textured duffle 30, 115–17, 158
colour, changing 40–3, 68
conversion chart 7
cords 75

corsage, rose 74, 118, 158
crab stitch 71
crossed stitches 35
cushions 28, 140, 152–5, 159

D...
decorative details 74–5
decreasing 44–8
double crochet 16, 71, 84, 86
double treble 17, 34

E...
edges
 beads 77, 136
 borders/edgings 32, 68–73, 96–7
 joining 56–9
embroidery 78–9
equipment 7

F...
fastening off 21
filet crochet 53–5
flowers
 cardigan trimmings 15, 139
 layered motifs 64–5, 156
 motif 99
 rose corsage 74, 118, 158
French knots 79
fringes 82
fur stitch 37, 147

G...
granny square 98, 140–1
griddle stitch 87

H...
half treble 16, 85
hat
 bootee and mitten set 72, 109–11, 158
 circles and stripes 61, 124–5, 126, 158
 seaside and shells 23, 129
hooks 7, 14, 24

I...
increasing 44, 46, 48–9

L...
lacet 55
lacy stitches 26–7, 32, 35–8, 92–5
lazy daisy stitch 79
leaves 74, 118, 139

linked stitches 34
loop stitch 37, 147

M...
making up 52
measurements 50
mesh 53–5, 69, 80–1, 92–3, 130–3, 146
mini ladder stitch 95
mittens, circles and stripes 61, 125–7
motifs 60–5, 98–101
 shrug 59, 140–1, 158

N...
notions 7, 52

P...
patterns, following 50–2
picots 32
pompons 83
popcorns 27, 100–1
pressing 66–7
puff stitches 19, 27

Q...
quadruple treble 17, 34

R...
relief stitches 27, 28–31
rib effect 31, 86
ribbon 7, 9, 34, 55
rounds, working 22
rows
 changing colour 40–1
 working 21
rug, rose-red heart 51, 147–8, 159

S...
sachets, pot pourri 53, 146–7, 159
scarves 20, 80–1, 119, 130–1, 158
seams
 crochet 58–9
 edgings 72, 73
 pressing 66
 sewing 56–7
sequins 77–8
shaping 43, 44–9, 69
shawls 38, 113, 114, 123, 158
shells 19, 26, 92, 94, 96
shrug, motif 59, 140–1, 158
size 50

slanting diamonds stitch 95
slip stitch 17
Solomon's knot 38, 123
spiked stitch 91
spirals 75
starting work 14, 57, 60
stitches
 basic 14–17, 84–5
 combination 19, 26–7
 diagrams 52
 lacy 26–7, 32, 35–8, 92–5
 placing 18–20
stripes 40–1, 89–90, 91
swatch, making 24–5
sweater, casual comfort 47, 144–5, 159

T...
tartan effects 80–1, 130–1, 158
tassels 83
tension 24–5, 50, 62, 72
texture 28–31, 86–7
throws 19, 140, 150–1, 159
ties (fastenings) 71
tops, summer 69, 77, 132–3, 134–6, 158
toys, bunnies 25, 104–6, 158
treble 16, 28–9, 35, 85
triple treble 17, 34
tubular cord 75
turning work 21, 22, 29, 35, 46–7
tweed stitch 86, 87

V...
V stitch 93, 94

W...
wave stitch 88, 89
woven effects 31, 80–1

Y...
yarn
 aftercare 5266
 changing colour 40–1
 crochet patterns 50
 holding 14
 joining/rejoining 39
 stranding 40, 41, 43
 suppliers 159
 types/textures 8–11
 variegated 115, 142